Giving Voice
to Traditional Songs

Giving Voice to Traditional Songs

JEAN REDPATH'S AUTOBIOGRAPHY 1937–2014

As Told to Mark Brownrigg

THE UNIVERSITY OF SOUTH CAROLINA PRESS

Published by the University of South Carolina Press
Columbia, South Carolina 29208

www.sc.edu/uscpress

Manufactured in the United States of America

27 26 25 24 23 22 21 20 19 18
10 9 8 7 6 5 4 3 2 1

Library of Congress Cataloging-in-Publication Data
can be found at http://catalog.loc.gov/.

ISBN: 978-1-61117-892-0 (cloth)
ISBN: 978-1-61117-893-7 (ebook)

This book was printed on recycled paper with
30 percent postconsumer waste content.

To my friends
Thank you for sharing and shaping my life

CONTENTS

PREFACE

Jean Redpath was a shy Fife lass who became an iconic folk singer—although, as was once said of her, "to describe Jean Redpath a folk singer is akin to describing Michelangelo as an interior decorator."

This comment is scarcely an exaggeration. Jean sang—and sang superbly —what she knew and liked. She left us with an enormous catalogue of almost seven hundred recorded songs, covering everything from folk, to traditional Scots songs from the seventeenth and eighteenth centuries, Scottish "bothy ballads," and traditional music in several languages; she also loved, sang, and recorded gospel music. In addition, she took time to champion a few recently composed ballads which she believed would be passed through generations of singers to become the traditional songs of tomorrow.

All of this, without reading a note of music. She picked up songs pitch-perfect by ear, then held them firmly in a memory which, for both lyrics and melody, was as retentive as a computer hard disk. That was how she learned as a child, and how she still responded to new discoveries in her seventies.

Despite this huge range of recordings, she was not simply a singer. She taught traditional song at several American and Scottish universities, covering activities ranging from participative group workshops and school outreach programs to formal university courses. She drew her students from, and performed in, many different countries, as far apart as Australia, Hong Kong, and South America.

An unbelievable journey for a shy, very bright girl who rebelled against family plans for her to be the first in the clan to go through university. Instead she left with, famously, five pounds (roughly eleven dollars at that time) in her pocket to sing at a friend's wedding in California . . . with no plans beyond that. In the event, she flew to Philadelphia to perform in a coffeehouse, where the manager's only interest was to keep her "on trial" and unpaid for as long as possible. He later disappeared with the club's takings, while she hitched a lift to New York and, with her guardian angel working overtime, found space on the floor of a total stranger's apartment in Greenwich Village. She shared this floor space with six other young hopefuls. Those who could get work sang and filled the fridge with the makings for peanut butter and jelly sandwiches; those who were still hoping ate them and did the housework and the laundry for the workers.

Jean's chance came at a hootenanny at Gerde's Folk City in Greenwich Village, where she was picked from the audience to sing, then offered a contract for a week's performances. She slowly built upon this and a second professional contract at the Caffè Lena, where she slept on a camp bed between the tables at night. When she could, she filled the communal fridge. When she couldn't, she ate from it.

By chance, she was at the right place at the right time. The 1960s folk music revival started in Greenwich Village and spread first to California, then across America, creating a huge wave of interest that underpinned many careers—of which Jean's was one, unfolding not without pain, and with much uncertainty. Jean said grimly: "I never quite had to sleep on a park bench, but it was close, real close, at times." As her career evolved, she took to the road, sleeping in all sorts of beds and back-killer sofas, as the people who had booked her tried to look after her. When they couldn't, and she could afford it, she booked into cheap hotels, including (quite unwittingly) a hooker's palace. Cue chair wedged at an angle beneath the door handle, a true Fifer, Jean had spent her money and was damned if she would leave before she got her night's sleep.

She was called in for interviewing at several radio stations—in these days, a pretty young single woman living on the road, with a half empty backpack and nothing but a glorious voice to offer, was a novelty. In true Jean fashion, she charmed with her singing and her humor, both the radio presenters and their audiences. As a result, she had an open invitation to drop in and go "on air" whenever she was traveling through an area—invaluable publicity, helping her to build a career. Which she did, rising steadily until she had performed at all the major folk festivals along with the greats and older seminal figures of folk and traditional music. Likewise, she graduated from singing in clubs to appearing at concert halls in most of the major cities in America and the United Kingdom—and elsewhere, including Australia.

Jean learned many of her songs during her family childhood in Fife, where she was part of a large extended family, most of whom sang or played musical instruments, and all of whom had an encyclopedic knowledge of every form of Scottish song from the "muckle sangs," or the long traditional saga songs, to the "bothy ballads,"* which were the rough and often salacious songs of ploughmen, shepherds, and the like. Her range of songs grew when she "sang for beer" in pubs with a student group during her studies in Edinburgh, and linked up with Hamish Henderson, professor of Scottish studies, and his invaluable archive of traditional songs. From many thousands of miles away, Hamish did his best to pull strings, call favors, and find her work in the early stages of her career. Jean's friends stayed loyal, always.

Jean's handling of an audience was unique, reflecting her background of traditional song performed for family and friends around a homely fireside. Jean was a magician with people and mood. Whether handling twenty fans in a village hall in Thurso, or one hundred in an old wooden church in New England, or two thousand plus in a huge concert arena, she had a way of gathering in her audience around her, creating the same intimate and homely atmosphere for which the songs had been written and performed for centuries. If she felt her audience was too serious, she would sing an upbeat ballad and tell some outrageous personal anecdote which would have them roaring with laughter. Then, by switching to a more serious and somber mood, she could leave them in tears. She was a master entertainer who seldom had a preplanned program but simply made her programs up in response to the mood she found in her audience that night.

Unlike many other busy performers, Jean was scholarly, painstaking, and obsessive in her research. She hunted down the traditional songs, tracing them back through centuries from the great old women singers of the past with their cracked and worn-out voices, who had learned the songs from listening themselves and were now happy to pass them down. Where there were paper references, she explored them, checking detail. Where there were people, she drew them into her performances, always asking "Have you heard a different version of this?" or "Does anyone here happen to know the missing lines/verses in that?" In the Appalachian Mountains, she found old Scots songs which had traveled there with the waves of Scottish immigrants, then been handed down from generation to generation by their descendants. Tracing the variations in lyrics or melody between the cultures fascinated her. She ploughed through reference papers, books, and early recordings, making herself expert on

* bothy: the building on farms that housed the unmarried males; bunkhouse

what she sang—and taught. Her liner notes on every song she sang—all 667 of her recordings—usually held a thorough analysis of what the song meant and the historical context in which it had been composed. She was as much an academic expert as a singer.

In particular, she became arguably one of the greatest authorities on the songs of Robert Burns. Apart from her own research, she worked with Donald Low in Scotland to record the huge sweep of known Burns's songs. In parallel to this, she worked with Serge Hovey in California to research and record Burns's lyrics to the original melodies he himself had chosen—as opposed to the more familiar tunes which his publisher had substituted with an eye to the potentially larger English audiences. These original melody recordings took twenty years to complete—not least because they were largely funded out of Serge's and Jean's pockets ("You don't do things like that, for money") and had often to wait until enough cash was available to hire the other musicians.

With such an incredible volume of high quality work over fifty years of performances and teaching, it should come as no surprise that honors were showered on her over the later years of her life. Honorary doctorates were awarded to her by several universities. She was not only chosen to sing for the Queen at the formal Silver Jubilee celebrations in Edinburgh; at Buckingham Palace she also was awarded an MBE, conferred by the Queen herself, for services to traditional music. She is the only folk singer whose portrait hangs in the Scottish National Portrait Gallery. She was drowned in diplomas and certificates from all sorts of Scottish history and Scottish language bodies—and their equivalent expat societies in America. Jean's approach to all of these was one of acute embarrassment: she may have spent most of her life in America, but she retained the native Scot's inability to accept praise gracefully. Scots find it easier to take blows than praise.

My own link with Jean was through an interview for the *Scots Magazine* in 2010. Waiting for the exact time when I should appear at the door of this much-decorated Scotswoman's house was one of the more nerve-wracking experiences of my life. In the event, she shook my hand, then said, "So, it's yourself," as if she had known me for years. There was no trace of the diva in Jean: "We dinnae do divas in Fife." She was the same no-frills, ordinary person who had left home to sing at a friend's wedding almost fifty years before.

We shared the same stark cultural upbringing and its strong social values, lapsed naturally into the broad Scots tongue with each other, and had the same sense of humor. The interview, designed to last thirty-five minutes, lasted more than two hours because I couldn't stop her talking. Then we changed location to a local pub for lunch and went from there to the old church in the fishing village of St Monance, where Jean wandered off into a corner and started singing, as she always did when she came to this empty space. I, who could never afford one of her concert tickets—she claimed I was too bloody mean—had a half-hour concert all to myself.

This was the start of a friendship which continued via e-mail. I nagged her mercilessly to gather together the various small bits and pieces she had written at different stages in her life and turn them into a proper book. Some of these writings appear as "Hindsights" throughout the chapters which follow: they offer a much younger voice and give a vivid description of what she saw and felt on various occasions. However, the promised autobiography never materialized until one night, around 11:00 P.M., she phoned from Arizona to ask if I would help her to write the story of her life "in my own words, as an ordinary woman, and not some distant diva dreamed up by a bloodless academic researcher."

As a retired bloodless academic researcher; I seemed exempt and accepted before she finished the invitation. That invitation gave the book its original working title: *Jean Redpath—in her own words.*

Sadly, by then Jean was recovering from her first bout of cancer and was still fighting the chemotherapy that had a devastating effect on her energy levels and her voice. We started running the interviews for the opening chapters by Skype, but the glitching, sound gaps, and pixilation drove us mad. Therefore, I traveled to Arizona, where she was recovering at the home of a longtime friend. For three weeks, we worked when she was fit enough to do so, running the series of interviews that provided the basis for the first eight chapters of this book. I quickly found that the way to get the best from Jean was to start her off with a series of structured questions, and, then, as she hit her stride, let her flow. If she wandered off course, as she did when she got tired, either she could be nudged back to the broad structure we had agreed to cover or the cassette tape recorder would be switched off, until she felt strong enough to start again.

Returning home, I worked up the tapes into chapter content and e-mailed the material to Jean, chapter by chapter—along with a list of queries for her to check out, such as people's full names, the detail of events, the accuracy of my translation and editing of what she had said. Her memory was remarkable, both for content and for accuracy. However, her residual interest in grammar and syntax from her English language course at the University of Edinburgh had to be sat upon occasionally, because it tempted her to rewrite what she had said on tape into Churchillian prose, obscuring her authentic Scottish voice. I insisted that we used what was on the tapes as far as possible, saying that her readers would expect her to sound like a folk singer, and not a retired Tory prime minister. Her reply was unprintable.

She came back to the house she had bought in Elie and made into her home for two months in the early summer of 2014. By now she was fighting a losing battle with cancer, but she refused to give in. She had come back home to put her affairs in order and to finish her book, and she was utterly determined to do this, come hell or high water.

We met for two or three days each week, spent the mornings going over Jean's editing and revision of the earlier chapters, the afternoons in working for as long as we could on the interviews for the final three chapters, and the evenings in doing our best to make the local wine merchant profitable. Jean did finish her book, in the sense that we completed the final interview in three stages on the day before she left to go back to Arizona "to get fixed." She died ten days later.

Despite her fame, Jean was a pleasure to work with, just an ordinary, friendly person with a brave and incredible story to tell, and a wonderful sense of humor that was never happier than when she was poking fun at herself. She chose not to go down the political protest route like Bob Dylan and Joan Baez, and she chose not to write any songs herself, arguing that anything she would have wanted to say was already said much better in the songs she sang. In these songs, her politics are clear: she hated the pointless waste of war, loathed political humbug, and was a staunch feminist. But, do you know what? One evening she sang to me, very tentatively, a couple of songs that she had written and both the lyrics and the melodies were beautiful. I have no idea how many other gems were written but kept to herself. Like all of Jean's music, these songs were in her head, and so they died with her.

I have friend who practices as a spirit medium in the south of England, and she e-mailed me many months after Jean's death: "I have a message for you . . . guess who?" The message was so typical, I have never doubted its authenticity.

Ghostwriter? Aye, right. Ask him who the bloody ghost is now.

Mark Brownrigg
March 2016

CHAPTER 1

Family and Childhood Years

I am often asked, why I was born in Edinburgh when my family lived in Leven in Fife.

It is almost as if by being born elsewhere, I was letting down the side. Brief pause for commercial: Fife is the only county in Scotland that was once an independent kingdom and we are never likely to let you forget that.

I discovered recently from my sister-in-law that because of high blood pressure my mother was taken into Laurieston Maternity Hospital in Edinburgh for six weeks before I was born on April 28, 1937. It would be nice to think it was the excitement and anticipation which was flooring her, but it could as easily have been a premonition of the challenges which were to come.

How quickly we got home, I never thought to ask anybody, but there is a lovely family story concerning my dad. He was working in Leven and couldn't get through to Edinburgh in time for the birth—in those days, husbands weren't expected to be there to hold hands and dance attendance. Anyway, when my aunt Elsie got back to Leven after a visit, he asked her, "How's Bluebell*—and what's the bairn like?" "Bluebell's fine," she replied. "But the bairn has a face like a skelpit erse."†

So it was compliments from the word go. Apart from being less than flattering, this kind of talk is typical of the Scottish psyche, which sees it as a sign of weakness to gush or praise, so that comment is generally brusque and inevitably critical. The love and pride may be there, but you have to look hard for them under the stiff upper (and lower) lip.

* Bluebell: My mother was christened Isabella but never known by any name but Bluebell.

† "But the child has a face like a smacked bottom."

We went home to live on the ground floor of a council tenement* in Leven, right at its gable end, where, growing up, we played in the close.† The first memory I have is not my own but came from my neighbor. The neighbors had recently moved in and I had just been turned out for the day to play, in what I am sure was white socks and black shoes, navy skirt, and white blouse. Neat and tidy as my mother would describe, with "a shilling's worth o' ribbon and a ha'pennyworth o' hair"—meaning a big white bow at the side of short straight hair.

Our new next door neighbor said to her husband, "Oh, Chick, come and see this bonny wee lassie"; then she came across to smile: "Hello, hen." To which I replied by sticking out my tongue at her, my latest and probably only trick. "You cheeky little bitch," she said. However, despite this unpromising start, we became good friends for many years.

My mother was one of twelve children and my father one of three. The paternal grandparents lived within walking distance, but I grew closer to my mother's family, possibly because she was always dropping in on them and vice versa, whereas my father had to be encouraged to go and visit his parents. My father's father was the last of the old patriarchs, sitting in a wing-backed chair, smoking a pipe and spitting into the fire, never missing. The pop of his lips when he spat was always followed by the sizzle as the spittle hit the flames. He used to snap his fingers when he wanted anything and my grandmother, who was a little slip of a thing, would rush and get it for him.

One night when we were visiting, my mother—quite uncharacteristically—said to me: "Away and kiss your grandfather good night." To which I replied, "I'm no' goin' tae kiss that. It has ower hairy a mooth."‡ He had one of these big drooping moustaches, and I wanted nothing to do with him. She didn't insist—I suspect she had her own views on that moustache and its owner.

* A council house, or local authority house, is public housing built and maintained by local councils to provide uncrowded, well-built homes at reasonable rents. A tenement in Scotland still has its original meaning of a multi-occupancy building.

† close: the gap between the blank gable ends of tenements giving access to the back of the buildings.

‡ "too hairy a mouth"

HINDSIGHT* 1.1

Some figures loom larger than life in our childhood memories. The one which jumps out at me here is my mother's mother:

> *I never could remember the details of her face, it was far too early for that, but Granny Dall was a huge woman, always dressed in black. One of my earliest memories is of her looming over the foot of my cot or bed. A huge figure, and I am sure she was smiling, but she was holding a teddy out in front of me and when I reached for it, she drew it away. It was all done in fun, she was only playing with me. But I am sure that if she hadn't stopped me from clutching that teddy, I would have remembered her with more affection than I do.*

I don't believe I ever really made the connection between that large daunting figure and the young girl sitting in the right front pew of John Henry Lorimer's classic painting from 1891, Ordination of the Elders in a Scottish Kirk, *a copy of which hung in most of the family homes.*

"That's your granny as a lassie," I was often told.

The girl in the painting was indeed the young Jane Kinnear who lived locally and was allowed to miss school in order to pose for the artist in Kellie Castle on condition that he teach her Latin and French, which he faithfully did. The elder closest to her, Robert Grant, was her grandfather.

I have other and more detailed memories of these early days. One of them has to do with Christmas. As an adult, I have always disliked Christmas, to the point of wishing I could go from December 23 to January 4 with no intermediate stop. I have listened to many explanations of this, but the one which fits best is etched vividly in my mind. I was a child of five or six and I was sitting on a pot with a basin under my chin, absolutely uncontrollable at both ends. The excitement of the approaching Christmas Day had got to me, and I can remember my mother saying, "Well, if this is the kind of nonsense we're having, there will be no more Christmases." That was enough to put anybody off.

* I have never really been sure why, but I have kept a series of notes for my own interest, almost as a spasmodic diary, usually written a few years after the event and gathering my own later thoughts on the subject. Looking at them now, they have a freshness, a more direct impression of events, than one has from recalling them as distant memories.

Another, in a similar vein, was when I was sent off to school for the first time with all sorts of warnings swirling round my head about how I had to shut up, sit down, not make a nuisance of myself, and always to do what I was told—the standard Scottish start-up pack for anything. After that first morning, I went home for lunch and my mother offered to take me back to school. I replied, "I dinnae need tae be ta'en back, I ken whaur I'm gaun'."* Thus began my independent lifestyle; I couldn't understand why one of the other kids went running round the classroom howling, when his mother left him—what was all that fuss about? However it was an independence which went barely skin-deep. Two days later, as I sat at the back of the schoolroom, I realized that my teeth were floating. I was bursting for a pee but, remembering that I had to sit still and not make a nuisance of myself, I tried to tough it out, only to have the same result as King Canute on his summer holidays.† I looked down at the puddle on the floor. In those far-off days of education, each child had a slate and a sponge to wipe it clean. I collected all the sponges I could reach from the kids around me and was mopping up when the teacher discovered what was going on. My mother had a summons to the school, and I was told that it was all right to ask to go to the toilet. But I often wondered what the poor teacher did with all those sponges.

There was very little by way of organized activity for youngsters. We were expected to entertain ourselves and did so in a much more relaxed and safe setting than even small towns can offer now. The only formal activity I can recall was a single evening when I attended the Rosebuds at the wee school.‡ Who knows what inspired any teacher to do overtime or what was the ultimate point of this exclusive little club, but there must have been about a dozen small girls sitting on the floor. I remember going there, clutching my two pennies in my sticky fist; the high point of the evening was when we got to crawl out to place our coins at the end of a

* "I don't need to be taken back, I know where I'm going."

† King Canute, a good and gracious king, reputedly got tired of sycophantic courtiers assuring him that he was all powerful as the king of Britain and able to rule the waves as well as the people. He asked for a chair to be set on the sand, in front of the incoming tide, then ordered the tide to stop and turn back. He got his feet wet, moved the chair back, and got them wet again. He then turned to the courtiers and said, "Know that the power of kings is vain, and trivial."

‡ wee school: primary school, teaching ages four to eleven

straight line. I was appalled when it became obvious that I was expected to go home and leave them there. I didn't go back.

When we were children, I didn't really see a great deal of my brother. Sandy was five years older, and at that age this is a huge gap. He was leaving secondary school just as I was starting it. There are echelons in childhood: he had his own friends and younger kids were just hangers-on, a bit of a pain. If you're still playing skipping rope and ball games against the gable end of the house and he's whacking a golf ball around the communal green which was behind the back of these houses, then you're not much use to him—although I did act as a retriever for him for a while. Mind you, I passed on the one which went through two panes of a neighbor's window and landed in a sink full of dishes. He didn't object too much to being instructed to clear up the mess, but he was seriously indignant at not getting his ball back.

That communal green stretched the entire length of the street and was the base for endless childhood games, the safe space for cowboys and Indians, tig,* hide-and-seek, and golf practice (see above!). Other communal games were played in the street itself: the pavements were permanently chalked out for paldies—or hopscotch—where old shoe-polish tins filled with earth were used to slide into the squares and mark our progress. The gable ends of the tenements were ideal for ball games, particularly "doublers," in which two balls at once were bounced off both the ground and the stone wall and demanded a good deal of juggling skill. So many of the chants used in those games are now forgotten, lost because kids no longer play them, and we would never have thought of writing down the words at that time.

> One, two, three a-leary
> I saw Wallace Beery
> Sittin' on his bumbaleerie
> Kissin' Shirley Temple.†

There was also the saga of Leven's May Queen summer festival, a parade and celebration toward the end of the school year which reached its climax with the crowning of the May Queen—probably one of the many remnants of tree worship found in northern Europe. While every other girl in the town wanted to be chosen as the May Queen—although these

* tig: tag

† Source: a traditional children's song

days she seems to be called the Rose Queen—I had my sights set lower, but with equally passionate determination.

HINDSIGHT 1.2: *Written about 1970*

I still remember the crushing disappointment at NOT *being chosen to be a fairy—doesn't every small girl see herself as a fairy, a ballerina, a sparkling princess, even if she is big-boned and built for stamina rather than speed?*

Somehow the other band of handmaidens, the flower girls, held much less appeal. Landing in that brigade smacked more of a consolation prize than of an honor to me. My mother, bless her talented hands, produced a pale lilac dress for the occasion, detailed throughout with pale yellow French knots which must have taken hours of time and patience. I was not to be won over by handwork; I knew that the ultimate was to be swathed in white net and given wings and a wand! I really don't remember much about the actual parade, although I am told I disappeared after the official function and was eventually found "down behind Cumming's shop, playing in tarry chips in that brand new frock!" Clearly, if I wasn't to be a fairy, then my interest in events was minimal.

Many years later, having achieved some eminence in my chosen profession, I was invited by the Leven committee to open the Rose Queen ceremony officially. The first year it was not possible because I was on the wrong side of the Atlantic; the second invitation coincided with a concert in Scotland, but still got a second decline-with-regrets response from me. This sparked the outraged question from my mother:

> *"Why are ye no gaun tae open the Rose Queen Parade?"**
> *"Because they wouldnae let me be a fairy, that's why!"*

The mistake that the original Leven committee had made in their selection, had clearly never been forgotten or forgiven.

We were never poor but neither was there ever much money around. For family holidays, if we got away at all, we went to my mother's family home in Largoward, halfway between Leven and St Andrews, up on the hill. That's where we met up with six of my mother's siblings who were still in Fife. Auntie Elsie was very close—I think there were only two years between her and Bluebell—and when they were young they looked

* "Why are you not willing to open the Rose Queen Parade?"

very much alike. This physical resemblance stayed with them, so much so that when they were running a boardinghouse in St Andrews, it was only at the end of the week when they were seeing people off that guests realized there were two of them.

My mother had gone to help an older sister, Nell, in the boardinghouse at one point and, when Nell left to get married, Elsie came to help. I can't remember how many years they ran that boardinghouse together, but they had a lot of fun with visitors. The only name I remember them talking about was that of an Indian professor called Promothenath Dasgupta (that's from oral memory!). He was a very cultured gentleman who, one night, nearly found himself getting a cold shower. My mother and Elsie were setting a trap for one of the students and waiting for him with a bucket of water when the professor walked by. He realized what was happening, of course, but just smiled and tipped his hat before saying "Good evening, ladies" and leaving them to their hijinks.

Food and lodging ruled my mother's adult life, because she was always either housing or feeding people. When I was about eleven, we moved from our two bedroom tenement to a cottage in the middle of Leven. It's not there anymore, because they razed it and put a public toilet in its space. Now I enjoy telling people: "Do you see that public toilet? I used to live there." The new cottage was a two-down, two-up sort of house which had lain derelict for years, and my mother was the one who had the vision—while my father looked ill at the prospect—of how it could be rescued and rebuilt. It belonged to the garage where he worked for many years, and became available at a time when we all needed separate rooms and a little more space.

We moved in after six months of the kind of work that you would normally experience only if you were on a chain gang or sent to prison for hard labor. There were earth floors in the basement, so we broke bricks and poured concrete. And before it was sold to us, there had been squatters in the cottage, so we had to clean and fumigate the place, sealing it up and burning sulphur in it—this was in the days when you fumigated a house yourself, rather than getting the council or an industrial cleaner to come and do it for you. Then we brought in ten-pound hammers (shades of John Henry!) to start the reconstruction work upstairs. We shoveled the debris out through the end window. After months of back-breaking work, the cottage was ready. One summer we had fourteen guests in it, mainly bed-and-breakfast holiday makers. We lived in the basement, and mother let out the habitable rooms to guests, some of whom came back year after year. No wonder, because we were five minutes' walk from the beach and two minutes from the town, and my mother was a wonderful baker.

Mostly, our guests were great fun, and some of them were fed lunch and dinner as well as breakfast. I surely had more fun than my mother, because I could goof off with the visitors, while she worked like a navvy. I kept in touch with some of these guests and in later life frequently turned up on their doorstep with my backpack to sleep the night on their living room floor or sofa. Shades of things to come?

Through all of this time, music was ever-present at home but was never considered a possible career. From a very early age my one ambition was to go to Atholl Crescent,* where the Edinburgh College of Domestic Science was located, and be a cook. Being taught to bake by an expert (my mother) and seeing her and her sisters involved in all kinds of catering ventures, I was far too young to think in terms (as I do now) of the restaurant business being the closest thing which still exists to indentured servitude. My answer to "And what do you want to be when you grow up?" never varied for many years.

Until one chance remark. I was being chivvied to wash the dishes and resisting and resenting as only a teenager can when my visiting aunt put her tuppence-worth into the argument. "By the Lord Harry, ma lass, if you're gaun tae be a cook, ye'd better get used to washing dishes."† Who will ever know what culinary delights died in embryo thanks to my aunt. So, have a care where you put your verbal feet—who knows on what dreams you may be treading.

At some point in my early teens, I remember getting restive about not having any money at all, only to be told: "What do you need money for? You have everything you need and most of the things you have asked for." A valid comment, looking back, but I didn't see it that way at the time. Like all teenagers, I wanted to have some weekly pittance which I could save, then spend when I chose to do so on something that I wanted, without having to ask permission.

* Edinburgh College of Domestic Science was originally opened in 1875 as the Edinburgh School of Cookery, where classes were open to the public for a fee of 1d. or 2d. By the mid-1960s the college had expanded to a student population of about six hundred full-time students.

† "if you are going to be a cook, then you had better get accustomed to washing dishes."

The money simply wasn't there. This strict upbringing has had a curious effect on me, teaching me never to buy anything unless I had the cash in hand, so that I have never been irrevocably in debt. For years, I seldom traveled without cash in my pocket—although that's also a reflection of the lifestyle I had chosen. Often I would arrive in a city where I knew nobody and, for many years, had no credit card—no bank would touch me: "A singer? Forget it!"

To an outsider, this archetypal Scottish childhood and upbringing might seem strange, devoid of love and support. That's maybe how it looks, but it's not how things were. We often played on the beach at Leven in the evenings and over the weekends. My father was slow to ire, but I recall the deathly stillness with which he received the news one day that some man on the beach had offered me a shilling. "Oh, aye. What for?" he finally asked, very quietly.

"Nothing" said I—having no idea what he was he was talking about.

In those days, I was never separated from our dog, a terrier/Labrador cross with a highly protective streak. It was years later before I realized that he was always stationed between me and any other person on the beach. But that wasn't enough to satisfy my dad. "Aye, weel," he said. "You jist gan' back the morn and see if yon mannie turns up again."*

It's a good thing for our family history that "yon mannie" never showed up, because my dad was following me in his car at a distance, and if anything had happened, I think he would have seen any reaction from himself as justifiable homicide.

Nobody messed about with Big Jim's bairns, as a teacher once found out, to his cost. My parents came home from a morning away somewhere, to find my teenage brother in tears over the dinner table. The neighbor who was keeping an eye on us explained that Sandy had been hit across the ear by one of the teachers—with a tawse no less, which could have left Sandy deaf for life.

The teacher in question was a bit of a nutter—he often stood on his long-legged desk chair to practice his golf swing in front of us. But hitting someone across the ear with a tawse was a step too far. My dad drove up to the school and demanded the man's classroom number from the headmaster. That evening we got his version of the exchange: "I can't tell you that, Mr. Redpath," the rector said. Then he added, "But I can give

* "Ah well, you just go back tomorrow and we will see if that man turns up again."

you his home address." Maybe he too was less than happy about the man's actions. Justice comes in many forms.

Murder wasn't done, but it was a close thing. The teacher in question started out with "Lower your voice, man, think of the neighbors" before my dad got into his stride. By the end of the debate, the teacher—and his neighbors—were left in no doubt as to what would happen to him if he raised anything other than his voice to any of my father's kids again. There would be a jail sentence waiting for him . . . after he got out of hospital.

Looking back, the move from the town house to the cottage was a big jump where personal space was concerned. For six glorious months, I lived right across the street from the school, so I could get out of my bed when the bell went and make it across onto the end of the line before the whistle blew. Then I'd nip back in at the eleven o'clock break for my breakfast. I was never very good at getting up in the morning—not at that age anyway. When I got to high school, I had to crawl out of bed in time to catch a bus. That was a bit of a challenge, until they made me a school prefect, and I could turn up late, throw my schoolbag in through the prefect's room window, and then saunter round to the front of the school to tell the teacher that I had just checked, and there were no latecomers sneaking in from that side of the building.

I wonder if she ever guessed . . .

My mother decided to stop doing bed-and-breakfast but, shortly thereafter, people from the local Coal Board office came and told her that their office was being transferred to Leven from East Wemyss; since there was nowhere for the workers to eat in Leven, could she take pity on them and "do something hot at lunchtime"? She started serving them soup, meat, potatoes and vegetable, and pudding, followed by a cup of tea and a biscuit for 2/3d,* which even in those days had to be the deal to end all deals. The word went out, and at one point she had three sittings, 12:30, 1:00, and 1:30 P.M., and as many customers as the little house would hold (which would be about twelve to fifteen people), adding up to forty or more dinners a day. All of this was cooked on a four-burner stove.

The hardest work I ever did in my life was a fortnight when my parents went off to Gibraltar to visit Sandy, when he was posted there, and my sister-in-law had just given birth to the first grandchild. I was left to provide dinners for forty-odds, five days a week, and also to keep three

* 2/3d: prior to decimalization in the UK this represented about 40c at 1955 exchange rates. At current rates those same 12 British pennies (now less than 25c) wouldn't buy a cup of tea.

driving school cars on the road, because my dad was running his own business as a driving instructor at that time. This meant peeling tatties at night, getting up at 6:30 A.M. to check the oil and water and tire pressure in the cars, then rushing around in one of them to deliver reminders and notes through the door to instructors and clients, because there were few telephones in those days. I was never so glad to see anyone as I was when my parents came back.

My father hadn't struck out willingly on his own. He had been with the same garage since he had left school, first as a "grease monkey," then as a mechanic, and then as one of the men who drove their tour buses. In the early postwar years, he drove the garage's tour buses through the Highlands and was much in demand by coach parties, because he sang throughout these trips. But even when he made it to managerial level, he was so conscientious that when he locked up and came home, he would switch the garage phone through to us, so that if some drunk phoned up at 2:00 A.M. wanting a taxi home, my dad would get out of bed and drive him. That's the way the man was built.

Somewhere around age forty-three, he came home ashen-faced to tell us that he had "got his books."* The garage for which he'd worked so hard all his adult life was switching to car sales rather than running servicing, taxis and buses. For my dad, the bottom had dropped out of his world—he knew no other work. But my mother's response was, "Thank God! You've been dancing attendance on that bloody garage far too long. You can do better. You've always wanted to start up a driving school, and now's your chance."

Dad started with no more than an old Austin—there were no golden handshakes or parachutes in those days—and for dual controls all he had was the handbrake. There was no driving school in Fife back then, and I think the nearest one was in Edinburgh. In those early years, my dad had a monopoly, and back home in Scotland I still run into people who say, "Your dad taught my dad (or my mum) to drive." He was as conscientious there as with everything else and built a steady business out of nothing. By the time he quit—he died at seventy, still running his driving school—he had bought twenty-seven cars, running them for two or three years, then trading them in again.

Although my mother and her sisters were all singers, my dad was the one who had the voice, but he was terminally shy. The only reason he had

*"got his books": been made redundant, fired

sung in his buses was that, sitting behind the wheel, he was facing away from his audience and could pretend that they weren't there. If he'd had to stand up, turn round and face them, he would have been unable to sing a note. I inherited both his voice and his shyness—in the early days at least. My earliest memory of singing by request in someone's house was that I would do it only if they let me stand in the doorway half out of the room, and everybody had to look away from me *and* also put the lights out. I wasn't being a prima donna; it was stage fright. I was absolutely terrified, a miniversion of my singing bus driver father. My performance piece back then? It was Brahms's *Cradle Song*.

While my dad had to be persuaded to sing, my mother was much more of a performer. She had always a party piece ready if there was a ceilidh. She never claimed to be a singer, but she could hold a tune perfectly well and had an amazing repertoire of everything from kids' songs to old Scottish songs, classic ballads and bothy ballads, Victoriana and piano-stool music to whatever music came off the radio in those days. She had an astounding memory, raised as she was in the school of rote memorization. If she heard anything, it stayed with her. My dad had a fair range of songs but preferred the current popular songs, like *I'll Walk Beside You,* which was recorded in 1939 by Count John McCormack, whose voice is with me still. Dad also played the hammer dulcimer—the only person I ever heard who could play slow airs on it. He was self-taught and had played for local dances in the old days. At that instrument, once again he had his back to the audience and was braver when he couldn't see anyone. At family gatherings, we had some great times with him playing on that dulcimer, but we could seldom get him to sing. Sometimes he would sing with me—but never on his own. He was incurably shy of performing, but he had a wondrous way with people.

My mother's side of the family were real characters. Jack was the youngest brother, the spitting image of Anthony Eden, and he had a good voice. He and his wife used to do duets on stage: they sang at each other in plum-in-the-mouth* voices, approaching each other from opposite ends of the stage and finishing up clasping hands to sing the final bars. I suppose they were imitating Jeanette MacDonald and Nelson Eddy. My mother's younger sister Elsie, who played piano, also sang in this strange "posh" voice. Even back then, I couldn't understand why people had to

* plum-in-the-mouth: Anglified and quite unnatural

sound so stiff and artificial when performing. Why couldn't we sing these old Scottish songs the way we always spoke?

My mother's brother Dod, or George, could not have been more different—he had a huge collection of bothy ballads and a decent voice with which to deliver them. He developed diabetes and, at a late stage in his life, had a leg amputated. That didn't change his earthy sense of humor. When I was back home in Scotland and met him in a family house, I said, "Well, you old bugger, I hope that new leg they've given you holds as much whisky as the old one did." Before I could finish the sentence, he had the prosthesis off and was holding it out: "See for yersel'" was his quick reply.

Then there was Aund, or Andrew. He courted the same lassie, Euphemia, for twenty-three years until one night when he dropped in on her and her mother for his usual Saturday night supper. Euphemia and her mother had the village shop, which was a step up the social ladder for him: there would be some money there, no doubt. The conversation had strayed into talk of the shop and the mother said, "Well, Euphemia, when you and Andrew are married, you'll have your bank account and he will have his."

"Of course," said the girl. At which point Aund said, "Och, I wouldnae want ye tae worry about something like that," and got up and left. Barely taking pause for breath, he found and courted another lassie for twenty-odd years, then married her. He had to, this time, because he got her pregnant—it was probably the only way she could catch him. But his story doesn't finish there. On the day they got married, Aund turned up at night as usual in his family house, where his sister acted as housekeeper for him.

"What are ye doin' here?" she asked, surprised. "I'm comin' home," said Aund. "No, no, no," she told him. "You're a mairriet man—awa' back tae yer wife." Andrew had been prepared to do the decent thing and marry the woman, but he hadn't got round to thinking about sharing his life with her.

Aund could play Scottish country dance music on the moothie the like of which I didn't hear again till I ran into Sam Hinton in California. Uncle Rob, was as good—and also self-taught—on the piano accordion. Geordie, my father's brother, was a pipe major,* and I had a cousin with

* pipe major: director of bagpipe music in a Scottish pipe band, whether military or civilian

a fine contralto. Within this musical context, if I grew up with a musical bent, then I didnae pey dear for it.*

All of my mother's family had their own collection of songs, which were trotted out at the family ceilidhs—there was no radio or television in those days, and people entertained themselves. And if anyone got stuck for words, or part of the tune in a song, one of the others would step in and help out.

Like my mother, I have a good memory for songs, and most of the Scottish songs I learned and carried with me were drawn from my mother and her family. I think I must have sung from an early age, because my mother was always being told, "Ye should dae somethin' wi' that lassie's voice." I think this was meant as praise, not a suggestion that my parents should be putting me under the cover of the budgie's cage to shut me up.

Suiting action to advice, at sixteen I was pointed in the direction of the only music shop in Leven which, as luck would have it, was half a block from our house. It sold sheet music, mouth organs, Jew's harps, maybe even a fiddle or guitar, and offered tuition on piano, fiddle, and presumably voice. The same man did everything, and I have vague memories of his running me up and down a couple of scales before he vanished into the front shop and came back with the sheet music for "When the Heather Gleams like Stardust on the Hills." Not the best of first lessons: to him, I was only money on legs. "You can pay me for that next week," said he, relieving me of my parents' hard-earned half crown† for the three-minute voice lesson. I didn't go back there—and neither did I pay him for that sheet music. No wonder I don't sleep well.

My mother was full of surprises and her memory covered a huge range of limericks—good and dodgy. I was usually protected from the suspect ones, but my sister-in-law told me that she and Bluebell were sitting and sewing peacefully at opposite sides of the fire one evening when my mother looked up over her glasses, which had slipped down to the end of her nose, and recited solemnly:

> There was a young lady called Maud
> Who said she was pregnant by God
> But 'twas not the Almighty

* I didnae pey dear for it: It cost me little.

† half crown: 2/6d or 13p in current money

Who had lifted her nightie
It was Rodger, the lodger—the sod.

At which point my mother pushed back her specs and returned to her sewing as if nothing had happened. I wonder often what oral and musical treasures died with her—or with her sisters, for that matter.

Nell, a little older, was the perjink* one in the family, and I recall doing a concert in my hometown in later years when, during my introduction to a song, Nell seemed to be sliding down in her seat. Her eyes were open, so I knew she wasn't asleep. Later I discovered that she thought that I was about to sing the words that *she* knew for the song and was trying to disappear, from embarrassment. I tried, God knows I tried, to get those words from her, but she would never tell me.

In school singing competitions, I always seemed to come in second or third to the same girl, Ursula, a friend of mine. Looking back, I think I already had a clear idea of how a song should be interpreted—and this didn't conform to what the adjudicator wanted. I was always commended for my voice, but I never won, unlike my friend who sang in that same plummy voice that made me cringe when I heard it in my own family—and she generally sailed through to take first prize.

I enjoyed school itself, despite always arriving late. Most subjects came easily to me, apart from chemistry. Even mathematics, for which at one point the teacher was only four years older than I. I remember her catching me staring out of the classroom window and demanding to know what I was doing. "I've finished, Miss," I said, and so I had—the answer was correct, too. I was watching the clouds, which have always fascinated me. Looking back, I think I was blessed with the brains but not the ability to work. I never learned to study, which was my downfall at university. Things came too easily to me at school, and it would have been better for me if the work had stretched me more.

As it was, I coasted through my classes until I had a mild case of rheumatic fever. In those days that meant being confined to bed. Disaster: take a healthy kid at the end of the summer holidays, when she isn't too keen to go back to school anyway, and put her into bed for a month, and you'll have an instant invalid on your hands before you know it. After six months, the doctor decided to send me back: "But no exams, no homework, no physical education." So I sat through all the classes and heard all

* Overly polite and careful of manners.

the material and then had to retake the entire year, while all my friends went on ahead. Going through that material for a second time pretty much destroyed any notion I had that one had to work for anything.

To make matters worse, I had also lost six months in the transfer from the wee school to the big school,* when we had to mark time because they were short of teachers in the high school. Together with my lost year, that left me eighteen months behind the normal age, both for leaving school and going to university. I was nineteen rather than the usual seventeen or eighteen for my first year at the University of Edinburgh.

Two years before, I had given up Latin to take geography, a subject which I loved. Now I found that to study English literature, I would need Higher Latin—and I had six months in which to get it. My Latin teacher, bless him, was the archetypal classics scholar, slightly stooped, and soft-spoken. His name was Andrew Black, and he gave me much more than a crash course in the subject; his quiet support and confidence in my ability carried me through: "Six months? That's not a problem, Jean, you can do it." After two years of never touching the subject, I passed the Higher Grade paper.

Before I went to university, I took driving lessons—once again at an age a little older than that of most beginners. My dad put me in the hands of one of his veteran instructors, Jimmy, a man who had once been reported to my father by a lady customer "for being impudent." When my dad said, "Oh dear, that's not like him—what did he say?" she replied, "Well, I was having a wee bit of trouble with the gears and had missed them a couple of times, and he said 'That's all right, Mrs. Paterson, just chase them into a corner and you're bound to catch one of them."

However, Jimmy did a great job teaching me to drive, then handed me over to my father who gave me an absolutely ruthless set of final lessons and wouldn't let me put in for my test until I could just about have passed the Institute of Advanced Motorists course. If I had failed, I think he would have gone into a monastery out of shame, but I passed, and I still look on it as one of the most useful skills I have taken with me from home.

My dad was very forward-thinking and got the use of some land from the council, a landfill site which was still settling. He put a square of tarmac on it, and, when he felt his students were ready, he turned this into a skidpan for final training. He had an old soft-top Austin (which had a low

*wee school to big school: primary school to high school

center of gravity) onto which he fitted a set of bald tires. Before the student arrived, we used to drive up there with two drums in his trailer, one full of old engine oil which we dribbled across the tarmac and another from which we heaved water all over it, making the surface even more treacherous. After the first terrifying slides, the students—including me—quickly learned from hands-on experience how to correct and control a skid.

When I got accepted by the University of Edinburgh, out of my mother's twelve siblings, my dad's three, and my sixteen cousins, I was the first in the family to go into further education. Sandy could have done so too, but he opted to take his national service, two obligatory years in the army, instead. Looking back, there was family pride in plenty over me, but it was never stated. I doubt my parents would have known how to open up and tell me what they really felt.

And so it was that I left on the train to head over the Forth Bridge to the big city of my birth and into a new career at university, with nothing more than a few gruff words of warning to stay out of trouble and behave myself. I honestly can't remember if my mother came with me to help me with my suitcase. I suspect that I simply followed the same path that I had carved on my first day in primary school—I knew where I was going and didn't need any help.

I had enjoyed school because it was easy—too damn easy—and because I could manipulate its rules to suit myself. Going to university was simply the next step in the path; it was what the family expected of me, and it never occurred to me not to go.

Nevertheless, you would think that the actual wrench of leaving home to go to university would leave strong memories of how I felt on that train going into Edinburgh, both about what I was leaving behind and what I would be facing in the future. The truth is that I don't remember anything at all about that trip. Everything is a total blank until I arrived at my room in the student residences and met with the girls who would become my friends.

Despite this, I was always aware at some level of the family's expectations for me. In a sense, I was carrying a flag for them. That feeling of clan loyalty kept me at university for at least a year after I would otherwise have blown my cork and left.

CHAPTER 2

Flying the Family Flag at University

Life at the University of Edinburgh started in 1956 in a small L-shaped room that I had to myself in Playfair Hall at Newington. Back then, all new students had to live in the university's halls of residence for their first two years, and our hall was one of five big Victorian buildings around a central court at the end of Newington Road. Near enough to university to walk, if you wanted the exercise. I took the bus.

I don't remember ever feeling lonely or cut off from family. Right at the start, I was taken out to dinner in a restaurant in Edinburgh by one of my mother's B&B guests, who used to manage the Pierrot* shows in Leven. He had said to her: "Tell Jean to give me a call when she comes through to the university; I will be happy to take her for a meal." I scarcely knew the man, and as a nineteen-year-old (going on fourteen) I had never been off the farm, more or less, so this visit to an Edinburgh restaurant was a bit of a challenge. My main recollection of the meal was of being introduced to olives, which I had never clapped eyes on before, and of firing them all over the table when I tried to stick my fork into them. I sat there thinking, "Oh shit, how do you do this?" There was a lot of "how do you do this?" at that meal.

Second, I quickly made friends in the residence. There are two ways of dealing with acute shyness: the first is to sidle in through the door and along the wall, trying to be invisible; the second has been described by a longtime friend as "Where most people creep into a room, you dive over the back of the sofa and start talking." Not quite, but this was the conscious decision I took on how to tackle my lifelong shyness, and it has become a strategy that I have followed ever since.

* Pierrot shows: Strictly speaking, the shows in Leven were variety shows, not the older Pierrot troupes, but my mother referred to them always as such.

Therefore, in the hall of residence, I walked in and introduced myself to the girls who were in the rooms closest to mine. Contact was made and two or three of these initial neighbors remained friends for many years—indeed I stay in touch with some of them even now. In particular, during my second year I befriended an American student whose room was almost next to mine, and it was her family who took me in when I immigrated to America in 1961.

So far as studies were concerned, I found university a huge change from school where I was a year older than my peer group and bright enough to score—fairly effortlessly—among the highest marks. There I had been a big fish in a small pond, but now I was swimming with fish who were the same size or bigger and brighter than I. This came as a shock and took a bit of getting used to.

Next, there was the ordeal of tutorials, where small groups of students gathered to discuss a specific topic in the course. These were terrifying. The first thing that struck me when I walked into a tutorial was that the American students talked all the time, whether they had anything worth saying or not; next, the English tended to commandeer the forum and were very much to the point and confident; finally, the Scottish students simply sat there and said nothing. We had never been conditioned to debate. Indeed, I would go so far as to say that my generation hadn't even been conditioned to think, just to memorize and then know our place and stay quiet. So I found myself way out of my depth, and tongue-tied. However, in time I learned to overcompensate, and I became a motormouth, able to talk about almost anything, whether I knew what I was talking about or not. This newfound ability became the means through which I have earned a living over the last fifty years.

Finally, probably worst of all, was the material I found myself studying. I had chosen a major in English language, because I have always been fascinated by semantics, the use of words, and one's emotional response to them. Semantics and linguistics were the main reason why I signed up for the language class. Much to my disgust, that particular course lasted for only six weeks, after which I found myself toiling through Anglo-Saxon and Old Norse. Dispiriting. This was not what I had come to do. I don't mind in the least reading the old sagas—but preferably not in the original. Things got even worse in second year when we moved into Middle Scots and required reading knowledge of German, which was a disaster. I changed courses in the middle of third year, because I could find no passion in, or for, these subjects. The tutor who was assigned to me was faceless—I can't even remember whether it was a he or she—that I couldn't bring myself to talk about my difficulties. In the end, on impulse, I targeted the head of department. Having heard him give a single lecture, I thought, I can speak to this man, and I did. More on this later.

On his advice, I changed to medieval studies, thinking that this would provide more of a bridge between the linguistic stuff I wanted to do and the literature I probably should have chosen in the first place. Looking back, perhaps part of the problem was that it was the English language I found myself studying, just as we had been taught English rather than Scottish history at school. I found myself rebelling instinctively against more of the same treatment. But there was more to my problems than this, a sense almost of alienation from the whole experience of university, of not belonging, of not being in the right place. Whatever the reason for my lack of interest in or commitment to the subjects, these were dreich years, academically.

From habit, I went home at weekends, but on a decreasing level. At first every other weekend, then, as I got more involved in things, less frequently. You cut the umbilicus after a while and establish a new social network within the university community. In my third year, four of us rented an apartment in a big old Edinburgh flat, out near Morningside, where we each had our own room. And in the fourth year, two of us rented rooms from a woman in the same area. Gradually, over these first four years I was getting more and more independent—just as well, given how my life evolved.

When I did go home, there was seldom anything asked. If there was a problem, it was assumed that you would get on with it and come home with straight As. Indeed if there were any queries, they typically addressed what were seen as shortcomings, or failures—all very Scottish: "Of course you passed your exams—but why didn't you get a better mark in that one?" So I don't think I bothered to talk much about anything and certainly not my lack of interest in the subjects I was studying.

HINDSIGHT 2.1: *Written in the 1970s*

Somewhere in those wood-floored corridors and stone stairways I met Wee Meg; four feet and eleven and three-quarter inches, tousled head, wide eager eyes. An elfish creature buried in some bulky sweater and the whole framed by the chaos of scattered books, posters, flags, records and empty coffee mugs that somehow characterized at once her room and her enthusiasm for living.

We traveled the country together as a twosome and in foursomes, summer and winter: Mull, early in the year with a week to cover one side of the island. Great banks of rhododendrons, sparkling sea, soft rain, and haggis boiled to sandwich heat over an open fire in the wet bracken (its twin we consigned to the deep with a stone tied to its tail).

I can still see the untidy bulk of her rucksack balanced incredibly on those childlike legs—all that could be seen of her as she felt her way painfully, barefoot, across the burn to the next campsite. We had rides on coal lorries, sheep lorries, and one unearthly journey in the shuddering, shiny womb of a brand-new aluminum-paneled furniture van. We slept in bus stations, railway stations, police stations, drove for hours, walked for hours, and out of this came a happy balance of hysterical clowning and silent rapport.

On one return trip from Stratford, she and I were walking north toward Carlisle when a police car passed us, slowed ahead, and turned into a layby. Meg was dressed for cold weather in heavy slacks, which, like most of her clothes, had to be rolled up many times at the bottom. The bobby returned our good-mornings and, after checking out Meg's huge untidy backpack and her rolled-up trousers, asked, "'Ow big was she when she started?"

Back in the hall, there was a corridor on the ground floor, with three or four music practice rooms which had upright pianos. Meg and I spent many hours making music there, her piano playing more than adequate for my knowledge of any of the pieces in the sheet music which was lying around these rooms, like "O My Beloved Father."

I became a member of two choirs and at one point found myself singing both Verdi's *Requiem* and Bach's *Mass in E minor*—one as a soprano, the other as an alto—all of this without being able to read a note of music. I preened myself, thinking that I was working from memory, until I discovered that it was extremely easy to sing almost anything so long as you were standing very close to a good strong sight-reader.

Around this time, I remember riding home to Newington after choir practice on top of a double-decker bus. We were humming a tune from *The Bohemian Girl,* probably "When Other Lips Their Tales of Love Shall Tell." Meg was harmonizing with me when a cultured voice behind us asked what we were singing. We turned to see a lovely old man, white-haired and with rimless glasses, formally dressed with a butterfly white collar, looking like someone from a time warp. He should have been framed, such a lovely head. The three of us had quite a conversation, and he was delighted to hear young people singing material which was dear to his heart. That bus trip was a lovely moment from these early years, and it has always stuck with me.

In second year, I discovered the Edinburgh University Folk Song Society through a lecture given at the Literary Society by Hamish Henderson, from the School of Scottish Studies. I had never heard of him, or of the school's archive of old Scottish songs and simply turned up to hear him give a talk on the oral tradition and traditional singers. This proved to be a life-changing experience, not so much because of the content of his lecture but rather because of his illustrations, one of which introduced me to Jeannie Robertson singing "The Overgate."

This was a song I had known all my life, but with a different tune and slightly different words.

> There is a ferm oot fae Crail
> It's neither big nor sma'
> Montgomery's the fermer's name
> And the place is East Newha'.*

I got very excited about this, sought out Hamish after his lecture, and never quite forgave him for responding to my own rendition with "Hmm, an interesting variant." It seemed so dismissive, not just of my mother's version—which had several verses unique to the East Neuk of Fife (bothy ballads are easy to localize, by changing place names or farmers' names to ones more familiar to the area)—but also of my excitement at discovering the musical framework which would turn my life around. And the best he could manage was that!

However, not for the last time Hamish went on to give advice which affected my whole life and career. He said, "If you're really interested in this material, you should go to the Folk Song Society." There I met Dolina Maclennan, Stuart Macgregor, Ella Ward, and Robin Hall, all of whom had roles to play in the revival of folk in Scotland. Dolina is fond of telling how, in the minutes of the society for the night I first turned up, she wrote a note: "New girl shows some promise." In any society, when someone new shows up members who are worthy of their salt will corner them and find out what they've got to offer. In my case, the voice was there, although it was very young, and what Dolina saw as "promise"

* This is my mother's version of "The Overgate," a bothy ballad that referred to the red-light district in Dundee, where agricultural workers went for their rest and recreation.

was a combination of both the new song material I had brought with me and the instrument I had been given to deliver it.

I started attending their ceilidhs in Ella and Simon Ward's second-story flat in Bernard Terrace. These were some of the best sessions in my life—although I suppose I should feel sorry for her neighbors. Our ceilidhs went on while there was still life in the guests and often finished with the pipes being played at 2:00 A.M. Bagpipes need plenty of space to spread their sound, and I can see why neighbors were nudged out of shape by having them played in an apartment block at that hour of the morning.

Hamish was always there, of course, glass in hand. His party piece was "Tail Toddle," during which he leaned forward from his considerable height of six feet three inches until the momentum carried his feet forward; somehow he always managed to get his head back and the impetus stopped before he hit the far wall. Never spilled a drop in the process! That's where I learned to sing "Tail Toddle."

Tail toddle, tail toddle
Tammy gars my tail toddle
But and ben wi' diddle doddle
Tammy gars my tail toddle.

Oor guidwife gaed ower tae Fife
For to buy a coal riddle
Lang ere she cam' back again
Tammy gart my tail toddle.*

It was also where Ella Ward, Stuart Macgregor, Robin Hall, and I came together and started singing as a folk group with the improbable name of The Night Hawks. How and when we actually started, I can't remember: it just sort of evolved that at ceilidhs we would sing together. From there it developed into doing the odd gig, and singing for beer—nobody ever thought of paying us. The only time I remember when the four of us were formally hired to get up on a stage together was as an opening group for Andy Stewart, at that point the Voice of Scotland. We thought: fame, at last.

*You don't really want a direct translation . . . but the summary is that Tommy had clearly introduced the young lady in question to the delights of physical passion while her mother was out shopping. For any obsessive translators, *gars* means "makes" and *but and ben* is "out and in." *Tail,* you can guess. Told you: innocence was better.

We learned a great deal. I sang melody, because I have no natural ear for harmony. I have to learn a harmony line almost as a separate melody, so I have hung out most of my life with people who could harmonize instinctively. Our repertoire was mostly the folk chestnuts of the 1950s, like "Michael, Row the Boat Ashore"—all material which was well known and widely heard on the radio. In this way we picked up some American folk songs as well as English and Scottish ones.

My great heroes at that time were the McEwen Brothers, Rory and Alex, who were among the first ever to get on television singing Scottish songs—an enormous step forward for traditional music. Many years later, when I was down in southwest Scotland, I phoned Rory and spoke to him. A delightful man, best known as a botanical artist.* I have never had the nerve to be a groupie, but I had so much pleasure and guidance from these singers that I am grateful to this day to have had a chance to talk to him however briefly, and to thank him, before he died. I still hear him in the background when I sing his setting of the Border rhyme "The Twa Rivers":

> Says Tweed tae Till, "What gars ye run sae still?"
> Says Till tae Tweed, "Though ye run wi' speed, and I run slaw,
> "For ae man that ye droon, I droon twa."†

I became increasingly involved in music during my university years. I was singing formally in choirs and less formally in pubs and folk clubs. Looking back, I spent more time making music—and shooting—than I did studying, because I had also joined the University Women's Rifle Club, which met once a week. This fitted perfectly with my idea of athleticism—lying in a prone position, .22 rifle shooting in an indoor range. It was cold but great fun and, because I was good at it, even greater fun. Problems arose when we moved out of doors, up onto Arthur's Seat and I tried a .303. The instructors counted the holes in the targets, because they could never find all my rounds. I used to tell them, "That's because they are all going through the same hole." That drew an old-fashioned

* Rory McEwen, *The Colours of Reality,* edited by Martyn Rix (paperback edition), £20.00, 224pp., 200+ color botanical paintings and black-and-white illustrations. Also available in hardback. London: Kew Publishing, 2013.

† "Says the Tweed to the Till, 'Why do you run so slowly?' / Says the Till to the Tweed, 'Although you run fast and I run slow, / For every man you drown, I drown two.'"

look, but, to back up my case, there were never any dead sheep lying around, so the missing rounds remained an unsolved mystery.

By the end of the third year I was really struggling with my academic work, not so much in terms of my grades as in being unable to generate any interest whatsoever in the subjects or even my own level of achievement. At its simplest, I found myself with no idea of why I was there.

This was when I had to look for help. As I mentioned earlier, I felt no sense of kinship with my assigned tutors and couldn't bring myself to talk to them about my troubles. Looking back, I am astonished that I reached out to Angus McIntosh to ask for help. But, once again, on the basis of a single lecture, I found myself instinctively trusting a senior figure, a professor and head of department. After his lecture, I went up to him and asked if I could make an appointment to see him.

Much later, when I apologized for taking up his time, he replied, "I went into teaching originally, because I was interested in students. Now that I'm head of department, I seldom see them. All my time and energy goes into administrative work—not through my choice, but simply the way in which the job has evolved. I am so relieved to discover that I haven't lost touch with the first reason I came here."

At that first meeting, he had no knowledge of my academic record but wasted no time in checking out both this and my course work. The next paper which came back from the tutor had an annotation on it from Angus: "This is not bad work; you are 19th out of 75 students, so you are doing just fine." That was the start. Angus not only rose to the occasion but became a lifelong friend.

Students panic or lose their way in studies all the time in universities. The standard treatment from any senior academic is to check, then reassure, then try to find a way in which to solve the problem—like changing course to medieval studies to take me away from the subjects which were turning me off completely. Angus made space to meet me several times and listen. I think he realized very quickly that conventional solutions wouldn't work, because he was dealing with someone who was slowly coming to the conclusion that she should be doing something else with her life. The problem wasn't so much the course as the whole context of university studies.

HINDSIGHT 2.2: *Recently, when I was searching for something else, I came across an old university examination paper, where I had stopped writing answers* *and simply written on every available margin of the four pages (see photo in the illustration gather). Clearly, it shows a crisis point, where I finally rebelled against university life and started out on the journey which has led me here. Yet I had completely forgotten about it. Strange to see these thoughts written in neat blue ink, after all these years, and stranger still to realize that everybody else in that room would have been scribbling like mad, trying to pass this very same exam. Here is what I wrote.*

I have a most peculiar sensation of unreality at this moment—complete and utter detachment. I suppose I've written about half a page and suddenly the hypocrisy of what I am sitting doing disgusts me. It's twenty-five to eleven and I don't think I plan to do any more. I have no right to sit exams with more or less the sole purpose of covering up just how little I know. I'm damned if I'll sit and flannel for two hours and waste somebody else's time in reading it.

As it is, there isn't and hasn't been the faintest sensation of nerves or remorse. What IS wrong with me? Have I just gone completely dead on this subject? It seems so bloody silly—translations, set phrases—what do I know about the way these poets' minds worked? If I could even think this was bravado (and I don't suppose I'm above that), I could admit, if only to myself, that I've been an irresponsible fool for weeks and that isn't much to be proud of. God knows I'm not proud of myself but I can't find it in me to be sorry.

What did Angus call it? "A deep unshakeable, positive integrity." Maybe. Somewhere inside there's been born a certainty of myself. Does this make any sense when I still don't know where I am going? But it's worth ten times the hell that is going to break loose when this little lot comes to light. To know what I am, even if what I am capable of has yet to be proven. Maybe I do face only my truth—but whose truth would I live by otherwise? "You can't please everybody"—so if you please yourself it's always a start and I don't mean on the level of being thoughtless of anyone else's comfort and peace of mind, but one's own.

Independent I certainly must be, and financial independence isn't so very far beyond me right now if the worst comes to the worst. My peace of mind is my own affair but this degree I owe to others. Funny way of showing how I honor a debt. Yet every admission brings a funny sort of release as if I'd conquered and gained control over another small stretch of rebellious territory. But the battle goes on, I'm still fighting like hell and wondering if, next time, I'll have any more luck with this stiff Fife neck. Pogo is right when he said: "Someday we may come face to face with the enemy and he is ourselves."*

* This was a slight misquote, under examination pressure. What Pogo really said is, "We have met the enemy and he is us." I prefer my own version.

What have I straightened out in the last months? Seems still to be "an organized state of chassis." This was a very fair exam too. Hell's teeth! Why can't I settle for half-way in some things when I sit on the fence all the time in others? Am I in danger of regarding it as my particular duty to oppose ALL *conventional and social pressures? Just as a matter of principle?*

There's so much to live for. I've spent the first hour of this stretch quashing an almost irresistible desire to sing—I would appear to have little cause to be so ridiculously happy and unconcerned. Completely unconcerned but NOT *uncaring.*

I've run out of margin space, but not time. How do I fill in the next two hours?

When I was in my early teens at school, after my time off with rheumatic fever, I started to stammer. My parents asked a doctor if they should bring me in, but he replied, "No, you're a little too close; wait until somebody outside the family mentions it." Eventually a neighbor—the same lady at whom I stuck out my tongue—said to Bluebell, "What's wrong wi' your Jean? She's stammering." I was hauled in for all manner of tests, including some with a psychiatrist, who returned the diagnosis that so far as he could see I was perfectly normal and he couldn't give any explanation for my stammer.

Over time, I have come to see this stammer as a sign of stress: when I am very tired and stressed-out, I find myself starting to stutter and searching for the beginnings of words. I've come to recognize this as a form of a parachute brake—*Watch what you're doing; you're pushing things too hard.* And at this very point in my university studies, I was conscious that I was starting to stammer again, to search for words.

Angus, bless the man, sat me down and talked through the options which were open to me. Nothing that I suggested was very sensible. Going as an au pair to France: "And then what?" he fired back at me. Going to Aviemore in the Highlands, which was just opening up as an outdoor center, as a dishwasher in the winter and a walking guide in the summer: "Well, that sounds interesting—but then what?" Angus didn't mess about: he was straight to the point. Then I added, "I also have an invitation to go out to California, to sing at a friend's wedding. Maybe I should just travel for a while?" This drew a thoughtful look, and, after kicking the idea around, he said, "Go home and get your passport ready." The invitation to sing at her wedding was from my American buddy, Marilyn, back in the halls of residence.

To get my passport in order might seem to be strange advice from a man whose first responsibility was to keep the brighter students working through his degree courses, but Angus never lost his gift of staying in touch with people, his ability to communicate with them, see things from their point of view, and then to understand.

I have blessed him many a time. It was also Angus who suggested at one point during the third and fourth years that I should go and see Zana Smart. She was the wife of the university chapel organist and a trained singer and voice teacher in her own right. This was one of the serendipitous encounters that have occurred from time to time in my life, just when I desperately needed something to happen.

I talked to her and told her that I thought I would like to train my voice. Her response was probably one of the most intelligent questions anybody has ever asked of me. She said, "That's wonderful. What do you want to train it to do?" Any other teacher might have automatically assumed that I wanted to be a classical singer and trained me accordingly. But Zana had the sense to realize that I didn't know what the hell I was asking of her. In those days, a classical singer clasped her hands under her bosom, took her stance with T-junction feet, tautened every muscle in her body, and launched forth. In folk singing, you just open your mouth and let it flow—it's a more natural form of expression. She kept me for over half an hour, running me through a phrase from an Italian art song, "Amarilli Mia Bella." She asked me to sing it, and I did.

Then she said: "Good, now try it again—lie on the floor." I looked at her oddly. It seemed a strange request. She repeated: "Lie down and sing . . . down on your back . . . there . . . like that . . . now sing." When I did, she asked, "Well? Did you feel any difference?" "Yes," I said. "I most certainly did." "Good. Basically all you have to do is to learn how to sing in a standing position, as relaxed as you were there," she said. "You're doing nothing wrong and won't damage your voice, singing as you are. Now I suggest you go away and sing for twenty years, and then come back."

Brilliant advice—however strange it seemed at the time. No voice matures until one reaches the mid-thirties, no matter what the singer wants to do with it. No young voice should be worked too hard, if it is still to be used with seventy-five years on the clock. Susan Boyle, the overnight sensation on the *Britain's Got Talent* television show is a case in point:*

* Susan Boyle on *Britain's Got Talent:* This TV show was designed to showcase young wailing wannabees, all glitzed up in their best and sexiest performance gear. When Susan Boyle, a dumpy older lady, appeared, there was much eye rolling accompanied by snide asides from the showbiz judges. Then she opened her

she was a good, solid mature woman, and when she opened her mouth on television, the voice came out fully formed. But it had taken thirty-five years to get where it was going, while she sang for herself and her family when she felt like it. In Zana's eyes, I was still a kid—which was why she was telling me to come back to her when my voice, the instrument, had matured. Her advice could not have been more appropriate to who I was, when I was, and where I wanted to go. I was lucky enough to meet her many years later and tell her just how much her guidance had meant to me at that very early age.

As for Angus and his advice to get my passport ready, the decision to leave my university course was never discussed with my parents. There were two main reasons for this. First, I figured that it was up to me to handle the problem: my parents had got me thus far, and it was my responsibility to take over and sort out my life. Second, the family had my future already mapped out as the first of the clan to go to university, and I suspected that their advice would have been, "Well, all you have to do is another nine months; why not just finish the degree and then worry about what you're going to do?"

Predictable advice—and quite possibly an injustice to them that I imagined it—but it was advice which didn't even start to deal with the problem facing me, and it wasn't what I wanted or needed to hear. How could they ever understand why I wanted to leave, or just how much I felt myself to be in the wrong place at this stage in my life?

It took someone from outside these familial expectations—Angus and Zana—to understand the fundamental nature of my disenchantment with university. Both sensing that here was an undergraduate who was perfectly capable of completing a degree but should not be made to keep her nose to the grindstone. Instead, here was someone who should be treated as an adult, with a good singing instrument that should be given a chance to develop itself elsewhere. University, far from being a springboard for me, was restricting and stifling.

My decision to leave university without discussing the matter fully with my parents tortured me for a while both during and after the event. However, by the time I was overseas and running hard, any guilt I felt

---

mouth and sang, leaving the judges shell-shocked, because she clearly possessed more talent than they ever had owned. They weighed the public's votes by the sackful, while the other wannabees sneaked off home, muttering darkly.

had to take a number and stand in line among the other issues—like simple survival—facing me.

The need to leave was so compelling that it might seem as if I had decided what to do after leaving university. Nothing could be further from the truth. Yes, I wanted to go and sing at my friend's wedding, and, yes, I wanted to take some time out to travel . . . but after that? Angus's insistent question *And then what?* still echoed in my mind. I had no answer, other than that if I was to search and find my proper place, my first step must be to raise the money to pay for my flight to California. Once there, I would take a time-out, try just living for a while, and see what fresh ideas presented themselves.

To start earning cash, I went on a summer tour of the Highlands with a Scottish country dance band. There were four singers with Angus Sutherland's band, two men and two women. We had a Mod Gold Medalist tenor;* the other lassie was also a Gaelic singer, and the other man and I sang old Scottish songs—two from each tradition.

I have one vivid memory from that tour. The gold medalist and I went out onto the Invergarry Bridge one night, above the river and by the light of a full moon, and he sang "Sine Bhan" ("Fair Jean") in a voice that would have melted the rocks, never mind a woman's heart. Next day his fiancée showed up. And I thought, "Aye, right . . ."

I had a lot of fun on that tour, but I was always aware that at some stage I would have to go home to my parents and tell them what my future plans were, now that I had left university. An ordeal waiting for me, fueled by both their disappointment and my own uncertainties, but it would have to be faced, and I tried to brace myself. At first there was mutual defensive silence; then, after a few days, when my father was driving me up into town he asked, "Have you decided yet, what you're going to do?" "Yes—I'm going to California," I replied. The poor man nearly drove our car into a wall. He knew nothing beyond the fact that I was taking some time out after leaving university. This was the first indication he'd had that I was thinking seriously of getting out of Scotland.

I went to teach in Kirkcaldy from September until February to raise the rest of the money needed to buy my airline ticket. Me, a teacher, after turning up at the last minute every morning when I was at school?

* The Mod is the main festival of Scottish Gaelic literature, song, arts, and culture, comparable to the Welsh Eistedfodd.

However, I needed the money, and this was the only way I could earn it. The alarm was set for bright and early—and I went into my first class with the head teacher's words still ringing in my ears: "Most of these kids are only waiting until they are old enough to leave school, so you'll never teach them anything. All I ask is that you keep them from breaking the furniture."

I felt a bit like a Christian in a Roman circus, getting my last pep talk before going out to face the lions. But I survived, grew tough, and learned to bend the rules creatively—like teaching the girls sewing and dressmaking, and encouraging them to talk about their boyfriends in the Friday afternoons when we should all have been doing arithmetic. All is fair, in love and teaching.

Yet, while I worked and waited, there was always a sense of uncertainty. Sure, I had left university, and I would be leaving Scotland as soon as I had earned enough to buy my plane ticket. But to what sort of life would that plane ticket take me? Over everything hung the black cloud of guilt at walking out on my parents'—indeed the broader family's—expectations. Of course, you take responsibility for your own life and make your own decisions, but that never leaves you blind as to the way in which your decisions can hurt someone else.

HINDSIGHT 2.3: *Written on August 2, 1970, who knows where or why?*

SCHIEHALLION, JANUARY 1961
I remember nothing of the drive to and from the mountain. I suppose we talked, but of what I cannot recall. It was magnificent weather—spring, three months too early, with delicate cirrus clouds across a translucent sky.

Scotland at its most beautiful—clear, rugged, strong, and capable of evoking such emotion in the turn of a corner, the breasting of a hill, that it caught the breath and clouded the vision.

I can visualize the road, the parked car, the laughing chatter as we climbed a fence and squelched our way across the low ground, leaving the sodden field for the coarse bracken and the short sheep turf of the north face. The sun had scarcely reached the lower slopes and in the shadow, the wind, keening in from the northwest, was a constant reminder of the moods of this mountain.

I had no company—no human company—for the rest of that climb. Arriving sweating and breathless somewhere short of the summit on the sunny south face, I think I sat for hours, the world spread at my feet. I loved this country. How could I plan to leave—for years maybe? What were the petty problems that had occasioned the decision to emigrate, compared with the passion that such a day and such a place could always rouse in me?

The sadness passed: I walked rather slowly back to the top of the rise and as the sheltered sun gave way suddenly to the ear-numbing northwester, I was swept with an explosive exhilaration. I ran, like a wind that knows no problems, no fears of a world unexplored. There was no thought of broken bones, twisted ankles in that wild, downhill careering—but Schiehallion understood and wouldn't let me come to harm.

I slithered, rolled, and tumbled to a halt, flat on my back, gasping and a little light-headed. My breathing steadied and I rolled over, arms flung wide and my cheek pressed to the turf. The world faded and I felt myself enfolded in some inexplicable, all-pervasive embrace. I could never, would never leave this country entirely. Through my palms, through my trembling legs, and close, close to my own, I felt the heart of the mountain beat.

On March 7, my mother came as far as Glasgow with me and put me on the Prestwick Airport bus. That memory lies somewhere between excruciatingly painful and numb. We were, both of us, trapped in the Scottish culture where neither of us knew how—or wanted—to open up and show the depth of our feelings for the other.

There was very little said; then, at the last minute, she pressed a five-pound note into my hand. In those days, it would have represented a good deal of money for her. Indeed, it was invaluable to me because, while I had earned enough to cover the flight and the cost of the bus to the airport, I had thought no further ahead than that. It had never occurred to me that I would need money to live on, once I hit the States. Without Bluebell's last minute gesture, I would have landed there with empty pockets.

I left her standing at the roadside in Glasgow, watching my bus move off.

It was a final image that haunted me but, in fairness, in my own mind I wasn't leaving forever. I was simply getting out from under my problems and fully believed that in eighteen months or two years, maybe four at most, I would be coming home with a clearer mind and purpose. I had no intention at that point of emigrating, only of completing the final steps down my exit route from the drudgery of university, while trying to block out the repercussions of this decision on my family.

I think I was in shock, in some form of self-induced anesthesia—*Can't deal with the situation; it's more than I can handle.* So you put your problems in a box and batten the lid down until such time as you can deal with or let the problems out, one at a time. In this numb state, I remember nothing of the flight. Only that, as we came in to land at John F. Kennedy Airport (Idlewild back then), the lady sitting behind me, who must have seen that I was on my own, leaned over the seat to offer me two quarters. "These are what you tip the porters," she said.

She might even have watched me on the bus to Prestwick and knew that I was green. It was my first experience of years and years of spontaneous kindness on the part of strangers, so typical of Americans. They are invariably outgoing and impulsively generous, and I have been a beneficiary of their kindness for many years.

I landed in America with eleven dollars in my pocket—the converted value of my mother's five-pound note—and by the time I landed in San Francisco airport, to be picked up by Neil and Marilyn (to whose wedding I was going), it was dark. They drove me from the airport to a tiny village called Woodside, in a valley about forty-five miles south. Having left Prestwick on a March morning, with the clouds down to the lum heids* and a steady drizzle, I awakened next morning to California sunshine, full spring, and everything in flower.

It left me in a total time warp, climate warp, head warp—the lot . . .

* Chimney heads or chimney pots, to vent the smoke from coal fires.

CHAPTER 3

Flowers and First Steps

Wakening in California felt as if I had died and gone to Heaven. After being cooped up for endless hours in a cramped and dismal metal bubble during two long-haul flights from Prestwick, then being driven in pitch-black darkness to Woodside by Marilyn and Neil, I opened my eyes to a blaze of blue sky and flowers. I found myself in a totally different time zone, a completely different and warmer climate, and an utterly different lifestyle.

It was a bit like being reborn. All the problems and disappointments I had left behind in Scotland were tied up in a package and laid away to be dealt with at some future date—or not at all. California provided a fresh start, and I was raring to go.

Marilyn's parents, the Jordans, had a farm, but not a working farm, like the grain and tattie farms I knew back in Fife. Harry Jordan worked in lumber and commuted to San Francisco every day, so he left the house at 5:00 A.M. to drive up the Bayshore Freeway. Pauline Jordan, never called anything but Mudds, did volunteer nursing work and was also an usher at the San Francisco Opera House. This opera-house role proved to be a marvelous connection for me, and I spent many nights working as a part-time usher up in the gods of the theater.* Looking back, I doubt Harry and Mudds ever saw each other, with her working nightshift and not getting home until after he had left for work. However their six kids suggested that they met somewhere along the line.

Their house stood on a slight rise, and the family's four or five Rambler station wagons were usually drawn up on the drive in front of it, leaving it looking like the forecourt of a car dealership. There was also a well-worn pickup truck which was given to me for transportation

* gods of the theater: upper balconies—closest to heaven!

around the valley and to the city, where I often went dancing. The sight of a young girl in a cotton frock driving this big truck probably freaked out some of the local taxi drivers, but I had a lot of fun with that vehicle.

The Jordans' house had plenty of ground around it—that's why it was called a farm out there—and this was where Harry kept his collection of exotic birds. These screeched endlessly throughout the day, adding bizarre noises to a scene already vastly different from Fife. Some of his birds were genuinely rare, like the Chinese silver pheasant. He had a golden pheasant too, but the silver pheasant blew my mind; it was such an elegant creature.

Mudds's father, Gramps, also lived in the household. In the early days he and Paul and Pete, the two younger boys, approached me and asked, "Do you play cards?" Some instinct prompted me to reply, "No, I don't play any kind of cards game except Patience." Wise move—one of the best things I ever did—because they were looking for a fourth for pinochle, and they were absolute fiends, card-playing terrorists. Thank God I had the sense not to get sucked into that!

Marilyn was number three of the six children. Oddly enough, although I had come to California to sing at her wedding, I have very little memory of the wedding ceremony itself. I sang "Mairi's Wedding" at the reception at Marilyn's request. This was an informal occasion, nothing like the weddings we had on wet Saturday afternoons back in Scotland, when the wifies were all dressed in their best. It was my first introduction to the much more casual way of life in California. Neil was a really nice lad, and he and Marilyn sponsored my immigration.

When I landed in California, Jim, the eldest boy, had just left home to go to university; Harriet the oldest sister had gone off on the SS *Hope*,* and with Marilyn now married, that left Eleanor, Paul, and Pete still at home. Pete, in particular, was delighted to have me there because he was under sixteen, which meant he had no driving license. The Jordan farm was far out in the countryside, so even the village was too far away for comfortable walking. Now if he wanted to go down to the Woodside store for ice cream or anything else, he knew he had a Scottish sucker who would slip behind the wheel and drive him there.

* A former naval hospital ship that was donated to Project HOPE in 1958; thereafter spent many years bringing help and teaching American medical procedures across the world.

HINDSIGHT 3.1: *Woodside Valley, written in 1972*

Fine, so it was 5,000 miles away from Fife—but this could as well have been on the other side of the world. Early morning, the air in the Valley still crisp and zinging, while the sun shone down in what looked like being another perfect, sunny day. They were all perfect sunny days here, because the San Francisco fogs never seemed to get past the line of hills between us and them. Prestwick now, like the memory of a bad dream which you only wanted to forget.

Riding high in the battered old truck Harry had given me, heading down to the village with Pete at my side. OK, so I had been hooked into driving him somewhere again—too early for ice cream this time—but I didn't care. I rolled down the cab window, let the clear and scented air blow round my head.

Then there it was . . . the gentle hills which molded the Valley, were suddenly covered by a sea of lavender blue flowers. Not bushy and rough, like heather, more a soft low carpet that clung to and up over the rounded slopes. That bright blue color, everywhere.

"What is it?" I asked Pete.

"Huh?"

"That wonderful sea of blue flowers out there."

He studied it, frowning. A 14-year-old boy has no use for flowers.

"Oh . . . them," he said at last. "Godetia, that's all."

"How do you know?" I asked.

He shrugged. "Because that's what our drive is called—Godetia Avenue. Then he stared through the windscreen again. "Hey," he said. "Can't you make this go just a little faster? Huh?"

The great thing about landing in a situation like this was that the Jordan kids were up for any kind of casual labor: the whole valley knew that if they were looking for a dog-sitter, baby-sitter, house cleaner, car driver, or groceries collector, they had only to call the Jordans and somebody would do the job for them. I walked in just as three of the older ones left, slipping seamlessly into a going concern. This solved my immediate problem of what was I going to do for work, with barely a nickel to my name. Within weeks, I had a regular clientele of my own, looking after young children and cleaning houses.

It didn't take me long to find out that cleaning houses was vastly preferable to child-minding. These American kids were . . . challenging. By far the most difficult kids in the valley belonged to a couple, both of whom were psychiatrists. Those kids were terrifying, running wild. I often wondered what happened to them when they grew up—Did they continue as they had started or did they grow into being perfectly normal and well-adjusted adults? There were few signs of that back then: they were one hell of a handful. Despite—or maybe because of—all that psychological support, that was one seriously wild household.

The eldest was Suzie, who was seven. I had barely started working there when I heard her chatting casually on the phone to a friend. Chatting *casually,* at seven? I could remember the terror I felt at sixteen, when the phone rang in our house, and I didn't know how to answer it. California was a different world.

I heard this seven-year-old chatting at length to her friend and saying, "Oh, and I have a new Scottish maid." I thought, no, I don't think I can live with that one. So I pointed out to her that, actually, I was working for her mother, and she just happened to be there. Suzie and I never did get round to sharing the same script. Battle lines were drawn on the day she dropped a two-pound ornamental candle on my bare foot, despite my explaining to her that this wasn't a good idea because there were so many small and delicate bones down there. She paused, thought about it for a moment, and then went right on with dropping it as planned. Servants were dispensable. My reflex action, even before I yelled out in pain, was to give her a backhander. I don't think anybody in her life had so much as raised their voice to her, let alone their hand. When she bounced off the wall, she looked at me in absolute horror, so taken aback that it never occurred to her to cry. If her mother had ever learned of the incident, she would have prosecuted me, but, dear God, that heavy brute of a candle hurt and I thought Suzie had left me crippled for life. It would be nice to think that my instinctive action helped to turn Suzie into a better adult, but I doubt that; it would take more than a single skelp to make much impression on that young lady.

Brad was the older boy. He scared the life out of me one day, early in my tenure as child-minder, when I found him lying on the floor, drumming it with his heels and his fists, his face dark purple. I thought he was having a major seizure. In fact it was a temper tantrum, about which I knew nothing—we didn't do temper tantrums in Fife, least of all in Bluebell's house, not if you expected to survive—and his mother came in to say "Now *Bradee. . .*" to try to pacify him.

The first time he tried this on his own with me, I studied him for a couple of minutes; then, in case he might do himself damage from banging his head on the hard floor, I picked him up by a fistful of clothing and carried him still kicking and screaming through to his bedroom and dropped him on his bed. At the doorway, I turned to tell him, "When you're finished, you can come out." That tantrum lasted for about twenty seconds, once he realized that I wasn't buying into it and that his usual ploy wasn't going to work. They were all very bright kids, but they had their psychiatrist parents wrapped round their collective finger.

At the opposite end of the brightness scale, they had a bone-headed Weimaraner who was about as well-disciplined as the bairns and added to the sense of anarchy about once a month by galloping through one of the plate-glass windows around the atrium in the middle of the house. The dog barely blinked, but his glass bill cost more than his dog food.

The youngest bairn, Todd, was an absolute delight, because he wasn't old enough to try anything on with me; instead, he just did what he damned well pleased. I went out of the house one day to see him thirty feet up in a pine tree. I have no idea how he got up there, but I knew if I shouted at him, it might scare him and he might fall. Nor could I go up there after him, because I wouldn't be able to carry him down if I ever got that far. I finally decided that if he had managed to climb up there under his own steam, then he could probably get down too, so I went back inside the house, hoping for the best. Sure enough, a few minutes later he came in, none the worse. But that wasn't funny, and those few minutes of waiting felt like hours. He was a precocious two-and-a-half- or three-year-old. He was never quiet and, one day when I realized that I hadn't heard him for a bit, I went outside to look. He was in the front yard with his small wheelbarrow—we were well off the quiet village road and perfectly safe—and he had found a stack of sawdust somewhere and was taking barrowloads of this across to stuff, one handful at a time, into the gas tank of his mother's car. It was too late to stop him now; the damage was done. I decided to let her find out in her own time.

On the day I was leaving, Todd went missing. I went out to find him and say goodbye, only to discover that he had climbed two shelves up on the garage wall—he could climb like a puggy,* that one—where everything was carefully stored out of the children's reach, and he had pulled down about a gallon of green paint onto the garage floor. Now he was

*"Puggy" has two possible translations: in Fife it just seems to mean "climbs like a monkey"; in more civilised parts of Scotland, a puggy was the small pug engine that hauled coal and iron ore from the mines up steep gradients on narrow-gauge rail lines to the ultimate distribution points.

having a wonderful time sitting in the mess, playing. Paint in those days wasn't water-based, so the human clean-up job would be horrendous. I thought, "Well, at least he's not drinking it; maybe just tell his mother that he's in the garage, playing, and leave fast."

Californian laidback lifestyle was exactly what I needed—simply to live for a while without responsibility. Sure, I was responsible for the kids, to know where they were and what they were doing, and watch they didn't come to any desperate harm but, working for a dollar an hour, I would go to someone's house, look after their kids for four hours, leave with four dollars in my pocket, and that was it. I didn't have to do any studying, I didn't have to worry about exams, there was no urgency to sit down and think about finding a new career for myself. These weeks in the valley gave me the time-out I wanted.

I met Bill and Jeannie Golder and their daughter Holly in the village after doing some house cleaning for them. They became friends, and we stayed in touch for many years until they moved, and I lost their new address. Jeannie was one of the older women who used to make me think at that stage, "When I grow up, I want to be just like her." There were many such role models in California, nothing like anyone I had ever met in Scotland. Jeannie was a larger-than-life character, with wonderful black curly hair, a lively sense of humor, and a great belly laugh. I often wondered how her daughter Holly got on, because there were many times when she must have felt herself to be in direct competition with her mother.

Everything and everyone was new to me. If it is possible to fall in love with a place and its people, then I fell in love with California. I didn't really see much of the Jordan family, other than the boys who were still at home. However the valley was full of British au pairs, and there was one lass from Liverpool and another Scots lass in particular who became friends. I was the one with the driver's license and the vehicle, so they would arrange their nights off—I could do what I liked—and I would drive them to the movies in San Francisco or to some place where there was dancing.

I have always loved and been involved in Scottish country dancing, even at the University of Edinburgh. Now, I found this invaluable as a form of social contact and entry. If you are ever looking for a gathering of Scots in America, the easiest way to find them is to search out the local Scottish country dancing group. Otherwise, Scots simply vanish into the undergrowth. There are no Scottish pubs or Scottish restaurants scattered around, even though there always seems to be an Irish pub.

That intrigues me, because we Scots are world travelers and have been for generations. When you meet it has always been "Whaur are ye fae? Scotland? Gi'e us yer haun'. Whauraboots in Scotland? Fife? Gi'e us baith yer haun's!"* Our sense of national identity is strong, yet we never seem to go out of the way to track each other down.

Over those first months in California, I did a lot of Scottish country dancing but somehow singing never crossed my mind. I stayed at the Jordan farm for six months, from March into August, and it isn't a time that I associate with any sort of public performance. One day, out of the blue, a letter arrived in the mail from someone in Michigan called Paul Endicott. I had never heard of him, but I discovered later that he was a manager of folk artists. His letter rocked me onto my heels: It didn't even say *"Would you like?"* but rather *"I have booked you into a club in Philadelphia on these dates for a two week gig at the end of August."* That gave me six weeks to get my thoughts in order. Did I want to be a paid performer? You bet I did. In high summer, I took off with a suitcase full of the cotton dresses I had made while teaching in Kirkcaldy—on the Friday afternoons when, instead of teaching arithmetic, I had taught the students to sew, and we talked about many things, such as which teachers were good-looking and which they fancied—things that enthralled fourteen- and fifteen-year-old girls. It was my most popular lesson of the week.

With my suitcase full of summer clothes, I headed off to Philadelphia, using the money I had saved from my casual work in the valley. Much later, I found out that Hamish Henderson had been at work in the background, although I never did discover how he knew of Paul Endicott. Endicott himself, I never met, but his letter went on to tell me that he had arranged a fee of $175 a week, which sounded like a king's ransom, after working for $1 an hour. There was no indication of who would be responsible for my travel, or accommodation, or anything else, but Endicott's letter finished by saying that he (through Hamish again) had also been in contact in Philadelphia with Dr. Ken Goldstein, who worked for Prestige International Records and who wanted to do a recording with me. I thought, "I am going to be rich and famous," and set off without a single doubt or misgiving. It is the oldest truism in the world: if something sounds too good to be true, it generally is. It became my first professional lesson, and it was learned the hard way.

* "Where are you from? Scotland? Let me shake your hand. Whereabouts in Scotland? Fife? Give me both your hands!"

I flew to Philly, my second plane journey but this time with more than eleven dollars in my pocket. I had squirreled away some money which covered the travel and left me something to live on for a few weeks, while still leaving enough cash in reserve to get me back to the Jordan farm in California. My original plan was to spend three weeks, maybe a month, in Philly.

From the airport, I checked into the YWCA in downtown Philadelphia, since I didn't know where else to go. That, in itself, was quite an experience. I spent my first night in the YWCA sitting up in bed and listening (I hope sympathetically) to someone who was either drunk or on drugs, or simply miserable, who poured out the story of her wayward life to me over the hours when I should have been sleeping.

Bleary-eyed, I turned up next day at the club, to find that I was "auditioning," which meant performing without getting paid, singing to an audience in a coffee shop for a couple of sets a night, while the club owner "made up his mind." My songs would probably have been drawn from the repertoire I had gathered from home and university, a mixture of traditional Scottish with the odd American folk song that I had picked up along the way. It certainly was unaccompanied, because at that point I neither owned nor could I play a guitar.

Having sung for three nights, with no indication whatsoever that there was going to be payment or any contract offered, my instinct was that the owner of the club was a chancer of the highest order, and I decided that the arrangement simply wasn't going to work. I phoned Ken Goldstein in Hatboro, which was close to Philly. He confirmed that Hamish had contacted him; however, the dates which Paul Endicott had given me hadn't been agreed to with Ken, who was teaching in Texas over that time. Nevertheless, he said, "Come up and we'll talk about it." I found my way to Ken's place by asking people for directions—something I have always done, because locals are usually incredibly helpful if they think you're lost and you have an accent which is completely unlike theirs. Especially when it's a Scottish accent.

Ken and Rochelle Goldstein welcomed me, quite literally, with open arms and the Goldstein household became my first professional short-term base or home. They had only the two girls back then, and Ken was one of these incredibly focused guys who couldn't work unless he was sitting at the kitchen table with the television going in one corner and two kids yelling in the other and his wife also trying to attract his attention in between. There he would sit, buried in a book, oblivious to everything around him. I was fascinated, never having seen anything like this before, first, because we didn't have a telly and, second, because if anyone had tried to read a book and ignore other people in Bluebell's house, they would have had their lug* skelped. Ken and Rochelle were a wonderful couple, so kind and hospitable.

Ken had spent a year in Scotland doing a Ph.D. thesis on Lucy Stewart of Fetterangus, and he knew a great deal more about the folk songs of the Northeast than I will ever know. He was delighted to find a singer who could also work with this unaccompanied traditional music. He didn't have a recording studio himself—although he possessed an incredible library in which I often got lost for hours—but he worked for Prestige International Records. With Rudy van Gelder as our sound engineer in a studio in New Jersey, which could have been a church hall, we cut that first record in seven straight hours. Normally you think in terms of recording sessions, then sitting down to listen to them, then going back to edit parts, but I knew nothing of this and simply sang for seven hours, and he got his LP out of it. Ken gave me a completely free hand in the songs I chose; he was perfectly happy to record whatever I wanted to sing. That recording session happened after he had come back from teaching at the tail end of 1961, when I was based in Greenwich Village at Miki Isacson's flat.

After that first contact, and agreement in principle to do the LP, I stayed with the Goldsteins for five days. No payment for my singing at the club was ever likely to be made (indeed the owner later ran off with all the funds), and it was still too early in my career for me to have learned to be a professional houseguest, so as the days passed I became increasingly edgy at placing these nice folks in a position where they were feeding me and giving me free accommodation—that was not their responsibility. I felt I should move out as soon as possible, and I decided to go to New York, having got a whiff of the big cities as opposed to the sheltered and cloistered existence I had led in California. Looking back, I think I was starting to feel my oats and to stretch my nearly nonexistent wings. I had still the wherewithal to get back to California, so I decided to use whatever surplus funds were left to go and look at the Big Apple. A BIG decision, made as casually as that. I still break out in a cold sweat when I think about it—and what could easily have gone wrong.

When I announced my intention, I don't think it occurred to the Goldsteins to ask me what I planned to do there. Ken and Rochelle were

* Ear.

a focal point for musicians who were on the move, particularly from the traditional music scene, and they simply did their best to help. By random chance, Bob and Evelyn Beers breezed by in passing with their little VW, which had Bob's psaltery—a pretty large instrument like my dad's hammer dulcimer, but plucked—in the back. When their VW left again it took me with them, squeezed into the back beside their instruments and rolling into New York City.

As we entered to city and were heading through one of the tunnels, Evelyn turned and asked: "Where can we drop you off?" "Is there a YWCA?" I replied. It was the only place I knew might take me in. They turned a little pale and Evelyn said, "Go there and you might never be heard of again." Maybe that was a little unkind, but they were looking out for me. Bob muttered, "We must know somebody she can stay with."

Here were two more people that I met by chance and who became lifelong friends. They stopped somewhere for Bob to make a phone call, then he drove me to No. 1 Sheridan Square, second floor, in Greenwich Village and took me up. As we opened the door, I heard a blast of bluegrass music, and I thought, "Oh how nice, a ceilidh, but why in the middle of the afternoon?" It was the Greenbriar Boys, rehearsing for a gig they were doing in a local club. In my total innocence, I had walked smack into the 1961 folk revival in Greenwich Village—and if that isn't serendipity, I don't know what is.

I have always said that I lead a charmed existence. There I was, dropping into New York City on a whim, knowing nobody, no job of any kind on offer, yet Bob and Evelyn delivered me right into the middle of exactly the place I needed to be— not only because of the music but also because of the apartment which became my second home, off and on, over the next few years.

Miki Isaacson's apartment was always full of people. She simply said "Welcome" and added me to the ranks of itinerant musicians who slept on her floor each night. She knew Bob and Evelyn, so there were hugs all round before they headed off to their own base in the city and left me standing with my suitcase.

Don't make the mistake of thinking that Miki's apartment was designed to be a guest house. You came in off the corridor to her studio apartment and on your right was a bathroom, on your left a Pullman kitchen—long and narrow—and then you walked into this "single end." There was a double bed and a couch, behind which many bedrolls and sleeping bags were neatly rolled up and tucked out of sight. There were usually eight of us in there—something which I didn't tell too many people back home at the time, because their immediate assumption would be that I had gone hippie and joined a commune. It was anything but; Miki ran her place like an army camp; she had to, or we would have killed each other.

At the time, all I registered was that here I was in New York City, with a place to stay. Miki wasn't a performer, but she loved the music and saw her own contribution as providing crash space for itinerant musicians. None of us had any money. That was the nature of the beast: if musicians were to work, then they had to travel; and travel in the United States is generally long-distance and expensive; therefore, they were seldom left with enough money from the gig to pay rent. Paul Endicott's letter was typical of the scene. You got a flat-rate contract which left you responsible for your own travel costs, food, and accommodation. Even when you were on your way to becoming established, there was seldom much of a margin left. So you learned to take any free accommodation that someone might offer. I became close friends with Miki until she died and used her apartment in Sheridan Square as my New York home whenever I was on that side of the country.

While the faces changed across the years, most of us became at least part-time regulars and formed almost an adoptive family, looking after each other. The ones who were earning bought food for the fridge and for everybody. If you had no work, you paid this back by doing the house cleaning and the laundry. We all contributed when we could, and learned to live on PB&J for most of the time.

The Greenbriar Boys didn't stay there, but only used the apartment for rehearsal space, because there was nowhere else where they could make that kind of music in the middle of the day. Johnny Herald, with his sharp elfin face, was my introduction to the high "mountain voice," the head voice sound that is so evocative of Appalachian music and country music. Ralph Rinzler was on the mandolin—they had changed personnel by the time I met them. He finished up as cofounder of the Smithsonian Folk Festival and director of Folklife Programs there. Bob Yellin was the banjo player, while Johnny Herald played the flat-pick guitar and did the singing. They made a great sound, and I have been a devotee of bluegrass ever since. Among the other regulars at Miki's we had Ramblin' Jack Elliott and Bob Dylan, who hit the big city almost exactly at the same time as I did. One of my early conversation stoppers was that I used to live with Bob Dylan: he was just a fresh-faced kid out of the Midwest who was in exactly the same position as I was, which meant mostly raiding rather than contributing to the communal fridge in Miki's apartment. We shared a gig at Gerde's Folk City once, but that came a little later.

With everyone struggling to make a breakthrough, you might have expected the atmosphere to be competitive and edgy. Nothing could have been further from the truth; it was incredibly familial. Without overstating it too much, as usually the only female among the group I regarded these guys as brothers. They were very helpful, not just then but also later in my career. If one of them got a gig somewhere, he would always suggest my name to the owner of the club or coffeehouse, trying to get some work for me. We were all in the same boat—if we hadn't been in Miki's apartment, we would probably have been sleeping in the park.

That apartment placed us on the edge of the main action, near The Limelight and Gerde's Folk City, the latter being the the focal point for anybody starting out. Living there, we bumped into everybody coming and going in the folk scene—like the Clancy Brothers, who were just starting to make it big at that time.

In addition to these better-known figures, we had one young guy staying with us who worked in a bank during the day and did his music at night. He was a brilliant banjo player, only eighteen, and he was basically trying to escape from his mother. He had arrived only a few days before me, and I have no idea how he stumbled onto Miki, but she had taken him under her wing like a born house mother. She said to him one day, "Have you put a clean shirt on?" "Yes, of course I have," he answered. "OK," she replied. Then, next morning, "Are you sure you have a clean shirt?" "Yes."

It turned out that he had three white shirts, which he simply cycled—he didn't know how to wash them—wearing each for a day, then hanging it up. We had a hassle every morning, to get him up and out to his work at the bank, and the first thing he did when he came back from there was to hang up the white shirt, get into his T-shirt and haul out his banjo. Unfortunately, he tried this at 3:00 A.M. one morning, when he had a tune running through his head and wanted to try it out. The result was a shower of books and shoes from every corner of the room. I often wonder if his tune ever made it, after a start like that. Or what happened to him; did he hack it as a performer or settle for being a bank manager?

Back then, I did an enormous amount of walking and got to know the lower end of Manhattan pretty intimately before I ever had a paid gig, because I couldn't sit in the house all day or I would have gone cabin-crazy. I had no spare money and could only live on what the guys who were working put into the fridge. But, looking back, we drew more than food from those who were doing gigs and keeping us in PB&J. We drew commitment and a very real sense of obligation: we owed them, and we would give our talent our best shot until we could finally make a contribution too. That familial bond not only fed us; it drove us on as well.

I landed in Miki's on a Thursday—curious how some things stick in your mind—and some of the boys were working at Gerde's Folk City over Friday/Saturday/Sunday, so we went down to cheer them on. Each Monday Gerde's held a hootenanny, so I decided to go there and try to get a chance to sing. You put your name on a list and an MC called out which of us had been picked to perform. If you were called, you did two or three songs rather than a set—although I wouldn't have known what a set was at that time.

I struck lucky and my name was called. Standing up, I sang through a couple of songs. On the second week I struck lucky again at the hootenanny, and, when I had finished singing, I was offered a job—or at least a contract—by Mike Porco the owner, for a gig at Gerde's six weeks ahead. The contract was to sing for six nights a week, since the club was closed on Mondays for the hootenanny. There were two performers who did two sets each, singing for half an hour. In effect, that made for four shows a night at the club.

I suppose I was a bit of a puzzle to them, singing without an instrument to support my voice. People were polite but puzzled at both hootenannies, because everyone always played a guitar for accompaniment. The unaccompanied voice was new to them, and a few weeks later, when I was fulfilling the contract, Brother John, the MC introduced me as a performer and gave me a quote on which I have dined out many times since: "Now I'd like you to welcome this young lady who sings a cappella; that means without music." He wasn't sending me up; that was his take on me.

At the start, I was so green that I simply stood on stage and sang one song after another and, not unless somebody in the audience looked completely lost, did I dream of stopping to explain what the words of the traditional song meant. It took me most of that first contract to realize that the American audience was struggling, not just with the unaccompanied voice concept, but also because I was singing to them in what seemed a foreign language. My solution to the first part of the problem was to borrow a guitar, purely as a stage prop, so that I would at least look the part when I walked out to perform. That kept everybody happy, even if I still couldn't play a single chord. Dealing with the language problem gradually evolved into my trademark chat between songs, translating the Scots dialect and setting out the historical background into which the pieces fitted.

Gerde's was a folk club, with a bar along the back. A wooden divider ran down the length of the room, leaving a narrow space to walk down to the bar with stools, and on the other side of the divider there were two rows of tables and a low dais up against a brick wall. When we were performing, there were no waiters or waitresses walking around serving; the audience members were expected to get their coffee or their drinks in the breaks between sets. With Mike Porco in charge, nobody would have dared raise a drunken voice, or they would have been out on their ear before they knew what had hit them.

With this setup Gerde's Folk City was intimate, and the performer was close and personal with the people who were your audience. Over the years I sang there many times, but I remember on the first occasion that a couple invited me to sit and join them at their coffee between sets. There was a very handsome silver-haired man sitting with them. We chatted away, but he wasn't saying very much, until he eventually spoke.

"Why did you sing only three verses of 'She Moved through the Fair'?" he asked me. "I didn't know there were any more than three," I replied. "There are four," he said. "How do you know?" I demanded. "I wrote it," he replied. He was Padraic Colum, the poet, and I got the fourth verse* from the author himself.

> The people were saying "No two were e'er wed,
> "But one had a sorrow that never was said,"
> And I smiled as she passed with her goods and her gear,
> And that was the last that I saw of my dear.

HINDSIGHT 3.2: *From notes to* Love, Lilt and Laughter, *recorded in 1963*

For a few months back home in 1959 and 1960, I was teaching, dealing largely with children who were regarded for one reason or another as "unteachable." Yet for all their emotional problems and low intelligence level, they had something that is often—sadly—lost in the course of education with their brighter

*He wrote the fourth verse about two years after writing the main poem, because listeners didn't realize that the woman in the poem was already dead.

15-year-old counterparts: a lack of inhibition and false sophistication, which made them refreshingly spontaneous and responsive. One of my most rewarding "performances" was to such a class, whose musical education was almost certainly limited to "pop" songs; yet "The Dowie Dens of Yarrow" and "She Moved through the Fair" saw tears rolling unrestrainedly down several cheeks and left me sensible of the power of music to unite people for a time at least on a plane of immediate emotional response.

For my first-ever week's contract, I think I got the going rate of $175, and I did my share of restocking the fridge back in Miki's apartment. I was working, and it hadn't taken me long to get my first contract. I was flying high, and anything seemed possible. But did I in any way see this break as getting my foot on the first rung of the ladder as a professional? If I am to be honest, not really. It was simply great fun—my God, somebody was willing to pay me for what I would be doing anyway! And singing beat cleaning houses. It took almost ten years before I realized that singing was in fact my chosen career, not just a fun style of living.

Maybe the folk scene contributed to this way of thinking, where singing for most of us was merely something that we did as part of our daily lives, a form of self-expression which was every bit as important as making money. The mandatory dress was street wear in the coffeehouses—I don't remember anybody getting up on stage in anything other than what they would have worn if they had gone there to listen to somebody else. There was a fair amount of grubby clothes, well-worn shoes, and hair to which Bluebell's reaction would have been, "That hair needs a good wash before you go out of here."

What jolted me out of this culture came later when I saw Richard Dyer-Bennet on stage. Although his voice was far too highly trained for what I would choose to hear delivering the material, he was a fine classical guitarist and always worked in a tuxedo. It was the first time I had seen traditional music presented in a large auditorium in formal dress, and I thought, "Hmm, I could do that."

Throughout these first months in America, I kept in touch with my parents by the old-style one-sheet airmail letters. Mostly I talked generalities, reporting that I had found a place to stay, had got a job, and that it was all very exciting. I never mentioned that I was living in an apartment with eight other people, all males—that would have absolutely freaked them out. Our airmail letters routinely crossed the Atlantic twice a month. When I had gone to America, it wasn't as if I had stormed out of the house or even that I had left for good. It was still in my mind that I would go back home in a couple of years. Therefore we swapped news about what was happening on both sides of the Atlantic. They were interested, I suppose, but still pretty bemused by my choice of career, reflected in their oft-repeated comment: "Aye, right, but when are you going to get a proper job, Jean?"

As for myself, when I got the Gerde's Folk City contract, I still had enough money in reserve to take me back to California, which I saw as my new home. I had walked blithely into the Big Apple and struck it lucky within two weeks, so I decided to see where my contract with Gerde's would take me. Only slowly did I began to realize that I had come here in August with a suitcase full of light summer clothing and that my first paid contract wasn't due until six weeks ahead. Late autumn involves a serious downshift in temperatures on the East Coast. If I wasn't turning right round and heading back to California, then I would be hanging around here until the early winter hit us, and I had no suitable clothes.

Not for the first time, or the last, Miki became my guardian angel. She was exactly the same size as I, and therefore I could borrow from her shoes, blouses, skirts, and jackets. Furthermore, her father was in the garment trade, and she took me to his warehouse where retail packs of three garments were often broken up for sample purposes, leaving the other two up for grabs. I grabbed. Between them, the Isaacson family outfitted me in winter clothing, which was no small thing. Without their help, I would have been in no shape to face the bitterly cold months ahead.

Miki was six or seven years older than I, in her late twenties. She had been a trained medical secretary, and had held down a job for a while; then she had gone off to a kibbutz in Israel and never really settled afterward. Not the happiest of lives, I think, but we were forging a friendship which would last for many years. Just as she had welcomed me into her life and apartment, she now waved me into her shoe cupboard and left me fully equipped to survive as many winter months as were needed.

One way or the other, I was ready to find out what the future would bring.

CHAPTER 4

Fun Way of Living

The feeling of euphoria never really left me over these early days—why should it, when I seemed to have struck gold within a couple of weeks of hitting New York City?—but gradually an element of realism began to creep in. My big money deal at Gerde's Folk City was six weeks in the future, with no earnings due until then, so it was back to eating PB&J from the communal fridge and pounding round the streets of Manhattan to keep away the cold and boredom.

This was a routine which wouldn't change much for some time. By the nature of the traditional/folk music scene, work was intermittent for everybody, no matter how we did our best for each other in terms of recommendations. There were more performers than there were coffeehouse slots available. You worked when you could, and, if the gig involved travel, then the vast distances of America ate up the fee from the gig, and you were left with very little to live on when you got home.

Like any family, we hung together and looked after each other. But the brutal truth is that we were, all of us—even Bob Dylan at first—living on the sharp edge of poverty. As for me, with no money coming in I was ultimately driven to dip into my reserve fund for getting home. What had seemed to me initially, on being given the contract, to be a magical solution was taking a longer to transform my life than was expected, nor was it comfortable.

Many PB&J sandwiches later, the one-week contract finally came round. I can't remember which songs I sang in my first sets at Gerde's Folk City, but you can probably find most of them *Skippin' Barfit through the Heather,* which was the first LP I cut with Kenny Goldstein just a little later. Kenny gave me free choice as to what I sang, so that would have reflected pretty much what I was doing at the time, and the likeliest songs would be "She Moved through the Fair," "The Gypsy Laddie," "Paddy

McGinty's Goat," "The Bonnie Lass o' Fyvie," "Rue," and "The Cruel Mother."

During this first contract, there came a second marvelous stroke of luck when I was given a really good review in the *New York Times*, sharing this with George Mgrdichian, the Armenian virtuoso who was playing in the Village at the same time.* He played the oud, an instrument which I have liked ever since.†

HINDSIGHT 4.1: *Robert Shelton's* New York Times *review, November 15, 1961*

A gazetteer of Manhattan night life could currently list authentic folk music from the highlands of Armenia to the lowlands of Scotland. The Scottish visitor is Jean Redpath, a big-boned, apple-cheeked, radiantly healthy girl. She is appearing at Gerde's Folk City, after a six months residence in San Francisco. Born in the town of Leven, Fife, twenty-four years ago, she studied at the University of Edinburgh. She has been a teacher, major-domo of a boarding house, driving instructor and odd time hosteller.

Miss Redpath would charm the audience with her repertoire alone—some 200 songs, enough to keep a ceilidh (folk jam session) going for hours. These include harmoniously poetic classic ballads, earthy bothy ballads from plowmen's shacks, mouth music in which Scots supply their own entertainment for dancing reels and strathspeys; songs of Rabbie Burns and a round of drinking, lyric love and children's songs.

Her voice is a clear, rich, beautiful mezzo-soprano, sure-pitched enough to sustain long unaccompanied numbers, such as a seal-charmer's song. She tried the song on a West of Scotland island, Barra, and reports that the seals responded. Also unaccompanied, in long arcing phrases are such arresting ballads as "Lord Randall," "Dowie Dens of Yarrow," "Wars of Germany" and "Willie's Rare."

Although Miss Redpath has no connection with the Scottish Tourist Bureau, she is a resolute booster of her land, its history, customs and, of course, its music. In a genially playful manner she conveys her fascination with the language of the

* As luck would have it, many years later when I began teaching at Wesleyan University, George was also there on the World Music Program, in yet another of the intersecting circles that went on over the next half century.

† oud: Middle Eastern pear-shaped musical instrument resembling a lute

Scots ("There's nae wey o' translatin' it") and flavors her onstage remarks with glottal stops and a thick burr.

Miss Redpath has found Americans to be warm and effusive, in contrast to her own people who are reserved. The lads and lassies in the audience obviously believe she has earned that warm reception.

The reviewer, music critic Robert Shelton, spent most of his time in Carnegie Hall and Town Hall, and occasionally dipped into the Village scene as a folkie. His reviews of music there effectively chronicled the 1960s folk boom. My first knowledge of the review was when somebody came in to Miki's apartment waving a copy of the paper and saying, "Hey, have you seen this?"

It's an old truism that there is no such thing as bad publicity, but Bob Shelton's complimentary comments were the best publicity I could ever wish for at this crucial stage in my career. That *NYT* review was followed by another in *Stereo Review* which was equally complimentary for my very first Elektra recording, and, thanks to the two of them, I never had to audition or explain to anybody who I was. A good review in a quality journal is a great vehicle for writing to someone and saying, How about a job? The only better job approach is two good reviews.

After Gerde's, my next job was at the Caffè Lena. Lena, the proprietor, was very hip and kept a close eye on what was going on in Greenwich Village, which was the epicenter of the 1960s folk revival. Singers were going from there around the folk circuit in the US to perform in the various festivals and coffeehouses. She watched what was going on in the Village, and she had picked up the *Times* review. She contacted me almost immediately, and I was singing in her coffeehouse shortly thereafter.

Looking back, I can't understand how anybody ever got hold of me for possible gigs in those days: I hadn't a phone number of my own or any fixed address. My guess is that Lena met one of the other guys from Miki's floor who said, "Right, I know where Jean is. I'll tell her to phone you." It is part of a glorious blur when I flitted high as a kite from job to job—and starved between them. I honestly cannot remember how I got any, let alone all, of these early jobs.

When I could, I replaced my reserve fund. When I couldn't, I dipped into it again to play my part in stocking the fridge or paying toward keeping myself warm. In those days you usually got a flat-rate fee, with no contribution toward travel or living costs. The Caffè Lena was the exception to this rule, and accommodation was provided—in the form of a camp bed in the coffeehouse after it was closed for the night and the tables had been pushed back. Not great, but I was under a cover and wasn't sleeping in the park.

I think I slept there only for that first contract. Afterward, Jean and Dick Weber, friends I made from the Skidmore faculty, always told me, "Come and stay with us," an invitation which I gratefully accepted. Skidmore College in Saratoga Springs, New York, is a liberal arts college and, I think, at that time it was all female. You make friends more easily when you're young. Over those early months when I was still new to the City, I made many contacts with people from Skidmore who became close friends for decades and in some cases throughout my life until now.

There were four young folkies who came along to every performance I gave at Caffè Lena. They sat at the front table recording every burp and hiccough I ever uttered—with Lena's permission and mine—through a microphone into a tape recorder that was the size of a small guest house and which sat on their table right under my nose. It would drive me mad today but, back then, it was great fun and part of the novelty and excitement of the scene. Even now, I have such a vivid memory of these four desperately serious young faces. Somewhere, Lord knows where, there are many open reels of these early Caffè Lena recordings.

Lena was very much into theater, as well as folk, and acted in many of the theatrical productions which she and her husband Bill put on. However, these productions didn't generate enough income to cover the cost of cast and rehearsals, not when there might be only four or five performances of the play, so, to raise additional cash flow, they started up the musical side of things as well in the coffeehouse. Lena not only ran everything; she also baked and therefore most of the food which was sold with the coffee was real home-baking. Today, the Caffè Lena is still the longest running establishment in the United States featuring folk music, although this now takes the form of a concert series rather than nightly performances. Sadly, Lena left us some years ago, and her husband died quite a while before her.*

After that first gig at Lena's, although I came back there many times in later years, it was down to making calls and chasing contacts that the

* The Caffè Lena History Project is dedicated to documenting the history and impact of Caffè Lena and commemorating the life and legacy of Lena Spencer. Book and CD set available at www. caffelenahistory.org.

boys from Miki's had made for me. One of these contracts was for a week's gig in St. Louis, and after I flew back to the Village from there, I had only nineteen cents left in my pocket. That was pretty typical so, away from home, I learned to eat even more lightly than at Miki's and to take any offer that would let me sleep on somebody's floor or sofa after the performances. The hard truth is that even with this intermittent work, I was always living on the raw edge of penury.

Trust me, there is nothing glamorous in the life of an itinerant musician out on the road. It is something that you have to do when you're young, before you start losing sleep worrying about where your next meal—and your next job—is coming from. Yet throughout all this hand-to-mouth living I was running pretty high. Why not? After only six weeks in the business, I had a review in the *New York Times*. When you're that age, your mind sees only the positives and finds a way of toning down and coping with the negatives. So far as I was concerned, I was getting regular work on the folk circuit as it was then and having a hell of a good time. I don't think I lost any sleep worrying about where I would be working next; the next job would happen of its own accord, because gigs seemed to have developed a habit of falling into my lap. Back then, I probably thought, "Doesn't everybody live like that?" No, they don't. Not really. Not even me, as I got older.

Around this time I went with a friend to the Chicago Folk Festival in January. If you want to feel real cold, visit Chicago in January. They don't call it the Windy City for nothing. I have never been so cold in my life, before or since. As these winds came whistling down the Chicago canyons straight off the lake, it felt as if they were skinning me alive.

Most of the folk festivals ran in the spring and the summer, with Chicago being the first of the year. The word went out that I was there, and I was asked to sing, so I got up and sang a couple of songs. As a result I made contact with Chicago folkies and got some work from that. In particular, I met and befriended one of the founders of the Chicago Old Town School of Folk Music, to which I returned frequently over many years. Dawn Greening and Win Stracke started that school in 1957 on North West Avenue and Dawn and her husband Nate became close friends and my regular stopping place when I drifted through Chicago.

Dawn was an education in herself, a marvelous role model. She was a big woman, at least six-foot tall and built accordingly. It was she who introduced me to the fact that you didn't have to be black to feel free and open about showing enthusiasm for a singer onstage. She was the one who helped me complete a culture change that had started within three weeks of landing in New York City. Back then, I had been taken by two friends to a gospel meet in Harlem. Growing up in East Fife, I had never seen black skin until I went to university, where one of my dancing partners was an African student. OK, in California there were a few black people, but in the Apollo Theater in Harlem I suddenly realized that we were the only three white faces among many hundreds of black people. Volunteer nurses were stationed about every ten rows down the aisles of the theater, and I wondered why—until the music built for around forty-five minutes, and the audience started to flake out in numbers all around us. It was almost like being at a Holy Roller meeting, with its frenzy and emotional group intensity. People were on their feet swaying, utterly transported to somewhere else, yelling "Yeay, yeay!" and "Amen" until many of them fainted and had to be carried away. One of the artistes that night was a young woman making her debut: Aretha Franklin was tearing up that auditorium. I get goosebumps still, just thinking about it.

If I hadn't been a Scot and just fresh into New York City, I would have been up on my feet and yelling with the best of them. I was completely blown away. This was a sound unlike anything I had ever heard before. Ever since, apart from the odd occasion when I was in direct competition with it, at a folk festival I would always find my way to a gospel tent when I wasn't performing.

Transported I might have been, but with my upbringing I had no way of expressing this or joining in the fun. I was trained by generations of douce* churchgoing women whose idea of riotous applause was to gently tap the fingers of one hand against the palm of the other. Anything further, like taking off their gloves to make more noise, would have been seen as vulgar and excessive. In the Apollo Theater I was already way over the top in terms of my upbringing, having clapped until my hands were raw. Yet, otherwise, I remained seated and silent amid the din, an observer rather than a participant.

Dawn took me over the final threshold and cured me forever. We had gone to hear Odetta in a nightclub in Chicago—now *there* was another BIG woman who could fill the front of any theater—and long before mid-show Dawn was leaning back in her seat at the table, shouting "Yeah . . . OK . . . Yeah!" with a total lack of inhibition, driving home the point that you didn't need to be a black face in Harlem but could be a WASP

* Polite, in an exaggerated or artificial manner.

in Chicago and still respond to a singer and her music as your heart and instinct drove you.

When that gospel beat got going, it was impossible to sit silent, to remain uninvolved. Under Dawn's tutelage, I let rip—a major step for me in getting away from the constraints and strict personal control of my cultural upbringing. She taught me that feeling could and should be expressed and that total involvement in the moment was both natural and acceptable—to hell with politely tapping fingers. Her example gave the final impetus to the start of my love affair with gospel music, which was to get me involved a little later in my life with singing and ultimately recording "God Songs" with a group of white and equally enthusiastic friends—the "blue-eyed gospel" records, as a friend once described them.

Back in real time, the guys from Miki's apartment were plugging away quite nicely. The 1960s folk revival was not the first of its kind, nor has it been the last, because revivals tend to come round once every twelve years or so as a new generation hits an age where traditional music, in whatever form it takes, comes onto their radar and is "discovered," creating a new wave of interest. However, there will never be another revival quite like the early 1960s, where traditional/folk music became the pop music of the day. The records which hit the charts and stayed there, like the ones from Bob Dylan and Joan Baez, were initially folk songs—before these two began to write their own songs and get involved in political protest—and were tapping into a deep-rooted public unease about growing issues like the Vietnam War and social and civil rights injustices.

Compared to many of Miki's regulars, I don't think I ever came anywhere near their stellar level, but I have no complaints. It has never occurred to me to do anything other than what I've done. The others were creatures of their time, whereas I was more a creature of the past. But we all rode that huge wave of folk interest.

In spite of working hard to stitch gigs together, even my reserve funds were running out. I had never seen this trip east as anything other than temporary, a few extra weeks to experience something that sounded exciting. It was time to go home to California, but I could no longer afford to fly back there. I decided to try and find someone who would share the cost of driving back across the US, and I struck it lucky once again when I found Marie. She was a folkie, devoted to the music, and had spent half the previous year drifting eastward, working her way through the various folk festivals and coffeehouses. Now, she couldn't afford to drive back on her own and, with the worst of the winter weather behind us, was looking for someone to share the petrol costs and the driving.

"I understand you are looking for a ride back to California," she said when we met after a gig. "I'm looking for a co-driver, who isn't totally broke." "You're on," I replied. "We'll split the petrol." We drove in her little Ford Anglia from Manhattan to St. Louis in February, taking a southern route to avoid any late flurries of winter, and there we picked up a third person to share driving and petrol costs, in Jim Kweskin.* He was performing there and he wanted to get back to Berkeley, so the three of us drove more or less nonstop from St. Louis to California. Three bodies, with Jim a tall thin guy, and three suitcases, two guitars, and an Autoharp all crammed into that small car. There was barely room in the back seat for the third person, when we rotated drivers. I'm lucky and have always had the traveler's gift, which is that when you're in a moving vehicle for which you are not responsible, you sleep. I slept, and, by the time we hit the California border, I was the only one of us left fit enough to drive.

It wasn't quite nonstop, because we got hung up for a little while in Williams, Arizona. Despite our southern route, we still hit winter weather and drove through snow in the southwest. Conditions were so bad, we came into Williams sideways down a hill, out of control on black ice, and we were very fortunate not to hit anything too solid. At the bottom of the hill, we had trouble starting again and discovered that we had damaged the fan and lost one of its lugs. It was in the wee sma' hours and the only place we could find which was both warm and open was the Greyhound bus station. Warm and open was the most you could say for it, because otherwise it was as soulless and as cheerless as you could imagine. You wouldn't want to spend much time in a Greyhound bus station in the middle of nowhere at 3:00 A.M. unless the alternative is to shiver in a broken-down car or walk the empty streets.

Around 8.00 A.M., we found a garage opening up. The workers' first reaction, after inspecting the damage, was that they would have to send off for a replacement part, which left us appalled. We couldn't afford repairs or hanging about for another two or three days while we waited for the repair to be done. In this dire emergency, Marie cranked up all her charm and set to work on the mechanic, who got out his welding tools and patched up the car enough to take us home. Throughout her

* Jim Kweskin and his jug band redefined and modernized pre–World War II rural music in the United States.

performance, I slept in the car—even through the noise of the repair. I had crept into the back seat after the bus station and hadn't been noticed when the car was put onto the inspection ramps. That repair cost us part of a night and part of a morning, but we still drove coast to coast in three and a half days.

When we got back to California, I returned briefly to the Jordan farm, but Berkeley quickly became my main base. This shift happened when I went into town for Scottish country dancing and ran into Ev and Marian Stanley. Marian was a fellow Scot, and the Stanleys had a small house in Berkeley. I got to know them faster than any of us would have chosen. During the country dancing that night, I felt a little strange, and when we went back to their home I simply fell over. I think I had strep throat, but the end result was that I was completely out of it for two or three days and in bed for a week. The size of their home dictated that my bed was a camp bed set up in the middle of their living room, so we got to know each other in a hell of a hurry. Despite, or maybe because of, this start, we remained friends for many years.

Around this time, too, I became friends with Malvina Reynolds, who was doing a radio show and invited me to come and talk to her. She and her husband Bud also lived in Berkeley, so I spent quite a bit of time with them too. The really spooky thing about Malvina was that she could have been a sister of my mother, because she looked almost exactly like her with her well-defined cheek bones and good facial bone structure.*

I learned a great deal from Malvina, who was a huge and powerful presence and another very political singer-song writer. She was quite a bit older than I, and it was odd that we got on so well, because I have never been political myself, except on certain subjects like Scottish culture. Malvina wrote "Little Boxes" in 1962, which became a hit song for her friend Pete Seeger the following year, and "Turn Round" which was a huge hit for Harry Belafonte. Alongside these, there were many others, including "There's a Bottom Below," dealing with the social problems of economic depression , and "It Isn't Nice," which became a civil-rights anthem, and some wonderful children's songs such as "Magic Penny" and "Morningtown Ride."

* My mother had another famous doppelganger. I remember once that a member of the family said, "I know who Auntie Bluebell reminds me of; it's that actress with the big mouth and the tousy [tousled] hair," and that was Katharine Hepburn.

On the West Coast, which was now my base, even part-time singing involved a lot of travel. Oddly enough, San Francisco itself never did have a folk club, although Berkeley, as a university town, was jumping. For my local gigs, I sang in coffeehouses there, but my other West Coast gigs mostly took me up north. I was often in Vancouver, where I got to know the folkies there, a fascinating bunch.* Occasionally, I got work which took me to the East Coast and, if I was anywhere close to New York, I would drop in and use Miki's apartment as my second home. We swapped letters, of course, but it was these East Coast gigs which helped me to stay in touch with her.

Work was steady, but I was never anywhere for any length of time, and there was generally a fair amount of space between the gigs. In these spaces, I did a lot of dancing in the Bay Area and in Mendocino, which is a beautiful place. Here there was a camp in the woods which could be hired out for anyone to use. For several years I went there to an annual Scottish Country Dance camp, where my cabin mate was a dance teacher from Vancouver and another Scot. I got my accommodation and dancing for free, because I sang there as part of the après dance entertainment. These camps were great fun, and so I always made a point of being back in California for early June. We were the first group to go into the cabins after the winter, so we had to get there at least a day early to sweep out the mouse turds and clean the windows. The same people came back each year, and we developed a system of who should bring what for the camp, so we had curtains for the windows and rugs for the floors. It made for high-class living in the redwood forest. The spearhead behind these camps was another Scots lad, Stuart Smith, quite a character, who judged dancing all over the country.

Mendocino itself is a magical place, with something vaguely reminiscent of Findhorn† in the early days in terms of its energy, which was quite special. It was built on steep cliffs that were frequently blasted by

* One of them, Murray Shoolbraid from Vancouver Island, has brought out a book in 2010 called *The High Kilted Muse,* which is a long overdue collection of bawderie, a subject which has never really been addressed since *The Secret Cabinet* of Robert Burns. Murray's sister taught Scottish country dancing in Los Angeles.

† Findhorn was a spiritual community set up near the village of that name on the Moray Firth in northern Scotland. At Findhorn all sorts of spiritualist and psychic aspects of life were explored: in the early days, particularly, there was a

high winds, with a huge rock stack out in the bay. One drizzly afternoon I walked down to the bay when it was approaching full tide and was moved, as I often am, to sing. When the waves came in, driven by the wind, they came surging round both sides of the stack, so the sea level in the bay built up really high from the combined swell, then sank down again. I turned round at one point and right on the crest of the wave were two old men's faces watching me: two seals that were listening to my voice. It was like taking a thump in the solar plexus, because the song I was singing was "Song of the Seals."

In those early days in California, I was just a dancing fool. In any city I visited, one of the first things I asked about was Scottish country dancing, because, apart from the dancing, it seemed to be the only place where Scots congregated. Back in San Francisco, there was a spell when we used to attend a country dance class run by Stuart, then head off to the Edinburgh Castle on Geary Street. This place had a small one-door- and one-window-width street frontage. It was, in the front, a Scottish import store (paradoxically, run by a New Zealander), but, when you went through the store and into the back, you found a twenty-foot bar, which gives you some idea of how big the place was. The whole bar was covered with British pennies (old money) and the juke box and the jukebox had Scottish music, including Scottish dance music.

Technically, you needed a license for public dancing in any place, but you didn't need a license for exhibitions. So that left us free to go from the dance class with Stuart to the Edinburgh Castle where there was room for two full sets down the middle of the floor. For years we used this both as an extra practice session and as a chance to relax and enjoy ourselves. It was, however, quality dancing, and long after we stopped, people were still coming into the bar to ask if they were showing dancing on a Monday night. I guess we did wonders for the bar's sales—if only because dancing was thirsty work and we drank a lot of beer ourselves.

Stuart's standard teaching cry was, "No spaghetti arms, please, if you're going to turn, stiffen your arm, give your partner something to work against." At that time I was dating a big guy called Dick, who had

---

wonderful and joyous energy about the place and the experimental work being done on both personal development and practical issues such as vegetable and flower growing. Findhorn still survives as a self-sufficient community, running workshops on all aspects of spiritual activity.

the flattest feet you have ever seen, but he was a really enthusiastic dancer. In one eightsome reel which I was dancing with Dick, I was doing a fast turn with a young man who had not really mastered the stiffened-arm concept. I locked my elbow, strengthened my arm, turned, and kept moving. He came off my arm like a stone out of a sling, hurtled straight across the room, and finished up in the lap of someone who was watching from the sidelines.

On another memorable occasion, Dick and his size fourteen boots* were doing a fast turn with me, when his feet went from completely out from under him. He pivoted on my arm, for a moment was horizontal until gravity took over and he crashed down, still hanging onto me and hauling me down on top of him, wreaking havoc with that particular dance.

Over this spell in San Francisco, I had several dance partners—maybe the ever-present risk of injury saw to that—with whom I went out for meals. With one of these, I saw most of San Francisco from the back of a motorbike, which also let us have some wonderful picnics in difficult-to-access places overlooking the Golden Gate Bridge, which couldn't be reached by car but could be attained by bike.

There was one wonderful dancer with whom I spent most time—I would have married him if he had asked me—but he had far too much sense to do anything as daft as that. We used to go up to the wine country, because there were always free wine tastings. So we tasted widely and well but seldom bought, and we left these sessions very relaxed to finish up at some place on a Sunday night where there was a dance. That was where I branched out into ballroom dancing, particularly the tango.

Not all of my sight-seeing adventures left me with memories wrapped in rainbows, however.

HINDSIGHT 4.2: *California, mid-1960s, having clearly entered into the spirit of the young American way of life*

The first moment of alarm came when the VW bus cut across the unpaved innards of a wide curve—traveling too fast on the down-grade to brake and take the turn.

* Back home we used to say that someone with big feet "had a good grip of Scotland." Maybe it was the different country which ran counter to this rule, but Dick didn't have much of a grip of the US that night.

Boy! That was lucky!

But the next bend leapt at us and the bus headed firmly for the edge, with intent to kill.

"Slow down! SLOW DOWN!*"*

No sickening lurch into somersaulting space—but a rock face at the other side of the road, rushing in at us. No protection. Hand down on the wheel again, screeching tires. Too much for the car. It went into a drunken waltz, the tail-end whipping crazily then, with the instinct for self-preservation of a learner skier, it lay down on its side.

The horizon swung and we were transported from a world of high speed, near frantic action to an eternity of suspense, screaming, tortured metal. No impact—no horns of oncoming traffic. Silence, bird song, and the gently rhythmic spinning of wheels.

"You all right?"

"Dunno—shoulder hurts."

"There's blood all over the place; is it yours?"

We climbed out of the passenger door, now our ceiling. I looked out to a still shot of cars stopped, a woman, wide-eyed with her fist over her mouth.

"Sit down. You're hurt—head's cut."

People came over, a police car turned up. They began to rock the VW upright again . . . "One, two, three . . . heave!" and it was back on all four wheels once more. Key in the ignition. Turned. The VW bus fired first time—what else?

While they drove the bus off the road, I walked back with the sheriff to where the tire marks left the hardtop and hung over the ravine. He pointed down. I looked.

"Guess we came within two inches of our lives," I said, my throat so dry the utterance came out as a croak.

"Guess you did," he said. "Beginner's luck. Jest don't try that trick again, d'you hear?"

Throughout those months there was a steady trickle of work, with lots of "resting" periods in between. Folk singing was not a profession with a weekly wage or a salary or even some form of guaranteed commission. To me, what I was doing was simply enjoying what I found to be a fun lifestyle. If there was work, I took it; if there was no work and no cash, then it was back to the PB&J sandwiches again.

When work was offered, you took it, however you were feeling. I once did a two-week gig in Vancouver while suffering from bronchial pneumonia. Although I'm not sure I realized what ailment I had at the time, I do know that I was having a lot of trouble breathing and that my temperature was way up off the scale. I used to get up around 4:00 P.M. in the afternoon and slowly paste myself together again until I was fit enough to go down and do the two sets between somebody else's two sets in the evening. Then I crawled home and collapsed into bed. You have to be young and living hand-to-mouth to pull a stunt like that. It was downright foolish.

Otherwise, I was too busy living to give any thought to asking if there could possibly be something that I enjoyed more than this free-wheeling life. Indeed it was ten years before it even occurred to me that what I was doing, singing, was in fact my career. Although I had left the Jordan farm to go to Philadelphia for a three-week gig, it took all of that time before I realized that I would never have to go back to house cleaning again.

I was just so grateful to be mobile and more or less independent. I had no home, but I had friends that I could always rely on, like Miki, who had a gift of making people feel that it was perfectly OK to be sleeping on her floor. That gave her pleasure too, because she saw it as something she could donate to the whole folk movement since she wasn't a singer herself. There were just so damn many of us with no roots, nowhere to stay. You do not mix the itinerant business with a front door and a rent or mortgage, or house plants, or animals. These don't figure in at all.

Much of my singing at the start was still a cappella although, as early as my third night at Gerde's Folk City I realized that the American audience was perfectly friendly and more than happy to listen to what I was singing, but they were puzzled, because this type of singing was unknown in the Village. That understanding had made me borrow a guitar simply to use as a stage prop, a form of visual aid for the audience. When people saw a guitar, they relaxed and said, "Oh, there's a guitar—so it's folk music," even if I sang two-thirds of the whole evening unaccompanied. It was a good lesson to learn, because a relaxed audience is easier to gather in and keep onside than a puzzled one, and, when you introduce an a cappella song, you can always persuade them, "Taste this, you'll like it; it's OK."

As a result, in the very early days I borrowed a whole series of guitars from fellow performers. I couldn't afford to buy one, and these other itinerants were too broke to part with their own instruments on anything other than a short-term basis. I did buy one ultimately, but when and how I can't remember. I still have that guitar somewhere; I think it's back with friends in Berkeley.

Now I have almost as many guitars as I have suitcases—and I can't play any of them. For lessons, I think somebody once told me, "You need to depress these three strings there, like that, to get an A chord," but since I have such big fingers, I couldn't get three fingers in there, so from the start I tended to use two. This can leave people very puzzled, trying to figure out which chords I am playing because I'm not using enough fingers. I listen with awe to a flamenco guitarist or a classical guitarist or any really good guitarist—one of my favorite performers, and one of the nicest men I ever met, was Doc Watson, who could do anything with a guitar. However, I have no desire to become an instrumentalist; the guitar to me is still very much a visual aid, a source of color change in a performance. Some songs are always easier to perform with a guitar, usually only as a gentle arpeggio behind the voice. That way, if I hit a bum chord, nobody notices. I also contribute to the school of thought that if three chords will do, why on earth would you want to use four?

On the wider musical scene, one of the things I did on a regular basis was to go to performances in New York with Bob Shelton, since he always had critics' seats in the same place in the theaters. Either in front of him or behind him was another critic called Henrietta Yurchenko, who wrote for a magazine and taught ethnomusicology at City College. If I was in New York City, I would go to Carnegie Hall or Town Hall and sit with Bob, Henrietta, and her husband Irving, and then usually have a drink after the performance. This way I saw most of the already well established concert performers who were coming through the City, and this experience played an important part in my musical education. I have mentioned Richard Dyer-Bennet earlier and his influence on how I ultimately dressed for performances myself. Richard was working with material which was dear to my heart, and he played a magnificent guitar. One evening it was not a concert hall but a nightclub I went to with Bob, the Blue Angel, to catch the debut of a young singer, Barbra Streisand. Her voice did little for me, but as I am a traditionalist, it was her material which didn't reach me at all.

These were the high spots. On the other side of the penny were some of the places where I had to spend the night after a gig. Once when I was working in Chicago, before I knew anyone there, I found the club where I would be singing and then went to the nearest hotel to check in. It didn't seem to be five-star by any manner of means, but it was watertight. The manager took me upstairs to show me my room, and, as he walked into the bathroom, he pushed the toilet handle and said, "Well, that flushes all right"—if there was any doubt, then I'm glad he checked. He left me standing there with my suitcase, surrounded by paintwork which was all black. That hotel wasn't the most cheerful place in the world, but the room itself looked OK. I went down and sang at the club that night, then came back to my room and locked the door. During the night, I heard the door handle being tried a couple of times and put it down to drunks wandering round and looking for their own rooms—a standard feature of hotel life.

Next day, one of the lads in the club asked: "Where are you staying, Jean?" "At the Maryland," I replied. "Oh my God, I hope you lock your door at night." "Well, I do, but why?" I asked. He winced. "When you walk round the corner of the square on your way home tonight, have a look at the neon sign."

This, I duly did and discovered that, when you turned round the corner, there was another building that cut the neon sign through its middle, blocking out the right-hand side of the two-line logo and leaving it to read—instead of Hotel Maryland—Hot Mary. I had booked myself into one of the biggest hooker hangouts in that part of Chicago. I locked the door and put a chair under the handle that night.

There were more door fumblings, but I came to no harm. Somebody Up There always seems to have been looking after me. While I know only too well that bad things happen to innocent people, I am one of the lucky ones who has never looked for trouble and have found very little of it in my life. Sure, it is not all luck; there are basic rules which you quickly learn. If you are in a strange city, do not walk close to any building after dark—there are too many doorways and alleyways where trouble could be waiting—and always keep your wits about you. Above all, don't smile at strangers. I tend to talk to anybody, anywhere, but I have discovered to my cost that if you smile at strangers it can all too easily be taken as a pickup. There have been a couple of occasions when I have had to explain to someone, as gently as I could, that I was terribly sorry if he misunderstood, but . . . piss off!

This itinerant lifestyle taught me a lot that I would never have learned if I had stayed on in East Fife. Although, perhaps not. On a later trip back home, I was staggered to hear someone talking about car-key parties in Largo. Of course there were car key parties in New York City, and probably in Berkeley, but Largo?* C'mon! No sex, please. We're not only British; we're fae Fife.

Back in California, I gradually moved on from staying with friends in Berkeley to having an apartment of my own in San Francisco's Haight-Ashbury neighborhood. Before I locked into singing full-time, the apartment was paid for by working part-time in the Scottish import store which fronted the Edinburgh Castle. Jack Speirs, the New Zealand owner, was aging and was quite happy to sit in the shop most of the day. However, the really brisk business was always conducted when the bar was open at night. I had no objection to keeping the shop open until the bar closed at 2:00 A.M., which meant for a roaring trade with drunks.

"Honey, have ya got anythin' in the Goldstein plaid?" "Well no, actually, but you might like this one. It's very pretty, you know." It was criminal, really, but I figured out that if they didn't have the sense to stay sober, it wasn't up to me to teach them why they should. Among the tartan tack, the shop's stock included a wide range of records, and I spent hours listening to Count John McCormack—Scottish shops tend to carry Irish stuff and vice versa—and the English lyric tenor Heddle Nash singing. No, don't ask me how an Englishman made it there, but he did and his was another fine voice that could move me.

Sometimes Jack listened with me, sometimes not. The somewhat-odd hours fitted into my lifestyle, and, in time, apart from working behind the counter, I did some of the buying for his shop. With my intermittent gigs, Jack knew I was likely to be gone for three or four weeks at a time. However, we found another Scot, Bill Cathro, a piper, who was trying to augment his income in much the same way as I was. He filled in at the shop when I was on the road, and, among the three of us, we managed to keep that wee shop open all hours until Jack got too old and had to sell.

That small apartment of my own in California provided the one point in my life where I could actually have house plants, and I became renowned for the African violets in my second story with its east- and south-facing windows. I couldn't have killed them if I had tried. I had every variety of African violet known to man and, ultimately, couldn't

* More correctly Lower Largo, a small coastal village in Fife that was the birthplace of Alexander Selkirk (1676–1721), the Royal Navy officer who was castaway on a Pacific desert island for four years, then rescued, and whose story inspired Daniel Defoe to write *Robinson Crusoe.*

even give them away. People begged me not to give them any more. All I had to do was split the flowers up and repot them, and they took off as if something was after them. I often wonder what happened to them, after I left. Did they take over that side of town or just wither away?

This easy-going lifestyle was soon to change when, out of nowhere, came an invitation to sing at the Berkeley Folk Festival. Barry Olivier, who was the founder and director of the festival for many years, had heard me on the radio talking to Malvina Reynolds. The folk circuit is a very, very small world. Hearing that I was living in Berkeley, albeit sporadically, Barry contacted me and asked if I would like to come along and sing at the festival. This was during the early years of the event. On the West Coast, we were far removed from the main thrust and churn of folk music in Greenwich Village, although performances by Pete Seeger and the Weavers had introduced the music here. So a new interest was mushrooming, a little in the wake of the East Coast explosion of folk, and setting up the Berkeley Folk Festival was the result of this.

There was a natural audience, for one thing. Berkeley is a university town, so there were thousands of students, with a lot of free thinkers and, at that point, an emerging counterculture movement in the hippies. The festival had taken off like my African violets, and to get an invitation to perform at that level was a huge step up for me, a real occasion. Performances at festivals meant exposure to large audiences, which usually led to a series of new contacts and new gigs. Being invited didn't always guarantee a shortcut into the big time, but it was a great way of marketing yourself as a performer. Yet another opportunity had fallen into my lap, the sort of invitation that you would never dream of refusing.

I didn't hesitate: I accepted. As for the performance itself, climbing onto the big high platform was—in more ways than one—a big step up from the eight-inch dais platforms I knew in coffeehouses and clubs. Then it seemed to take a very long time to walk across that stage to the microphone. Next, instead of the tightly contained small audiences of thirty to forty people in a coffeehouse, and not many more in folk-club gigs, there was a huge open space and a sea of about four thousand faces of folkies and their families. While you are still swallowing heavily to be standing in front of this amorphous mass, because the stage is outdoors your voice is greatly amplified, what is meant to be a nervous greeting comes out as a bellow which makes you jump out of your skin at first. Any sense of intimacy and control of the audience goes straight out of the window, before you even start to sing.

How did I cope with such a total change in environment? I'm not sure: no doubt there were nerves and stage fright, but back then I was flying high. I wasn't thinking, "Whew, I've never faced this before—how do I deal with it?" It was simply another experience, another exciting challenge. Something new. As I stood there, shaking, I think my main feeling was, "Let's have a crack at this one—and learn as you go along."

I remember the classical arena at Berkeley as being a very attractive place to sing, but there was so much going on around me that I can't say if I got any great sense of satisfaction or not. It's all a bit of a blur. The festival lasted for several days. Malvina was also performing there—she was local—and there were plenty other rising names appearing. Lots to see and hear. Festivals are notorious for agents and managers to be scouting around, looking for talent, but I was so raw that career never figured in my thinking. Once I finished singing, I simply hung around to listen to the other performers as yet another folkie in the audience.

That first festival was great fun. I did the Berkeley Folk Festival in 1962, went back there in 1963, and then did the much bigger Newport Folk Festival in 1964—another huge leap in audience size from even Berkely talk about a sea of faces!

Once again I had struck it lucky: after Berkeley the festival invitations started to come in hard on the heels of reviews and word-of-mouth recommendations—the Philadelphia Folk Festival, for one, was another whopper. Without fully registering it, I had passed another threshold in my singing. The more I appeared at festivals, the more regular and widespread became the invitations to work in coffeehouses and clubs. The old fun-loving part-time lifestyle began to change, and I was increasingly busy, beginning to live for long periods on the open road, traveling from gig to gig.

I had slipped seamlessly into being a full-time singer and was well and truly on my way, but I was still enjoying these new experiences too much to realize this is what had happened to me. I had still to recognize that this was my chosen career.

After all, singing wasn't really work. Was it?

Jean's mother, known as "Bluebell," with Jean and her brother Sandy.
All images courtesy of the Jean Redpath Estate unless otherwise stated.

Jean and Sandy as older children

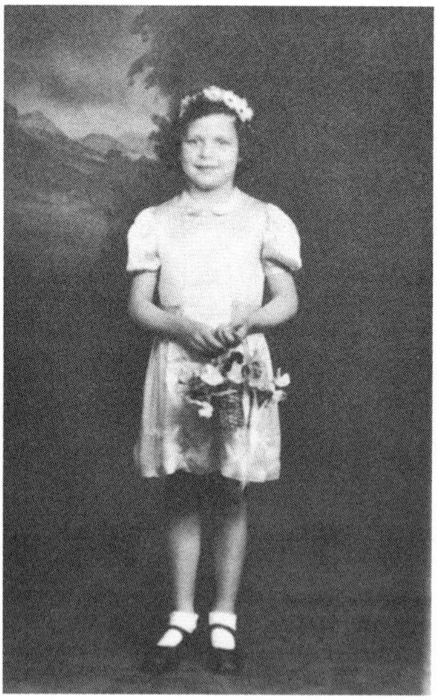

Jean as a flower girl, getting ready for the May Queen parade in Leven

Jean's father, Jim, and her mother, Bluebell

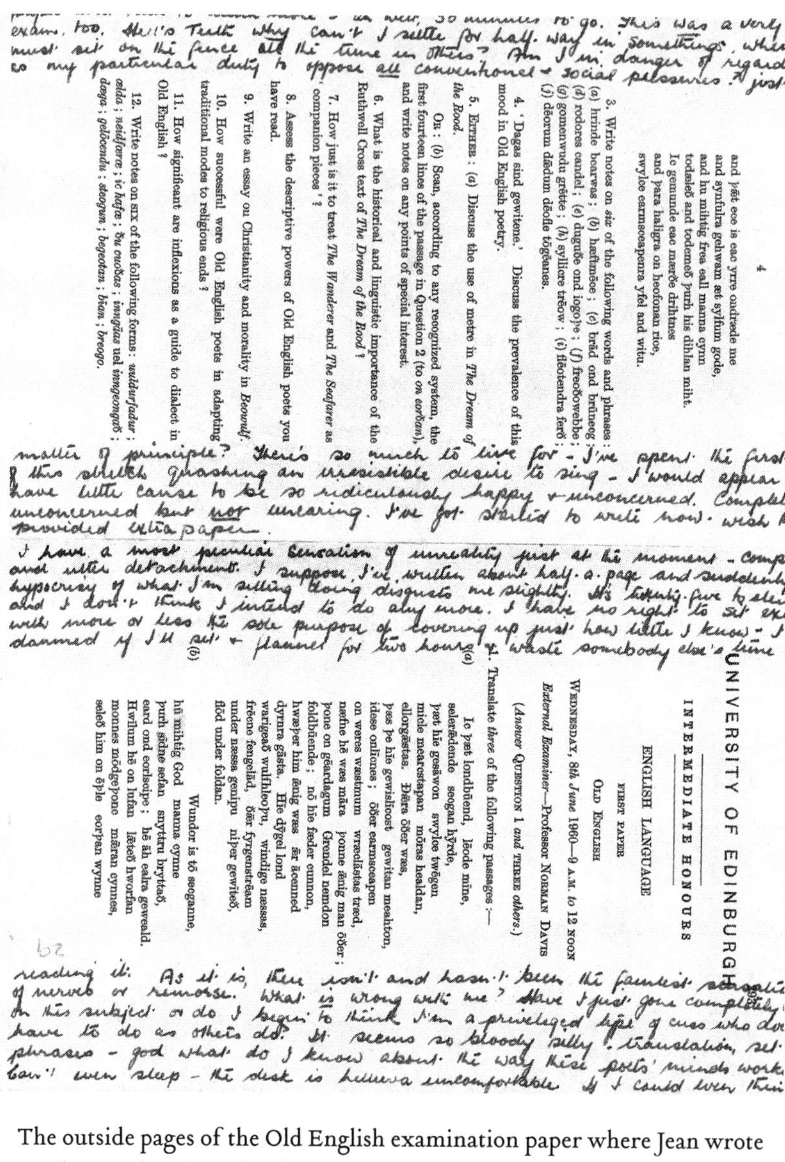

4

and þæt ece is eac yrre ondræde me
and synfulra gehwam æt sylfum gode,
and hu mihtig frea eall manna cynn
todæleð and todemeð þurh his dihlan miht.
Ic gemunde eac mærðe drihtnes
and þara haligra on heofonan rice,
swylce earmsceapenra yfel and witu.

3. Write notes on *six* of the following words and phrases: (*a*) hrinde bearwas; (*b*) hæftmēce; (*c*) brād ond brūneeg; (*d*) rodores candel; (*e*) duguðe ond iogoþe; (*f*) freoðowebbe; (*g*) gomenwudu grētte; (*h*) syllicre trēow; (*i*) flēotendra ferð; (*j*) dēorum dǣdum dēofle tōgēanes.

4. 'Dagas sind gewitene.' Discuss the prevalence of this mood in Old English poetry.

5. Either: (*a*) Discuss the use of metre in *The Dream of the Rood*.

Or: (*b*) Scan, according to any recognized system, the first fourteen lines of the passage in Question 2 (to *on eorðan*), and write notes on any points of special interest.

6. What is the historical and linguistic importance of the Ruthwell Cross text of *The Dream of the Rood*?

7. How just is it to treat *The Wanderer* and *The Seafarer* as 'companion pieces'?

8. Assess the descriptive powers of Old English poets you have read.

9. Write an essay on Christianity and morality in *Beowulf*.

10. How successful were Old English poets in adapting traditional modes to religious ends?

11. How significant are inflexions as a guide to dialect in Old English?

12. Write notes on six of the following forms: *wuldurfadur*; *ælda*; *neidfæræ*; *ic hafæ*; *ðu cuoðas*; *inngāas* uel *inngeongað*; *dæga*; *gelōcendu*; *steogun*; *begeotan*; *bīan*; *breogo*.

UNIVERSITY OF EDINBURGH

INTERMEDIATE HONOURS

ENGLISH LANGUAGE

First Paper

Old English

Wednesday, 8th June 1960—9 a.m. to 12 noon

External Examiner—Professor Norman Davis

(*Answer* Question 1 *and* three *others*.)

1. Translate *three* of the following passages:—

(*a*)
Ic þæt londbūend, lēode mīne,
selerǣdende secgan hȳrde,
þæt hīe gesāwon swylce twēgen
micle mearcstapan mōras healdan,
ellorgǣstas. Ðǣra ōðer wæs,
þæs þe hīe gewislīcost gewitan meahton,
idese onlīcnes; ōðer earmsceapen
on weres wæstmum wræclāstas træd,
næfne hē wæs māra þonne ǣnig man ōðer;
þone on gēardagum Grendel nemdon
foldbūende; nō hīe fæder cunnon,
hwæþer him ǣnig wæs ǣr ācenned
dyrnra gāsta. Hīe dȳgel lond
warigeað wulfhleoþu, windige næssas,
frēcne fengelād, ðǣr fyrgenstrēam
under næssa genipu niþer gewīteð,
flōd under foldan.

(*b*)
Wundor is tō secganne,
hū mihtig God manna cynne
þurh sīdne sefan snyttru bryttað,
eard ond eorlscipe; hē āh ealra geweald.
Hwīlum hē on lufan lǣteð hworfan
monnes mōdgeþonc mǣran cynnes,
seleð him on ēþle eorþan wynne

... 30 minutes to go. This was a very ... exam, too. Hell's Teeth why can't I settle for half-way in something, when ... must sit on the fence all the time in others? Am I in danger of regarding ... as my particular duty to oppose all conventional & social pressures? A just ...

matter of principle? There's so much to live for – I've spent the first ... of this stretch quashing an irresistible desire to sing – I would appear ... have little cause to be so ridiculously happy & unconcerned. Completely unconcerned but not uncaring. I've got started to write now – wish they provided extra paper.

I have a most peculiar sensation of unreality just at the moment – complete ... and utter detachment. I suppose I've written about half a page and suddenly ... hypocrisy of what I'm sitting doing disgusts me slightly. It's twenty-five to eleven ... and I don't think I intend to do any more. I have no right to sit exams ... with more or less the sole purpose of covering up just how little I know – I'm ... damned if I'll sit & flannel for two hours & waste somebody else's time

reading it. As it is, there isn't and hasn't been the faintest ... of nerves or remorse. What is wrong with me? Have I just gone completely ... on this subject or do I begin to think I'm a privileged type of cuss who doesn't ... have to do as others do. It seems so bloody silly – translation, set phrases – god what do I know about the way these poets' minds work. Can't even sleep – the desk is hellova uncomfortable. If I could even think ...

The outside pages of the Old English examination paper where Jean wrote her Declaration of Independence across its eight vertical margins. Courtesy of the University of Edinburgh.

Jean's father, Jim, admiring the pass certificate given to one of the first students of his driving lessons.

Jean singing in a radio studio in the very early days

Jean with a guitar probably borrowed for the occasion in the early 1960s

Jean performing in an unknown coffeehouse in the late 1960s

Jean taking a break from tax forms in Tucson, Arizona. Courtesy of Betsy Sandlin.

Jean working on the Burns recordings with a terminally ill Serge Hovey

Jean getting into the spirit of Thanksgiving with her longtime friend Betsy Sandlin. Courtesy of Betsy Sandlin.

Jean with a summer-school class at Airthrey Castle, University of Stirling. Courtesy of Whyler Photographs, Stirling.

Alec and Hazel Barbour, close friends of Jean

The presentation party for Jean's honorary doctorate at the University of St Andrews

Jean in her study at Elie in 2010. Courtesy of the author's collection.

Jean walking a trail in Arizona's Catalina Mountains. Courtesy of Betsy Sandlin.

Jean performing in Cambridge, New York, for her friend Benjie in earlier years. Courtesy of Betsy Sandlin.

A portrait study of Jean in the early 1980s. Courtesy of Janet Swanson.

CHAPTER 5

Living on the Road

The flurry of invitations which followed the Berkeley Folk Festival kept me busier than usual for the next few months. I found myself on the road almost constantly, singing in coffeehouses and folk clubs across America. However, this activity didn't bring in much extra money; I was still on the treadmill of a standard flat-rate fee, out of which I had to pay my own travel and accommodation. That didn't worry me, because I saw singing less as a means of earning money than as a way of paying for a lifestyle which I enjoyed—new places, new faces, new experiences. People were paying me to do what I loved doing, which was to travel around the country and sing.

A similar wave of new work followed my second Berkeley Folk Festival in 1963—including an invitation from the festival committee to appear in the big Newport Folk Festival. Berkeley was big enough, both in its growing reputation and its audience size—but the Newport Folk Festival was huge, in a totally different league, with fifteen to twenty thousand in an audience against the four to six thousand at Berkeley. I was thrilled to bits to be invited. This was a major honor, the Big One, and Newport was one of the best showcases in the music world.*

Surprisingly, not even a festival this big ever cared what you were going to sing; you were simply invited to perform, and the selection of songs to fill your slot was entirely up to you. For my usual run of coffeehouse gigs, I often made up my program on the hoof, in response to the reaction of the audience. If they seemed to be getting too quiet and introspective, I slipped in an upbeat song to get their feet tapping, and, if I felt things were getting a bit too boisterous, I would bring in a song designed to raise a lump in the throat or bring a tear to the eye.

* Newport was "the acne of the folk festival world," as an interviewer once informed me, his enthusiasm getting the better of his vocabulary.

However, even with my limited experience of folk festivals, I knew that this sort of intimacy and impromptu program-building simply wouldn't work. For Newport, I needed something more structured. I turned to a couple of jotters I had started to keep, where I had written down what experience had shown to be nicely balanced sets of songs for twice-an-evening performances—sets not only balanced in terms of mood, but also in terms of the broad vernacular in their content. By now I realized that I was singing in what amounted to a foreign language to my American audiences, and even the titles of the songs had often to be explained as part of introducing the song and its content.* This could take up to ten minutes of translation and explanation before I started singing, so in planning any set of songs I had to keep the length of introduction in mind, as well as changes in the mood I was trying to create.

I'm sure I used some tried-and-trusted set for the audience in Newport, where my most vivid memory is of the sheer number of people listening. I was conscious of the faces in the first fifteen to twenty rows, but after that, as the audience stretched out in front of me for about a quarter of a mile, individual faces merged into a vast amorphous mass of pink and brown.

I was shaking in my shoes. There was a huge and very high platform, raised to make performers visible to those at the back in that vast level-ground audience, and I had to climb up steps to get onto it. Being so high above ground was daunting in its own right, let alone in front of that sea of faces, and I had to draw on all my experience as a performer to launch into "Song of the Seals." The weather did its best to help my planning, because we were right on the coast, and I could smell the brine of the sea and a haar† creeping in as I sang.

As is always the way in an outdoor concert, you are simply performing to a vast growling beast out there, and your voice disappears into the air. In contrast, even in the biggest indoor auditorium there is some sort of enclosed space which provides a feedback of sound and feeling, which in turn creates some form of psychic connection between the performer and the audience, allowing real creativity in mood and feeling. In an open-air festival, there are too many people, no truly enclosed space in

* Even then, the most frequent reaction to my explanations was, "Gee, what a cute accent. What did you say, honey?" There were times when I felt I needed an explanation for my explanation.

† haar: sea fog

which to hold their attention and the sound, and too much movement and distraction. They listen and observe rather than become involved—which means you have to settle for performing to them rather than trying to gather them in. You are reduced simply to doing your best to sing the song, often competing with other noises and movements.

Obviously, it was an honor to be invited; it was a thrill to be there, and there were all sorts of singers and other people I knew from having bumped into them on the coffeehouse circuit, but Newport was the start of a strong sense of reservation bordering on dislike that grew up within me at the prospect of singing to large audiences and out of doors. It wasn't where either I, or my songs, truly belonged.

However, there was a fun side too. I remember that Dave Van Ronk,* another performer, and I went out of the festival grounds to get some food and drink, and when we returned the festival's security people wouldn't let us back in. I thought Dave would do his usual thing of turning it into a fight, so I stepped in and in my best Scottish accent said, "Well, actually, we are performers; we went out through another gate, and we're due back on pretty soon." Maybe they understood, but more likely it was the usual magic key of my Scottish accent. They waved us in, and the standard comment, "Gee, what a cute accent," followed us.

Another vivid memory from that Newport festival was of hearing Dock Boggs† perform for the first time. The festival grounds were right on the shoreline and subject to sea fog. When Dock got up onto the platform to sing, a haar came rolling in—huge thick banks of it. They had a blue spotlight on him, this little old guy sitting on a folding wooden chair. Suddenly, he was completely blotted out and all you saw was a blue bank of fog, out of which came this high Appalachian mountain voice singing "Oh, Death":

> What is this that I can see
> With icy hands taking hold of me
> I am death and none can tell

* Van Ronk became a legendary folk and blues singer. He was born in Brooklyn, and his classic recording was *Folksinger,* but there are also the superb recordings *Inside Dave Van Ronk* and *In the Tradition.*

† Morgan Lee "Dock" Boggs was another towering figure in the folk and blues scene. Two of his 1920s songs, "Sugar Baby" and "Country Blues," are included in the 1951 *Anthology of American Folk Music.*

I open the door to heaven and hell
Oh Death, O Death, please spare me over till another year.*

It was unreal. These first four descending notes supporting the words *Oh Death* raised the small hairs on the back of my neck. I never heard that song again, until I found it in the movie *Songcatcher.*

Apart from Dock and Dave, I think Dylan and Baez were performing there too: these festivals tended to haul in everybody who was anybody in the folk circuit—as well as a lot of folk who were on the rise and trying hard. Somewhere out there in the world, I am on an early Newport festival LP, because one or two of the songs I did at that festival were recorded.

It was at the Newport festival where another major development took place in my career. During most festivals, lots of managers and agents dropped in scouting for talent and generally making a round of contacts with their business links in mind. All of this was peripheral to me at the time, because I was there only to sing and to enjoy myself. But after my set—he had the sense to wait until I got over the worst of my stage fright—Manny Greenhill, who was Joan Baez's manager at the time, approached me.

"Do you have anyone representing you?" he asked. I looked at him blankly. "Who does your bookings?" he prompted. "I guess I do," I replied. "But I don't really see it as making bookings. I just get one job after another, when I can." "Well, if you would like a manager to do that for you, we should talk," he said. All of this happened backstage, if there was such a place at a huge festival like Newport, in 1964. At the time, did I realize what a major change this would bring to my singing and my life? I doubt it. Back then I was flying high without a care in the world, and I think I just accepted it without much thought, as in "Oh, right, OK."

Looking back, I see things differently. There I was, having barely wet my feet in the profession, when I got the offer of decent management. I bless Manny for that—for not just clocking up new bookings, but also for having a much clearer idea of what I was trying to do than I had at this stage of my career. I was truly lucky—or blessed—yet again, as so often in my life. It is almost as if my path was prepared for me, even before I hit the earth squalling. I never chose singing as a career; it chose me. I just

* "Oh Death" is a traditional Appalachian song.

sang, and it never, ever, occurred to me to do anything else. And when I needed help, it was always there. On cue.

Throughout all this, I was keeping in touch with my parents. What little I did tell them about these folk-festival invitations wouldn't have made much impact on them because, at that stage, festivals were not even a glint in an organizer's eye back in Britain. It took years before they made the transition across the Atlantic. Writing home during these early years was never easy, because our letters were still overshadowed by their feeling that I had let down both myself and the family by not completing the Edinburgh degree course. Therefore my letters home were no more than carefully edited surface chat, filling the one-sheet airmail letter form, simply a gesture toward staying in touch. Likewise, my mother's letters back to me only outlined what the family were doing. While the contact between us never broke down, it was always guarded, edgy.

Yet many years later I discovered that she had kept whole bundles of these letters of mine. That really rocked me: simply knowing where I was and what I was doing must have meant much more to Bluebell than I realized. My discovery provided yet another example of how the Scottish culture of holding back and firmly controlling real feelings can so easily distort a relationship. All parties are left second-guessing—and the guesses can be way out of line. In our case, how many years were wasted in this daft fencing?

Having Manny as my manager didn't so much transform as regularize my life as a singer. It was a huge release to have him take over all the hassle of getting bookings and negotiating fees. Until then it had never occurred to me that I was in any form of bargaining position; I was just happy to get work of any kind. With Manny in charge, I discovered that what I was getting paid for a gig went up, even if I had still to cover my travel and accommodation.* The latter often took care of itself if someone from the other end said, "We'll sort out a place for you to stay." Folk club organizers were well aware that most performers were hard up, and they knew that we would always be grateful to arrive and find that bed and breakfast had been arranged with a family or a committee member. As being on the road became my life, I found myself becoming more and

*Since travel costs and accommodation were still the same, these higher fees for gigs left me making a better margin and some real money for the first time since I had come to America. Thanks, Manny.

more the recipient of this sort of hospitality, at times shading into a state I usually describe as "being a professional house guest."*

As well as booking gigs, Manny introduced me to Jac Holzman, the founder, chief executive, and driving force behind Elektra Records, and in the years from 1963 to 1966 I made three LPs for them. The first two LPs were made very close together in the early years of working with Manny; the third came after a break of two years when I was just so busy on the road that spending time in a recording studio was never an option. Jac was one of those wonderful larger-than-life guys who thought nothing of doing everything, including flying his own plane. One of the strong memories I have of doing these first two LP recordings out East was of being flown over Manhattan by him and looking down into the deep street canyons which my feet had once pounded in my PB&J days.

Outside these brief visits to the recording studios, life was simply more—a lot more—of the same. Being on the road became my home. In terms of singing live, I found that my usual brief explanation of what a song title meant and what context a song fit into when it was written was slowly developing into a longer and more relaxed chat. Somewhere out on the road I saw someone else do this, and, as with so many other things, I began to build something similar into my own performance. Imitation is the sincerest form of flattery, as the saying goes.

The man whose delivery style impressed me so much was Sam Hinton, an oceanographer in San Diego.† I watched him work at folk festivals and liked his wonderful laid-back chatty approach. When Sam did a set of any kind, he chatted a lot, explaining what the references were and telling some kind of wee story on the side. This fascinated me, because it was a natural development to what I was already doing. I began to develop my dialect translation into a broader explanation and a chat between songs.

* I stole this line from a young woman who was tending bar at a party which some friends gave, and they were chatting her up and asking what she did when she wasn't tending bar, She replied, absolutely deadpan, "I'm a professional house guest. Where do you live?" That was enough to scare everybody off!

† Sam Duffie Hinton (1917–2009), American folk singer and marine biologist, worked at the University of California, San Diego. He wrote many books and articles on marine biology in his day job and recorded "Buffalo Boy" and "The Barnyard Song" for the Library of Congress in 1947. His other commercial recordings include *Singing across the Land, The Real McCoy,* and *The Wandering Folk Song.*

This kind of introduction grew to be my trademark, although it evolved over a period of years rather than overnight. And not without pain. Once, in a hall I overheard someone mutter at the back of the audience, "I wish she wouldn't talk so much, and sing a bit more instead." Before I could answer, someone else in the audience whipped round and said, "If all you want is her singing, go out and buy the CD." Not only was it better riposte than I might have come up with, but it was also the kind of put-down that I could never have delivered to a customer.

Manny's bookings took me to all sorts of gigs. One that I shall never forget was when Manny booked me for a summer evening outdoor program on the outskirts of Boston. I was working from the back of a flatbed truck as part of an experimental venture to take music out to members of the public when the kids were out of school and everyone was at their wits' end wondering what to do with them. I and a couple of other singers were sent, we were sent as musical missionaries to one of the lower-income sections of Boston.

Nobody ever invites missionaries or knows what to do with them once they're there. You could have cut the suspicion and latent hostility with a knife. It was a strange and off-putting feeling, standing with a microphone on a truck and with absolutely nothing at my back. For the first time, I truly understood why the old-time gunslingers used to sit in a bar facing the door with their backs against the wall. I got more and more edgy as a bunch of fairly wild kids started running round behind me; every so often, the mike would die, because they had unplugged it. At the same time, sitting out there on grass banks was a muttering and restless crowd. I had been dumped in a place where nobody was expecting me or had the faintest understanding of what I was trying to do. To make matters worse, a horrendous lightning storm was building up and everybody was on edge.

The energy of the place was crackling with static of all kinds. The last straw came when a stone bounced across the flatbed truck, then another, then some more. I was disposable, but I couldn't afford to replace my guitar—a new one I had bought recently. Still singing, I put the guitar away in its case, and not only did I do the rest of the program a cappella, but I also made it through the rest of my material as fast as possible. I gave up on introductions, and I even dismantled the microphone during my last song in order to let me and the rest of the crew get the hell out of there as soon as I was finished. Hindsight 5.1 gives a graphic description of my feelings at the time

HINDSIGHT 5.1: *Dorchester, Mass., August 26, 1970—years later and the memory of that gig was still burning brightly*

OK, kid, grin and brace yourself—here we go. Forty-five minutes and you're off the book. "No, I'm not part of a group. I sing by myself." Are these people ready for a soloist? Oh, Christ, not again! Why do these bloody mikes always scream?

Shut up, you little bastards, I'm probably enjoying this less than you are. John, for God's sake, can't you at least keep the brutes off the stage? Do I mind stopping for a bit to let you fix the mikes? Not at all, go ahead. Take your time. Add another piece of staging, lift the mikes so the kids aren't blocking the sound. Take as long as you like—it's all coming off that forty-five minutes.

Respite's over. You have to go back.

Keep the racket down, will you, there's only one of me.

No point in appealing to any better feelings in this shower—carry on regardless, you've only got 35 minutes to go.

What the hell was that?

I dunno if that was a rock or not, but one more and I quit—check be damned—and go home. Then . . . fuck 'em all, they're not going to get the better of me! Another rock, huh?

First priority—get my guitar out of sight. If anything hits me, sure I'll probably heal, but I can't afford to buy another instrument. Your fault, not mine, but you're going to have to settle for unaccompanied.

You're getting rattled, kid, and you can't clout that red-headed little brat clowning on the stage. No point using sarcasm, it'd be lost.

Tell me, John, I know what's going on down here—but I can't see beyond the third row. Is there anyone there on the hill, and if so, are they actually listening?

That was bad. Sounded like a whine to me. God, it wouldn't take much to start tears. Where's your sense of proportion? And your sense of humor? You never had rocks on the stage before—it'll make a great story. And I'll bet it's the first time the culturally deprived of Dorchester ever sat through an a cappella concert.

Concert? That's a laugh. Why don't you quit? God knows, but I've never walked off the job yet—not for this lot either. Can't tear a strip off them over the mike, I'd probably have a riot on my hands.

Jesus, would I like to lay that little bastard across my knee!

John, I'm going to do one more song and then quit—I've had it.

Maybe this is a pure myth, this idea of mine that there's always the few who are listening and it isn't fair to take it out on them. Cool off, kid, dismantle the mike while you finish this song—it'll make you feel better and you're not going to change this world in one night. Chalk it up to experience—six years ago a gig like this would have demoralized you completely.

How do the kids driving the truck and handling the sound equipment cope? They're a nice bunch and they've been doing this for two and a half months! I'm outa here . . .

Even looking from fifty-years-plus distance, that gig was sheer hard work, a nightmare with nothing particularly rewarding about the performance. Give Manny his due; he had bought into what he thought a worthwhile idea—and indeed it was—but a solo singer of traditional songs didn't fit into that kind of missionary slot. A group of instrumentalists with foot-stomping material would have carried the audience a whole lot better than a young unaccompanied female singer. I told him, "I really don't want to do another one of these." Manny held up his hands. "You won't," he promised.

OK, so I survived, but it was another—very large—straw that was building up to a veritable haystack of dislike of open-air performances. Even a tent is easier than open air when it comes to handling an audience. So much of what I try to do depends on making contact, almost individually, with however many people are there. Building any kind of intimacy is impossible when everything you are putting out goes almost straight up into the open air. This has very little to do with actual sound; a good soundman and a good set of speakers can make sure that everybody in the place hears the music. However, that type of projection creates a very different wavelength from the one I am talking about, which is more emotional, introspective and, on some levels, almost psychic. When I talk about feeling, smelling, almost tasting the atmosphere in a room, it is not just a case of "working the crowd" by singing material that they are familiar with; what I am always trying to do is to take them a little further than they have been before. To do that, first I have to find out where they're starting from, what they're capable of, and then how far I'm capable of taking them. If you get a crowd which is "wired" already and knows your repertoire and already looking for comedy and nonsense between the songs, then the challenge is to quiet them down and take them as close to tears as possible. If, however, you start out with a tight-laced and silent audience, who would rather just sit there quietly and be entertained, then the challenge is to loosen them up, make them laugh and—hopefully—make them sing.

Traditional song is much easier to do in an intimate setting, because its roots lie in singing to family and friends around your own or somebody else's fireside. My preference for contained spaces and smaller numbers doesn't just reflect my development as a singer through the coffeehouse circuit. It also reflects the music I am singing and what I see almost as my brief, which is to give people something that they haven't heard before or, if they have heard it before, to get them to learn to hear it with slightly different ears. It is a mix of intimacy, friendship, interaction, and even teaching. This is what sparks me as a singer; that is why in the later stages of my career my preference was always for a smaller venue—the smaller the better. Of course there is an economic element to this choice. I no longer depend on the income from a two-thousand-seat auditorium to keep me solvent for the next few weeks, which leaves me free to follow my preference to get up close and personal with my audiences. It is so much easier as a performer to contact, control, and move people when you can almost reach out and touch them, which is the essence of traditional music in its traditional setting.

Yet there is another dimension to this. I have always been aware that I was simply one more singer in a long line of female singers who have kept the traditional ballads alive. There were times when I was performing that it felt almost as if I was merely the instrument through which these old singers were still delivering their songs. I heard their voices, so clearly, in my head. So clearly that, when first I recorded the songs I had learned from them, I was often appalled when I listened to the recording, because what came through the speakers was so very different from what I had heard in my head. It took me a long time to realize that what was missing was maturity; I hadn't lived long enough or had enough of the rough edges knocked off me to understand fully what I was singing and, therefore, to be able to sing the song exactly as I still heard these others sing it. It's all very well to learn the tune and the words and get choked up by the emotion of the song, but it takes more than that to bring the song to life. It takes living through the experiences these old singers were singing about: they knew these hurts and feelings from their own lives and were able to project them into the song. Now that I have lived long enough to be a river-tumbled boulder with nothing but the essentials left, fully understand that it is the essence of loss, the essence of misery, the essence of grief and death and of all the things that we struggle to deal with as humans that one must put into the song. You can only bring it to life when you too have lived through what its lyrics and its melody are talking about.

At age twenty-three, what the hell did I know about these things? But I did my best to follow these old singers who, by their performances, had illustrated where I was supposed to be going. I copied some of the pronunciations, some of the phrasing, some of the emphasis that Jeannie Robertson used, that Lizzie, her daughter, used, that Lucy Stewart used if I had been particularly moved by one of their ballads. I did my best to swallow, absorb, and digest their songs and singing into my bloodstream; then I tried to reproduce the same performance myself. I was always very conscious that there were many of these old voices behind me and, at times, it felt as if I was channeling—but, back then, this would not have been a popular thing to say. When it really works, there is nothing quite like the feeling of having several hundred people suddenly go very still in the middle of a ballad—that's when you know you have got them all to go to exactly the same place at the same time. I cannot define what that place is, but I surely know it when I feel it, because at that place and at that point in time it is almost as if I'm not there but somebody else is—one or more of the many older voices. They still live on, buried somewhere, in their songs.

At the open-air performances, no part of this experience was possible. In the early days there was no such thing as doing a sound check on the speakers and saying, "Wait a minute, there is too much reverb, or far too much bass; can you adjust please?" You just walked over to the microphone and did your thing. Luckily, as an unaccompanied singer, I always heard what I was doing above the speaker which was relaying the sound around me; I never had to stick a finger in my ear like some performers. But the whole sound system thing can be so off-putting. Nowadays, I always specify in my contracts "the less machinery on the stage, the better." A mike is essential; my spoken voice does not project, and my accent makes it impossible for people to get on the same wavelength and understand what I'm saying for at least ten minutes. When I'm using a mike I don't have to work so hard to speak or to project enough voice to fill a hall. That way I can keep everything at the same kind of intimate level of delivery, and I don't have to switch from a soft-spoken voice to a Wagnerian singer's voice—that would be too much of a jolt for any audience, I think.

In complete contrast, working with a radio show is different. You get up in front of a live audience, yes, but the prime object of that kind of show is the outgoing radio transmission, so there is an absolute wall of mike stands, music stands, and monitors in front of you. You have to do your best to ignore them and be as natural as possible. By now, I had more or less learned to handle this. Henrietta Yurchenko, one of my two New York music-critic friends, also did radio work and had pulled me in fairly quickly to be interviewed on radio. I guess I was newsworthy, because it was unusual for kids to do what I was doing in the early 1960's. These days, it is commonplace for young people to head off to South America or elsewhere with nothing but a half-empty backpack, but that was unheard of fifty-five years ago, especially for a young woman on her own, heading off into the blue. For me, exposure to radio shows had come almost immediately, and I started doing radio interviews early on.

Part of the attraction, I am sure, was my broad Fife accent. Americans loved it, and even if I had been reading the telephone directory, they would have found it fascinating. However, my natural accent slowly built into an unusual problem. Living and working in America, all the voices around me in the music industry were American, and I began to develop almost an American voice myself.* It is the curse of having a musical ear—I don't read a note of music and have to learn what I sing by ear, so it is not surprising that I tend to react to and reflect the accents coming in. Back home, I quickly become pure Scottish again, but as soon as I returned to the United States, I morphed quickly into being American-Scottish, simply reflecting what an ear that is attuned to music was picking up.

Back out on the road, with Manny almost certainly pulling the strings, I got an invitation to sing at both the Philadelphia Folk Festival, another of the biggies on the East Coast, and at Mariposa, which is the folk festival in Toronto. Those two gave me the complete set of the Big Four: Newport, Philadelphia, Mariposa, and Berkeley. There were others, like Fox Hollow in Petersburgh, New York, and I was at most of them several times, but Mariposa was the best of the bunch, because you had to get there by boat, which meant that anybody who turned up had to be seriously interested, otherwise why get into a boat and pay the extra ticket money to get out to the island?

At that early stage in my career, I couldn't afford to get too precious and tell people, "I don't like singing out of doors." I needed the exposure of these big festivals for the work and the money they brought in later.

* At one stage I used to worry that I would lose the Scottish tongue, and my throwaway line, "I am going back home to brush up my accent," was one-third funny and two-thirds serious.

The first time I complained, from memory, was quite a few years later when Manny got me invited to the Birmingham, Alabama, festival. When that was first mooted, I grumbled, "It's in the South, so it will be hot, and it's out of doors."

You employ a manager to have a more realistic picture of your personal financial context than you have yourself. My tentative revolt was quickly suppressed, in my own best interests. Manny loved my voice—but he loved it even more when it made cash registers chime for both of us. "Well, the Alabama festival is out of doors, but your concerts are in a stone church, so everything will be cool," he replied firmly. Discussion ended.

True to his promise, that festival turned out to be wonderful. I got the best of both worlds, because I had the days to wander out of doors for as long as I could handle the heat, finding out what was going on and listening to other people. Then, when I had to work, at least I was indoors, where it was lovely and cool.

Of course I had fun at these outdoor festivals but, over the years, my aversion built up toward this kind of gig. The final straw, even though it makes me smile now, was the New Orleans Jazz and Folk Festival. This event was in a tent, which was fine, except that, while I was singing, I realized that I was only 150 yards away from the gospel tent, in which about 400 people were really rocking. Even if there wasn't a floor on which audience members could stomp their feet, the noise was just infectious. Then, as if that wasn't bad enough, somewhere during the course of my fourth or fifth song, a Trinidad steel band marched past the back of our tent. When this sort of thing happens to you as a performer, you can only swing with it; there is nothing else you can do. But I tell you "Eileen Aroon" never sounded quite the same again, not after having "Just a Closer Walk with Thee" in one ear and a Trinidad steel band beating out syncopated rhythm in the other. The solo voice has demands of its own. Much of what you are doing depends on what you are trying to communicate through your voice, and you don't have a lot of choice if you are mainly concerned with just trying to be heard.

By 1965 I had been home again, going back to Scotland briefly to find that the same kind of folk circuit, not so much in coffeehouses as in folk clubs, was popping up in Britain. These folk clubs were inevitably held in pubs, where you had to learn a whole different set of survival skills to cope with the problems of places whose main objective was to sell alcohol. W.C. Fields should have added to his famous quote, "Never compete with children, and small dogs, *and drunks*." You cannot compete with a drunk, because he knows neither logic nor social embarrassment. In some places, you have to depend on the management to try to keep down the worst of the noise and disruption, while in others you can only ignore the chaos and get on with what you're doing. You are often left to handle the challenges on your own, and your singing becomes almost a subsidiary repertoire. Your main repertoire, if you want to be able to concentrate on your singing, has to include a stock of tried and tested one liners which help you establish control. You learn to cope with drunks by using a wide range of comments, ranging from "Good evening; how are you; I'm glad you're here," to "No, I think you've missed the point; what's supposed to happen is that I'm going to sing, and you're going to listen, and if you finish before I do, then wait for me."

This battle for control always has to come out with the performer's smile, because it is very easy to lose a whole roomful of people if you get too snotty. Only once did I make that mistake, and I learned the lesson the hard way. If the disruptive group is known to and is part of your audience, then you do not take them on. The first time I did, I lost a whole roomful of people before songs, during songs, and after songs. Even when I left the stage, the same icy silence followed me.* As I walked off, I thought, "Well, that wasn't comfortable but it was a damn sight better than the noise I was competing with before I spoke." True, but that kind of response is not something you want to demonstrate often, because reputation travels, and bad publicity travels even faster.

Even on that first trip home, I got myself booked almost immediately into the folk circuit in Britain. Before I had unpacked my suitcase, I was off again on tour in England, to discover a very different culture than that of America, because some of these folk-club pub venues were pretty grotty. You got paid for singing and it was usually up to you to control the crowd, if it became restless and had been drinking. That's where I served my new apprenticeship, learning to control drunks while keeping the audience onside. So far as most pub management people were concerned, they were making money from selling drinks to the people whom the folk event had drawn in. To them, we were background music—and the main problem I have with that is that I have never considered myself

*Small communities in particular take an indulgent view of local drunks "Och, it's only oor Billy, an' he's an awfae lad for the drink" ("he likes to take a lot of drink"). Get a bit sharp with drunken Billy, and the whole community sides instantly with him.

background music. It took me a while to grow into voicing that opinion. When I did, I found that it came as a surprise to most people that they were disrupting the singer's performance by their noise. The decent ones generally quietened down; the rest merely said "tough," and carried on.

I spent three months in Britain on that first visit, the beginning of a routine that lasted for at least forty years of commuting back and forth, coming to Scotland usually twice a year, getting straight off the plane and hitting the boards, on both sides of the Atlantic . Manny had nothing to do with the British side. Initially, I handled my own bookings, after building up some knowledge of the network of people who were organizers in the different clubs. Then this changed abruptly, and without planning.

One night when I was singing in Thurso—a great favorite place of mine—I was accosted by a woman who became my British manager. I had been singing a kid's song and had asked the audience, as I often did in my performances, "Has anyone here heard of the second verse or does anyone know any other verses?" It's a marvelous way to discover new material because, with a couple of hundred people present who know and like this type of music, there is a fair chance that somebody has heard the song you are talking about or knows the verse you are looking for. At the time there was no response; then, as I was winding down after the performance, having a beer with some friends at a table, a voice boomed out over my head: "Incidentally, that song you asked about, it's a children's song from somewhere at the beginning of the twentieth century and the second verse is . . ."

Almost spilling my beer, I did a double take to find an assertive lady standing over me. It was a typical entrance for someone who became a lifelong friend, as well as a manager. Her name was Henrietta Munro, and she and her brother ran an antique shop in Thurso. Her life had been typical of her gender and age group in that she had been summoned home from a job in Fleet Street, London, to look after an aging mother. She was one of a kind and had far more ability and drive than she was using in her life up north. In the course of the next eighteen months, she took over my bookings—all done by snail mail in those days or by picking up the phone.

With this new outlet for her energy, Hetty kept me as busy back in Scotland as I could handle. When I came off the plane, I had barely time for a cup of tea with my parents before she had me traveling on both sides of the border. This kind of touring could be done by road, whereas in the US that is seldom possible. In the beginning, I wrote to my dad: "I need a car; do you have anything in mind?" In reply, he found a big hunter-green Humber with real wood paneling and leather seats, which probably did several gallons per mile in those days when petrol was cheap. It was the ideal solution, a big solid car which helped me get through an extended tour of one-night stands and weekends, shuttling clothes, a guitar, records to sell, myself, and possibly company, down south and back.

On these multigig tours, I found my own places to stay—and some of them, I wish I hadn't ever found. The one that made the biggest impression was in Manchester. I arrived at the venue for the gig in the middle of the afternoon, after driving most of the day down from Newcastle, to find that every place was closed. It must have been the local half-day holiday, but by then I was starving, and all I could find open was a Chinese restaurant. By the time I left that establishment, I had become almost an honorary member of the family.

When I went in I asked, "May I have tea?" They brought me a big mug of Builder's tea.* "Oh, I am so sorry," I said. "I meant green tea." From their smiles, I don't think anybody had ever asked for that before. The owner was delighted and, when they brought through the food, I also asked for chopsticks. At that point, I could have asked him for the keys to the restaurant and he would have given them to me. As I ate the meal, I found myself wondering how it must feel to be offering cultural food in a place where nobody has a clue about its subtleties and wanted only sweet-and-sour chicken and chips.

That meal had to be eaten as most of my larger meals have been eaten, somewhere between two thirty and four in the afternoon, so that I was running on fuel but not on a full stomach by eight, nine, or ten at night. When I finished, I went back to the bar where I was going to be singing; they didn't do accommodation but directed me to a hotel just round the corner. I got there to discover grimy stained-glass windows and swinging doors and brass which hadn't been polished for maybe twenty-five years. I went in through the side door, carrying both my case and my guitar—you couldn't leave anything outside in your car in a place like this—and immediately I fell over a disemboweled piano.

Picking myself up, I walked through a grubby corridor which took me into the bar through another side door. There was one table, where two old boys and an old girl with a mouthful of teeth like odd cups were

* Builder's tea: brown tea made from tea bags, with milk and sugar already added

sitting. She leered up at me when I walked in and said "Good afternoon, dearie" in the sort of deep and scary voice someone would put on for a radio show or a bad Gothic horror movie.

I walked over to the guy behind the bar, who had a greasy cloth and was wiping down the bar counter, paying me no attention at all. "I'm told you have rooms," I said.

"Oh, aye?" Wipe, wipe, wipe. "I need a room, please. Have you a free one?" Stopping wiping, he craned over the bar to check me out from head to foot. "Are you on your own?" he asked. I got the implication, and, drawing myself up to my full five feet eight inches, replied in a polite clipped voice, "I am looking for *one* room, for *one* person, for *one* night."

He got the message: "Oh, aye. We can do that," he said.

Taking my suitcase, he led me up one flight of stairs. These weren't too bad, but by the time we reached the second flight we were crunching over bits of plaster on the steps. "We're havin' a bit o' work done," he said over his shoulder. When we got to the top landing, it was festooned with strings, from which hung some very gray sheets. "That's bathroom in here," he said, trying to open the door. It wouldn't move. "Somebody in there," he added, and ushered me into a room which had wall-to-wall beds—two double beds, so close together that you couldn't get between them, and crammed so tightly against a couple of wardrobes that you couldn't open the wardrobe doors. There was half an inch of grit and grime on everything. One of the windows was open at an angle, leaving a black mark in the curtain where the dust had blown in.

I turned the sheet down—at least they seemed to be reasonably clean—and asked him. "How much are you charging?" He told me—it wasn't very much but still more than this was worth. The last thing I wanted to do was stay there, but it was an hour and a half before I was due to start work and I had been driving all day. I needed a bath—for this grade of hotel, showers had not yet been invented—so I sat on the edge of the bed and chain-smoked until I heard the bathroom door open. As I rose to go through, I heard children's voices, and the bathroom door closed again. This happened three times, as somebody processed a chain of kids through there, and, when I finally managed to get in, the bath had a black ring about eight inches deep, and the floor was covered with kids' clothes and wet towels.

I had to do something. I used one of their towels to clean the bath, then spread the cleanest of the other towels inside the bath, to keep my skin off the bath surface as much as possible. I bathed in four inches of barely lukewarm water, which at least helped to revive me a little bit, then went to work—taking my suitcase as well as my guitar with me rather than leaving them back there.

However, deliverance was at hand in the form of a friend who showed up unexpectedly at the gig, having heard I was performing there. "I thought I would take you home," he said. "Oh what a good idea," I replied. Nevertheless, I felt that I should go back and at least offer to pay the man in the hotel. I was prepared to argue that I wasn't going to pay full rate for a room I had never slept in but, to my surprise, he looked up from wiping the bar with the same greasy cloth and said, "No, that's all right. You don't have to pay. You never used the room." So I headed off before the woman upstairs found that somebody had been using her towels which, I reckon, were cleaner after their bath with me than before.

That room is etched forever in my memory—the bathroom particularly—but there have been many other rooms where I have worked very hard to avoid any skin contact between myself and the sheets. The gig itself went fine—nice pub, good audience, and a friend who provided a much-needed escape route, but when you were on tour like that accommodation was always hit or miss.

I didn't always have bad experiences. I once worked with the Spinners* in Liverpool, and two local singers, Jacqui and Bridie, sent word to me that their house was available, and I was welcome to stay, although they themselves were on tour at that point. Their friend came to collect me; I slept in pristine sheets and had my breakfast made for me in the morning. In Britain as in America, folk is a very small circuit and a very familial one.

Against this, there was another place in London I will never forget. The folk club was run by a husband and wife team who lived in a house which seemed to be four rooms stacked one on top of the other. It was a strange building where two rooms were above street level, and two (including the kitchen) were down below. The wife disappeared with a group of people after the gig, and the husband was stuck with looking

* The Spinners: a Liverpool folk group and one of the first to have multiracial band members. They started as mainly a skiffle band with a mostly American folk repertoire, then broadened to include English sea shanties (following up on the suggestion of a seaman) and English folk. They became central to the revival of folk music in the UK, where one of their own compositions, "In My Liverpool Home," has become a modern classic.

after me. He made me something to eat, which was fine, then showed me the bedroom. The bed was buried under laundry and heaps of clothes. When he turned the sheet back, both the pillowcases and the sheets showed evidence of serial occupancy over, I would guess, about six weeks. I thought, "There is absolutely no way on God's earth that I'm going to sleep there," so I spread some of the clean laundry on top of the bed and slept on it under my jacket and without taking my clothes off. Next day, I drove back to Newcastle, and a friend there—the same Meg who went hiking with me as a student—asked me: "What do you need?" "A bath," I replied. "And after that, I want to burn my clothes."

On all these visits back to Britain, I always stayed for a while with my parents, who were now living in a house on the promenade in Leven where there was plenty of space for me. If I had gigs, I radiated out from there, taking off from Leven for two or three weeks at a time. Looking back, I don't think they ever really understood what I was doing, until I was getting my name in the Scottish papers or happened to show up with a new recording. While they never said much, I suspect they concurred with the optician in Leven who had looked after the family's eyes from day one and who, when I met him in the High Street at a point well into my singing career asked, "Aye, Jean. Is this you hame again on holiday?" When I was back, to the locals I could only be back on holiday—whether I was working my butt off or not. "Aye, Tom," I replied. It was easier to go with the flow than argue. "Are ye still singing?" "Aye." "Is it no' aboot time ye got a job?" he demanded.

For most Scots, the puzzlement was always, "What's this singing for a living rubbish?" My parents never fully understood where I had "gone wrong"; to their minds, I'm sure there was a lot of pride in much later days, after I began to get some academic accolades and public recognition, but I suspect I was a bit of a mystery to them most of the time. When I left Leven to go and sing in Thurso, then do another gig in Aberdeen on the way south, I left them shaking their heads as my car disappeared up the street. Or when I said, "I'm off to Halifax," they just nodded. Maybe they were prepared to give me my head, so long as the police didn't come calling for me while I was away.

When I got back to the United States, Manny had moved his base of operations to the West Coast and had an apartment in Santa Monica. Joan Baez was already under his wing and also had an apartment there where I could stay while visiting. She and I never coincided in Santa Monica although we often met at folk festivals.

Manny was a political creature, and this often made me feel guilty about not being in the least political. Any views I have are always capable of being expressed strongly through my music—whether antiwar, where there are plenty songs to tear your guts out about the absolute insanity of wars, or feminism where there are plenty lyrics that relate to strong feisty women. On issues such as these, yes, I have strong opinions, and I suppose that you could call them political, but I have never taken them to the point of banner waving.

Nevertheless, Manny would never let me leave without having something to think about. He had a wonderful lively mind, and I suspect I amused him a lot. He was great to work with as a manager. He kept me busy, he kept me solvent, and, apart from that one miserable gig on the back of the flatbed truck in Boston, I don't think there was anything he brought in that I didn't want to do. Manny was knee-deep in the folk movement, and part of his reason for moving to the West Coast was to be in better touch with whatever new wave was emerging out there.

His bookings kept me almost perpetually on the move, so that I was never in one place for long enough to think about recording. Finally, the third Elektra LP was scheduled in Los Angeles after the company opened an office there. I knew nobody in LA at that time. Jac Holzman wasn't there but was directing things from afar this time. He had a secretary called Vera Hertenstein who took me under her wing during the times when I wasn't working in the studio.

I was staying in a motel about twenty blocks from where she lived, and that's where I first ran into the concept that if you were walking on a pavement in Los Angeles, then you were obviously a vagrant or had malice aforethought, because I was twice stopped by the police for doing just that. There is no bus system in LA, and I had no car, not even a bike; how else was I going to get anywhere? So I walked and the police circled the block a couple of times and then pulled over to ask me what I was doing. I explained in my best Scottish accent, and it worked for me each time; I would have had a lot of persuading to do, without it.

Simply living on the road and traveling from gig to gig in both America and Scotland kept me busy, busy, busy. Yet somehow three new developments managed to enter my life, each with their own commitments. Firstly, my long-standing interest in gospel music evolved into performing it and ultimately recording some of our favourite songs with a group of like-minded friends in Chicago. Yet another place to swing into, for yet another reason. Then, second, I found myself invited to take up an artist-in-residence post at Wesleyan University, which involved teaching as well as performing traditional songs both to a school outreach program run by the university and to undergraduate classes. This was a different beastie to my teaching in Kirkcaldy, both in terms of the interest level of the students and of my own new and intense commitment. Damn it, I had *so* much I wanted to pass on, all the stuff I had learned the hard way from a decade of performing.

More of both new ventures in the following chapter. For the moment, it is enough to say that I was performing all over the US on weekends, then thrashing back to teach school kids and university students during the week. I felt a bit like a ping-pong ball, getting batted back and forth across the country.

My carefree early days of part-time singing and Scottish County Dancing were long behind me. Living on the road between performances or staying with friends and using them as a base when I was in their part of America had become a way of life. The penny was beginning to drop, at long last, that singing was not so much a way of life as my chosen career.

There was no sudden epiphany. I had already recognized a few years before that I was pretty much a resident in America, having immigrated on a visa under Marilyn and Neil's sponsorship when I came to sing at their wedding. At no point did I consider dropping everything I was doing and going back home to Scotland. Why should I? To do what? Even singing full-time on the UK folk circuit, I could never make as good a living as I was making in the States. I was better working in America, and, somewhere along the line, it got through to me that singing in clubs wasn't an accident anymore and that I would be doing this for some considerable time to come. If this was a career, then I was having a good time and seemed to be well established in it. I had never doubted that singing was what I was about; now there was a growing sense of permanence rather than the feeling of living from day to day.

Nevertheless, as a busy professional singer, this meant that I was moving pretty fast, always on the run, trying to be both a teacher and a performer. This didn't leave much time for self. Looking back, it should come as no surprise that, during these years, the third and less successful development was that I got married and divorced.

What drove the marriage was pretty much cultural expectation. I was twenty-nine years old, and I found myself thinking, "By this age, I am supposed to be married, settled and having a family." It was a poor idea. He was one of the joint owners of the Edinburgh Castle, and I had known him over many years, between working in the shop and coming there for Scottish country dancing sessions. One night I said to him, "Why don't you ask me to marry you?" He blinked, then asked. I accepted. We married, and that was a bad mistake. It didn't last. It never had a chance, because I was so seldom there.

At the time, I simply told my parents that I was getting married. My mother was more than a bit piqued that it wasn't going to be a church wedding. That rocked me back onto my heels. "Look," I told her. "I've spent my whole life listening to you railing against the kirk, and saying that you wouldn't have anything to do with it." A silence, then, "Aye, that's right," she said. "And you always told me you would never set foot in it?" I said accusingly. "No, I wouldn't," she agreed. "Well, how do you reconcile that with . . . ?" "You could at least have got merrit in the kirk,"* she snapped. "No' just a registrar's office." Bluebell and logic often parted company, when logic stood in the way of what she had always believed. For all her tirades against the church, she herself had gotten married there, because that was the respectable thing to do for her generation. Weddings and churches were the natural order of things, whatever you thought about either. End of story.

Whether marrying in church would have made any difference, I very much doubt. Marriage isn't simply an arrangement of convenience. To maintain any marriage, you have to be there for each other; presence is the lifeblood of any relationship. I was too busy moving, too busy being a successful established singer whose work was starting to be recognized to be there at all—unless I was dashing in and out between flights.

Robert was a good man, and we remained friends until he died. It was a hard way to learn that to the list of insupportables for the wandering minstrel, like pets and house plants, one can add marriage partners.

*"merrit in the kirk": married in the church

CHAPTER 6

Moving into New Ventures

Gospel music had taken me over, from my baptism by total immersion at the Apollo Theater back in Harlem in the early 1960s. It broke forever the constrictions of my Scottish upbringing—blasted them away.

I had been brought up to perform—and listen—to singing with intense introspection. In the traditional Scots muckle sangs* there is much repetition, and the song is totally formulaic, almost hypnotic, because there is no hurry, and there are anywhere from eighteen to forty-seven verses to allow the audience to settle down and listen to this story without having to wonder what's going to happen, because they know it is going to be tragic anyway. For the singer, delivery of the muckle sang and its changing moods takes intense focus and controlled emotional involvement. However Scots also do brevity probably better than anybody else. I usually describe short songs like "David and Jeannie" as the equivalent of a Japanese painting; the singer gives you only two or three tightly controlled brush strokes of story and mood, and you are left to fill in the details and gain understanding through your own experiences of life.

> What was on your mind, bonnie Jeannie?
> What was on your mind when you changed your bed to mine
> Were you tired o' lyin' your lane, bonnie Jeannie?
> It was a' for love o' you, bonnie Davie
> It was a' for love o' you, but I see my folly noo
> For you've gi'en me cause to rue, bonnie Davie.†

* muckle sangs: literally, "big songs"—the long traditional ballads that told a story which was generally rooted in real events from long ago; often a form of oral history

† Traditional Scottish song

Switching from this kind of introspection to gospel music, the whole point of which is rhythm, group movement, group singing and group harmony, has the same releasing effect of giving you permission to do all sorts of things you have never done before, both in singing and in expressing emotion. In addition, it is bloody great fun.

My involvement in gospel quickly moved from listening to singing. I ran into Lisa Neustadt and Helen Schneyer at folk festivals in Philadelphia and New England. Lisa was a teacher who didn't wander all over the place like most singers I knew, while Helen lived in Washington, D.C., so I met her when I was singing there. When we got together, we would get ceilidhs going in hotel rooms, dormitory rooms, restaurants, or community halls at festivals. The singing would just start spontaneously. My whole working life was woven round solo singing of songs which were seldom intended for multiple voices, whereas gospel is crafted to be easily memorized and sung immediately by as many voices as possible. This contrast was as sharp as night and day, but I had no problem whatsoever in making the switch—and doing it joyously. My favorite place in any festival when I wasn't on stage and working was the gospel workshops, so I had already spent a lot of time singing gospel music, holding the main melody line and letting the people around me do their own thing. Since my work left me based in Boston* for a while and since Lisa lived there, we started singing quite a few of the gospel songs together.

She had a wonderful instinctive sense of harmony, which left me with the main melody, and we gradually collected some other like-minded people and musicians she knew. At some point, we decided to record. The Angel Band that we set up was a pickup group which seldom worked together in public and normally only got together for a recording. We did this often enough to produce a series of "blue-eyed gospel" LPs.

A second and truly fulfilling new direction came to me when I was approached and asked to present my music academically. In 1972 I was invited to be artist-in-residence at Wesleyan University in Middletown, Connecticut, fitting this in between commuting back and forth to performances across America. The invitation came through a town-and-gown

* Thanks to the famous—and real—American hospitality, I have been based for time periods ranging from months to years at different places, including San Francisco, Berkeley, Boston, New York City, Chicago, Providence, Sarasota, and Tucson, residing with many different people and going back and forth as my work took me across the country.

program which was trying to bridge the gap between the university and the community. Wesleyan ran an extensive range of music studies and, within this area, they got funding for a new world music program. They wanted to use this to fund musicians to come in and do a mix of courses at the university plus work in local schools. They decided to go for both Anglo-American and Afro-American music and brought a young man from Ghana who was a dancer and a drummer. He taught classes at the university and worked in a high school in the town. Similarly, they brought me in to run a ballad course at Wesleyan, then work three days a week in an elementary school.

Quite a challenge, covering everything from school kids to degree students. Flattered as I was, that thought made me pause before I agreed to be involved. One of the things which appealed to me was that, for the school part of the project, I hadn't been placed there solely to teach music but also act as a cultural resource, available to kids working in every subject area, so that they could ask, "How is this done in Scotland, and what's different about how we handle it here?" A real challenge to my ingenuity, as I found myself covering everything from carpentry, to stained glass, to bus trips to dinosaur museums, to having them build a Loch Ness monster out of papier mâché. We even built—with a friend's help—a small wooden building (see photograph) inside one of the classrooms and used this as a post office, a bank, and a shop; the Scottish Tourist Board gave me a whole mess of posters to put up in it, and from somewhere I got a lot of old Scottish banknotes* for the kids to use.

This grade-school project worked really well in parts; some of the teachers were right into it, while others saw me only as a free period for themselves. Through all of this, I sang with everybody and the only thing I ever asked was, "Please, I don't care where we sing, but don't put me in the music room."

The school had a young headmaster—maybe even younger than I—and he told me, "If it isn't illegal, immoral, or starts a fire, go do it." The only time the teachers got really exercised was when I organized a

* These were real banknotes from old banks which had been taken over in the early 1960's. The money intrigued the kids. American money is all the same size, but at that time we had seven Scottish banks—the Bank of Scotland, the Royal Bank of Scotland, the Commercial Bank of Scotland, the Union Bank of Scotland, the Clydesdale Bank of Scotland, the National Bank of Scotland, and the British Linen Bank, all issuing their own notes.

treasure hunt which raged right through the school, as two of my classes of kids were running wild. Whatever the other teachers thought about it, the kids at least had a wonderful time. And so did I. Maybe part of me has never really grown up.

Why my resistance to taking classes in the music room? This was instinctive on my part, but that resistance was set in concrete after I talked to Jean Dodds, who was the music teacher there and who, with her husband, became a good friend. Jean told me of her own experience when she had started out in that school. She said, "I had the class come in, with a tape recorder sitting on the window sill and playing some lively music. The kids sat on cushions on the floor of the music room, so that it was easy to clear it for movement. As they came in, I said to them, "Just take your cushions, sit anywhere, and face the music." So help me, they all lined up in straight lines, facing the closed piano. And I thought, "They are only seven years old; what the hell have we done to them already?"

I still rate it as one of the greatest achievements of my life, to start with a class of seven-year-olds imbued with this kind of training and mentality in their approach to music, and four years later have the whole bunch of them—boys as well as girls—belting out the songs I had taught them without any thought of key or piano or anything else. OK, so I cheated a bit to get them onside, because there are plenty Scots songs of the politically incorrect variety, and kids love anything or anyone kicking against the system. The first time I started into something like

> When I was a wee, wee tot
> They took me from my wee wee cot
> And put me on my wee wee pot
> To see if I would wee or not . . .*

I swear that they looked heavenward to see if I was going to be struck down by thunderbolts. If any came, they missed me.

Whatever the reason, the project worked; the proof of the pudding† was that I was there in that outreach program for four years. What was meant to be a one-year residence became a two-year residence because,

* Traditional Scottish children's song

† The full expression is "the proof o' the puddin' is in the eatin' o' it"; it is an old Scots saying which translates "the proof of the pudding is in the eating of it" and means that if the pudding has been eaten, then people must have enjoyed it. It is now, of course, well known in the United States as well.

although Wesleyan ran out of money for my teaching assistant after one year, they decided to keep the project going if I didn't mind working without an assistant. I didn't; I could handle the kids on my own. At the end of the second year, although they didn't get the grant renewal to keep my own job going, they found money somewhere else and the project continued. The crazy thing was that this became my work during the week while on the weekends I might be as far afield as San Francisco doing a concert.

In the middle of all this, I found myself benefiting from yet another wonderful act of American spontaneous generosity. A friend bought me a car. "You can't do that!" I argued, my Scottish upbringing rebelling. "You can't plane-hop all over the country, then get back to Connecticut to teach, without being able to drive" was the reply.

That was the beginning of my love affair with a wee yellow VW Beetle, which went on for twenty-one years. It was my stalwart friend, in good times and bad: I retreated to it more than once in tears after a hard gig, when I was exhausted from the endless traveling on the road. It became almost my home on wheels and I was heartbroken when it finally became too old to repair.

The college-teaching side of the Wesleyan project was fascinating. In the first class I ran there were six undergraduates. I held it in my apartment, saying, "I can't see how walking into a brightly lit classroom at ten in the morning and talking about a classic ballad is ever going to work. So why don't we hold the class at my place, after you've had your supper?" They would arrive around seven in the evening and we spent a couple of hours going through the material. The muckle sangs are all about death, disaster, matricide, patricide, incest, betrayal, and similar uplifting stuff. This fact drew a comment after the course had been running for a month: "Aren't there any cheerful songs at all?" a student groaned.

"No," I said. "As a matter of fact, there aren't too many cheerful ones."

Struggling to stay ahead of my undergraduates taught me a lot about traditional music, which up until then I had only sung and never studied academically. One of my students, fairly free with her opinions, dropped in for old time's sake to my classes a couple of years later and said to me, "Boy, you have sure got a lot more content now than when you started." I thought, "No wonder; I knew sweet damn all when I started."

It seems ironic that I was now working a lot harder at putting some academic foundation under the songs I was singing than I had ever worked as a student in Edinburgh. Enter the missing passion! Not only had I found something dear to my heart, but I had to work my tail off, learning enough about the background and structure of the traditional ballad to be able to analyze and explain the songs to third- and fourth-year students in a degree course. It also provided a nice balance for me, since the other half of the town-and-gown program was to get seven-year-old kids singing anything at all, be it Scottish or not.

Apart from teaching, my life as a singer went on. In 1972 I made a record for Folk Legacy in Connecticut. Sandy and Caroline Paton owned the company, and they had a lovely acoustic studio. This LP proved to be another fast job, where I needed only a few second takes. Sandy, who was also the sound engineer, used to call me One-Take Redpath, and I knew from the start that we would work well together. He and I went off with a list of fourteen songs to try and decide, on our own, what should be the first and last song on each side, so that the LP hung together. We came back with exactly the same running order for the songs, which showed us that we had the same feel for balance and content. Great minds think alike—yes, I know that quotation goes on to say that fools seldom differ—but the rapport felt so good, we went for it. That record was *Frae My Ain Country** When you do enough recording, you soon find out that the path is seldom as smooth and fulfilling as that one was.

For instance, I would have killed for the use of that studio again when I launched into a major project with Philo Records and Bill Schubart.† We recorded in New England, in northern Vermont in a converted barn where the soundman was downstairs and the studio was upstairs. The building creaked in the wind, and we had to stop when it was raining or when a large truck passed on the main road. The whole experience was

* *Frae My Ain Country:* From My Own Country; Folk Legacy 49

† Bill was a memorable character—well over six feet tall and built in generous proportion. On one occasion, he was coming from a board meeting for the Council of the Arts in Vermont when he was so frustrated and so hot that he stopped his very large car in the middle of a bridge and jumped—suit, shirt, tie, the whole lot—into a swimming hole underneath that he and his brother had used as kids. Up above cars screeched to a halt as people thought he was trying to commit suicide. Then he surfaced, climbed out, probably having emptied the swimming hole by the splash he made, shook himself like a dog, climbed back into his car, and drove off. He said later, "The only thing I regretted was not having taken my brief case with me."

an exercise in patience by everybody involved—engineers, singers, and instrumentalists alike. Everything would be flowing beautifully, and we would be thinking "This is it," when, out of nowhere, the roof timbers would begin to creak and groan, and we had to do at least that verse again.

Although I had started out as an unaccompanied singer, I was now becoming accustomed to working with a whole range of musicians: some I saw only once at the recording; others came back again and again to become friends. One of the earliest was the cellist Abby Newton, and I worked with her as often as possible, because I have always liked the blend of voice and cello. That instrument sits nicely with the timbre of my own voice. This friendship led to another LP. A boyfriend of hers at that time was a classical pianist, and together we decided to make a record of Joseph Haydn's Scottish folk songs.* Having heard only classically trained voices sing these songs, I thought it was time to redress the balance, to put more emphasis on the Scottishness of the material, and to sing the words as they should be sung. The three of us had a great time, working on this project.

Amid all this recording activity, I was approached by Serge Hovey—again courtesy of Hamish Henderson working behind the scenes. Serge had been researching the songs of Robert Burns over a period of twenty-three years, trying to identify the original tunes to which Burns had set his lyrics. This research had left him with 323 Burns songs which he set to the original melodies and arranged for every combination, from solo voice and piano to two pianos, string quartet, and even a small orchestra.

How did this major new venture happen? Out of the blue, like so many things in my life, came a letter explaining what he had been doing and saying that he was looking for a singer to work with him in making the new recordings. We met up at the School of Scottish Studies in Edinburgh in the summer of 1973, during one of my trips home. Serge, who was a tall lean guy of about six foot three inches, showed Hamish and me what he had in mind on one of the pianos. I was intrigued by the broad sweep and challenge of the project and never considered asking for details or guarantees. I simply thought that he was looking for someone to record these songs with him in the United States, and I would be in the US, so why not? "This is what I'm doing," Serge finished up, at that first meeting. "Would you be interested?" "Yes," I replied.

* *Haydn: Scottish Songs,* PH 1082

No other answer seemed to be relevant, but then I have always had a tendency to jump off the high diving board without checking first that there is water underneath. All of the fine tuning, negotiations, and running head-on into each other about how things should be presented came after I was pretty well committed to the project. I can remember vaguely wondering at the time how I was going to fit this in between long sessions of teaching myself and my students classic ballads, encouraging grade-school kids to sing, recording gospel and folk with Philo Records, traveling all over the country to coffeehouses and concerts on the weekends, plus commuting to and from the UK folk circuit several times a year. I would fit it in somehow, I decided, and as quickly as that, I became locked in to a major recording project which took us twenty years.

All of these new activities were making my life as a performer more and more complex. Toward the end of the 1970s, Manny said to me that he thought I needed somebody who could spend a lot more time on me and take more interest in developing as well as promoting my career, which was moving into all sorts of new areas. As always, Manny saw things more clearly and more quickly than I did: I was now working in different countries, was increasingly involved in recording, and had moved into the academic field and continued to perform as a singer. What had been a great business relationship had run its course.

We split as friends, and I began to search for a replacement. I was talking with Columbia Artists about a possible contract when Iddy Olson, who was one of my original ballad students at Wesleyan, turned up in Connecticut, job hunting. She was by then—and is still—one of my best friends. One evening I said to her, "While you're looking for a job, how would you like to help me organize my life? After all, you know as much as anybody about what I am doing, and how I like to perform."

It is vital that whoever is doing your bookings has a good grasp of both your style of music and your own preferred way of working. Without Iddy's help, I would probably have signed up to a stable like Columbia Artists that would have worked me long and hard. Sure, I might have made a great deal of money but, I suspect, I would have burned out within ten years. The whole credo of the big management companies was keeping their artists busy and profitable because, obviously, they were getting a cut. In contrast, when I finally got very tired of being on the road and decided to take a prolonged break from performing, Iddy understood and picked up the reins again with bookings as soon as I felt ready to come back.

Yes, it happens to all performers, I suppose. From being ready to travel anywhere to get and fulfil a gig, you hit a point after years of constant travel when you just can't face any more of the grind of being in perpetual motion between performances and living and working when most people are asleep and sleeping when most people are out and about. There comes a time when just being normal appeals far more to you than staying on the performance treadmill.

That's when you should put your career on hold and step back to give yourself some personal space and allow your batteries to recharge. Ignore this kind of weariness at your peril, or you are likely to drift into going through the motions rather than engaging with your audiences or the songs. I badly needed that break. I never lost my love of the music or stopped singing; I simply became disenchanted with always being on the road.

HINDSIGHT 6.1: *Chicago, mid-1970s*

Meanwhile, the rest of human life—and all its problems—went on. Life on the road can be lonely. You meet people, form relationships, but with a career that was sending me from one end of America to another, nothing seemed to work out in the longer run. That can hurt like hell. . . .

That awful fifteen minutes at the foot of the stair. Miserable silences, passionate outbursts, strange removed clinical searching for the right thing to say—for anything to say.

Would that goddam taxi never show up? Maybe there was confusion from my phone call, that Scottish accent again, but working against me this time—why do you always get a mechanical operator on the phone, when you are least able to cope with the disembodied voice saying "Will you spell that, please?"

Another ten minutes. No words, just tension, the dust on the stairs, the cigarette butts on the floor, all examined in careful eye-avoiding detail. My head ached. Hot sticky hallway. Unreal—this isn't happening, it's all a very bad movie sequence. Why do I feel nothing?

Christ, where's that cab? The apartment door only opens halfway—there's a stack of bottles behind it, there are boxes everywhere, books, furniture, old radios, more bottles—all covered in finger-gritting dust, all leaning inwards, ready to topple, crash. It's felt like a lifetime in that shrinking space since last evening, with insufferable heat, unbearable silences. And the cat, a spirit of malevolence, the smell of it everywhere, resenting me.

I can't do it anymore, go back to the quiet nights, or the giddy gaiety of too many beers. Or to last night, with its too many tears.

"There's nothing wrong with you. . . ."

Only that you lied to me, like I'm doing now. Everything's wrong with you, chaos, claustrophobia. You don't measure up but, honesty be damned, I can't tell you that.

Checker cab—blessed escape. "Goodbye, I'm sorry." At last I can leave. "There's nothing wrong with you." Except that you can sleep in that tiny oasis of a bedroom, with dirt and disorder crowding on every side, piles of clothing leaning, waiting, behind closet doors. And that cat, ears flattened, teeth sinking into the soft flesh of my palm. Traitorous affection all around me. I am half-running now, fleeing.

Where am I going, driver?

Anywhere—I don't know. A telephone, the airlines terminal. Let's see, who will have me? Oak Park, New York, Belmont? The next bit of my life depends on the drop of a dime, but this I do know: home is not here. That's it, driver. Find me a telephone. . . .

Singing for a living is hard work, despite all the glitz and glamour. Throughout my career, young women have come up to me, saying, "Oh, I would love to do what you're doing. What have I got to do, to be like you?"*

This question was asked so often that I developed a formulaic reply. It ran, "Great, delighted that you are interested. What do you need, to do what I'm doing? I'll tell you. You need twice the normal amount of stamina. Being a sprinter is no good, you have to be a long-distance runner. You need to be able to eat anything, anywhere, at any hour of the twenty-four, as is available—or not. You have to be able to sleep anywhere, under any conditions, at any hour of the twenty-four, for as long as is available—or not. After that, if you've got some talent, it helps—but it isn't crucial. Without the other three you're not going to make it anyway."†

* Over the years that has shaded off into them saying, "You remind me of my Mum." Now I get, "You remind me of my granny." Your audience renews itself, you don't; you just get older.

† Looking objectively at this reply, I can see that it illustrates just how much the years of performances and endless travel had changed me. I told these kids the plain unvarnished truth. When I was young and flying high, I would probably have told them to hitch up their skirts and go for it.

It wasn't the most popular answer, but at least I had shaken them out of any starry-eyed belief that this was a romantic way to live. It isn't. It is not just about singing, performing; it's bloody hard work and a most unnatural lifestyle. It happens to suit me to a T, but it is dangerous to walk into it without a few words of genuine warning. Did this hard-nosed advice scare some kids away from singing as a career? I doubt it. If anybody had told me that at the age of twenty-four, I would have ignored them; so too would anybody listening to me who had real talent and real drive, so no damage was done. It has to be a passion and what you really want to do, otherwise you are going to have a pretty miserable time.

Glamour, no. Yes, you are in the public eye all the time. You are wearing fancy dresses, and people are clapping their hands together to applaud your every song, but that's just the shop window—inside can be a whole lot different.

HINDSIGHT 6.2: *Written in the late 1980s*

It is part of a performer's life that each and every fan wants to wax enthusiastic, which is lovely, but if you are on the receiving end, and exhausted, it can be difficult to handle. When all you want is peace and quiet, the combination of endless traveling and being constantly stopped by nice people who then praise you until your toenails splinter inside your shoes can crack anybody's professional discipline. Being nice and approachable twenty-four–seven is hard to do without the odd slip. In this case, thankfully, the fan kept her sense of humor rather better than I kept mine. . . . Madam, if you read this, you got me at a bad time, and I'm sorry.

There I was, barely landed and still tired and sweaty from a long flight, when I was accosted by a woman from Scotland who had also just arrived and was enthusiastic to the point of embarrassing me. "I saw you in concert in Edinburgh," she said. "And it was wonderful and I was on the same plane and I thought "Oh, boy! I've been on the same flight as a celebrity. I kept whistling wee Scottish tunes but you didn't turn round."

Nice in its way, but she went on, and on, and on. In an effort to stop the effusions I interrupted: "You've just flown across the Atlantic? I'm surprised that you're still on your feet!" The words were said without thought. I was bone-weary and had simply retreated to my default position of being a Scot who could take anything but praise. All I really meant was, "Where do you get all this energy from after that flight?" It came out all wrong, because I was starting to feel sorry for myself. However, she chose to take my words literally—and her response was tongue-in-cheek.

Getting down on her knees on the floor, she touched her forehead to my hand. "Is this what you mean?" she asked, with great good humor. Her reaction, in sending me up, left me laughing. Touché. I had been well and truly upstaged!

I always worked in a dress. In the early days, simple cotton summer clothes—a cotton skirt and a white shirt. Then I graduated to dresses and, as soon as I could afford them, into long dresses. They hide a multitude of sins, for one thing, but, more important, they demonstrate to an audience that you are taking both the songs and your performance seriously—while sidestepping the whole culture of the trained voice, the T-junction feet, and the hands clasped under the bosom.

I don't know how anybody can sing in that position, where there isn't a relaxed joint or muscle in the body. The natural stance for me is a very slight slouch, the knees flexed, taking all the pressure off while leaving me perfectly balanced, so the only thing I have to worry about is the intake of breath. This stance is not particularly attractive but, if you're wearing a long dress, it cleans up the lines. My costume, if you want to call it that, was considered and refined over the years.

One of the things that helped to refine it was a concert in Elgin in the north of Scotland, round about the same time that I had bought a dress I rather liked from Cummings in Leven. As I walked onto the stage in it for the first time, from the back of the hall, I heard a woman's voice wailing: "Aw . . . there's ma froak!" "You don't half know how to demoralize somebody before their opening song!" I called back to her. This got a big laugh out of the audience, but it was a salutary lesson. From that point on, I started to get my dresses made. Recognition is all very well, so long as it goes further than wardrobe recognition.

Academic recognition is always nice. The next new development in my career was on account of Robert Innes at Stirling University. I had stopped working at Wesleyan at the tail end of 1976 and was doing only the odd academic workshop here and there, when I was invited to sing in a university town. This was a format which Iddy was trying to develop, where the booking would include a ballad workshop on campus on Friday, followed by a full evening concert at the university or its associated town on the weekend.

Bob Innes was setting up a summer-school program, "The Heritage of Scotland," at Airthrey Castle on the Stirling University campus. He had heard of my work at Wesleyan and contacted me to ask if I would do a week's class in Scottish song to run alongside three fiddle classes (in the Northeast, Shetland, and Highland traditions), and a Scottish country dancing class. Alastair Hardie, Tom Anderson, and Angus Grant were playing the fiddle, and Jessie Stuart was running the Scottish country dancing. That was a fascinating program, and it ran successfully for ten years, during which I arranged my work schedule in the States to leave myself free to come back each year to take part.

Toward the end of the 1970s, I was doing more concerts on both sides of the Atlantic than folk clubs. This development marked a tidal change in the folk scene. By then there were fewer coffeehouses: that whole phase had lasted for a while but was now ebbing fast. The massive interest in folk couldn't and didn't last forever. With the disappearance of the coffeehouse circuit in America I began to sing in some strange places, such as museums, many of which have wonderful auditoria—although after doing this for many years, I began to wonder if it was safe for me to be singing in a museum, because the risk of being kept there as an exhibit was becoming too great. However, such a venue did give me the unique answer to my question about how to find the auditorium: "Follow the main corridor down to the whale and turn right," I was told.

I also sang in churches, particularly in New England, where a church might be the only communal space for a village or small town. Those old buildings were great for performances because they had been built with acoustics in mind and the wooden surrounds gave them a lovely sound.

The same was true of Scotland. I remember one concert in Langholm in 1998, one of those great nights where choosing a program in response to audience reactions produced something memorable. I was in great form—in storytelling as well as singing—and the audience was loving every minute. The concert went on long after it was meant to stop, but nobody left, and I was pumping adrenaline. Somebody should have hooked me off long before the end. When I finally did come offstage, it was to a surprise. The sound engineers had decided that they were going to record the whole thing without telling me, knowing that being recorded would have made me much more inhibited. When I came off, they gave me the thumbs up: "Fantastic!" they said. "We've got every minute of it!"*

* *Jean Redpath Live!,* JR LIII. Both the concert and the "secret" recording were arranged by Pete Heywood, one-time editor of the *Living Tradition* magazine, which covered traditional song.

Not all of my singing over this period was performance-based. Serge Hovey and I began working on his Burns project at his home in Pacific Palisades, near Santa Monica, and gradually, as my friendship with Serge and his wife Esther grew, this became another local base for me when I was passing through or dropping in to work, because it was a recording commitment which went on for many years.

I explained to Serge that I was more than happy to sing the songs, but I didn't read a note of music. As always, I would simply learn to sing the songs by ear. To a composer of film music, used to working from his scores with a group of musicians, that couldn't have sounded great, but we had to find a way of working together. "All I need is the words," I told him. "Then if you play the melody three times over to me, no chords, no harmonies, I can deal with it from there." As a result, somewhere I have a large collection of tapes with either Serge or his son Danny saying in their strongly accented Californian voices lines such as "Whaur will Bonnie Annie lie?," followed by a single line melody on the piano repeated several times.

I would start out with perhaps twenty-six songs on a tape and play it over and over, immersing myself in it totally. Eventually, when I was working at something else in the house, a tune would pop into my head, and I would find myself humming it and wonder, "What on earth is that?" Then, like an echo in my head would come a disembodied Californian voice saying "Whaur will Bonnie Annie lie?" Alternatively, if someone said "Whaur will Bonnie Annie lie?," up would come the tune.

I had no say whatsoever regarding the songs on the first recordings. Serge chose them, his choice being dictated by the songs for which he felt he had a final arrangement. In the early days, his arrangements for many of the 323 songs were still very much works-in-progress. Like me, he was leading a very full life, and the songs had to wait in the wings until he had space and reason to work on them. Until now, there had been no point in his sitting down to do full arrangements, but finding a singer for his project was the final impetus he needed.

We had found a way of working together, but as we moved into the recording phase, fresh problems began to arise. Serge was a perfectionist, and everything had to be gift-wrapped and bow-tied before we went anywhere near a studio. There was none of my usual approach of "Well, let's run it and see how it works," knowing that if somebody didn't like it we could simply back up and do it again. That was not an option for Serge. For one thing, money was always a problem. Both he and I were doing this for nothing, but we couldn't expect professional musicians to come in and do it for free. So we never started an LP until there was enough money behind us to pay for the pianist, a string quartet, and any other relevant instrumentalists. Recording complex arrangements live is problematic because, unless you are dealing with a well-rehearsed orchestra, somebody is always going to blow it. Then you have everybody sitting around while that one person sorts it out, before you all have to do it again. To eliminate any risk of wasted time, energy—and money!—everything was recorded in "layers," which left me singing with a piano, laying down the basic track. We got voice and piano down first; then Serge would bring in the strings for two days and add these; then he would bring in the wind instruments for two days and add them. The end result was a studio-built recording, which was a real trial to me. It is not a part of my recording career that I remember with any real pleasure or satisfaction. The layered approach meant that I had no opportunity to connect with and react to the other instruments and, worse still, I struggled to cope with the places in the song when the instrumental voices would take over from mine. It was strange to me to sing, then stop abruptly for a count of thirty-two bars or more (to leave space for the missing instrumental layer), then be brought back suddenly into the song again by the piano. This whole process felt unnatural and took a lot of getting used to, but I figured that if Serge, as composer, could swing with the fact that I wasn't standing there with a score in front of me then I, in turn, should learn to deal with what was needed in these studio recordings.

What we did lock horns about was his tendency to wait for three bars before the delivery of the punch line in the song. After we had tried this a number of times, I looked at him and said, "Serge, I can't do that. It's against every instinct. If you're going to tell a story, that's not how you do it. That's not timing; it just sounds weird." I can be pretty noisy when I hold a strong opinion, and he was the composer whose score I was bucking against. Irresistible forces did meet immovable objects on occasion and sparks did fly but, mostly, we found a way to sort out our differences to the point where we were both happy with the final result. However there are some songs on the Burns records that I will never sing again.

We recorded our first Burns LP in North Ferrisburg, Vermont, in that same barn where I had worked on the Philo Records project. From memory, two or three of these LPs were done there, from 1973 through the rest of the 1970s and into the 1980s. It took us twenty years to make the seven LPs, mostly because of the money issue, but also because Serge, that remarkable man, was coping with ALS, or amyotrophic lateral sclerosis, which made him progressively less mobile and ultimately bedridden. Throughout his decline, we worked. I admired Serge enormously: he was a role model for plain bloody grit, and I doubt I will ever find anybody else remotely like him. He absolutely refused to quit, and he absolutely refused to compromise his vision of what he was trying to do.

That Burns collection has been the subject of more strong opinions than anything I have ever recorded. Reactions come only in extremes: it is either "I love those; they're the best thing you have ever done" or "What did you do *that* for?" The latter group of people are usually Scots who have their own inflexible image of the national bard and how his songs should sound, regardless of the actual tunes that were running through his mind as he wrote his words.

The only time I have been subjected to physical violence—not quite violence, but it came close—was during an informal Burns evening in Scotland. Someone proposed, "Perhaps Miss Redpath would close the meeting with 'Auld Lang Syne'?" I rose but, having been working with Serge, the tune which came off the top of my head was the tune Serge's research had shown to be the one Burns had in mind.* The audience struggled along with me for about one verse and chorus until somebody who was considerably more territorial and considerably less sober than the others put his shoulder in and pushed me off the mike, saying, "Ach, ye've got the wrang tune." Looking back, this was funny rather than threatening, but it does show just how firmly attached folk are to the familiar. The rest of the hall switched with relief into the known version but, out of sheer bloody mindedness, I soldiered through to the end with Serge's less familiar tune. The irony was that someone came up to me afterward and said, "I have never heard that other tune before—it's lovely; where did you get it?"

The problem is that most of Burns songs have been "improved" by many people, including his own publishers, over the last 250 years. George Thomson has a lot more to answer for than anybody else.† He was primarily concerned with the music and had formal performances (with

* That tune is close enough to the one everybody has in mind to be recognizable, but not so close that one can sing along with it.

† George Thomson (1757–1851) was born in Fife, although his treatment of some of Burns contributions to his *Select Scottish Songs* makes me hesitate to advertise that fact.

an English audience) in mind. He routinely changed Burns's choice of tunes to ones he thought would appeal more to such ears and, through repetition over the years, these have become the melodies by which Scots recognize the songs. In contrast, the American market mostly accepted Serge's choice and arrangement of original tunes; therefore most of our sales were there. Nevertheless, considering how expensive they were to make, I suspect some of these records still haven't cleared their initial outlay—nobody ever saw much by way of royalties. Serge certainly didn't, but that wasn't the object of the exercise. If you're money-driven, you shouldn't be doing this sort of work anyway.

Through all of this, Iddy's bookings kept me busy: the longer I was around, the better known I got to be, and invitations came from further afield. With the demise of the coffeehouse circuit, given my own preference for smaller audiences, most of Iddy's bookings were now for colleges. These normally had funds, some kind of auditorium, a built-in audience, and usually the possibility of running an academic workshop on classic ballads. Sometimes the booking was made through a member of the college staff, who would collect me from whichever airport I flew into, as happened at Idaho Falls. I remember at the Idaho Mormon College , where Alasdair Fraser and I were doing the gig together, something we had often done before.*

I arrived first and the young man collecting us asked, "Do you mind if we wait for an hour to collect Mr. Fraser from his flight?" "Of course not," I replied. So we sat down and had a cup of something, then picked up Alasdair. We drove out to the college, with me sitting in the front of the car and Alasdair in the back. As we arrived, the nice and helpful young man said, "We thought that, rather than having you in a position where you had to ask for a ride anywhere, we would just leave you with the college car." He looked over his shoulder to Alasdair and asked, "You do have a driver's license, don't you?" At which point, I had to grind my teeth rather hard. When we got out of the car, Alasdair muttered under his breath, "Well done, Jean. If that had been Sally [Alasdair's wife], he would have been given his head in his hands to play with."

* Alasdair is a wonderful fiddler and almost a Fifer (he comes from Clackmannan). He worked on several of my CDs. He now works with a cellist called Natalie Haas and a group called Skydance. He runs regular fiddle schools or fiddle camps not only in Skye and elsewhere in Scotland but also in Spain and California.

There was no point in making an issue of it: the young man's social gaffe simply reflected cultural differences. In his Mormon community, it would never have occurred to him to ask a woman if she had a driver's license, because that was not her place in life. Feminism had yet to strike there. Get ready to share your car keys, guys, or buy a second car.

I enjoy meeting new people. I remember an encounter in Los Angeles when I had a gig in Santa Monica. I had taken myself out for a meal around 3:00 P.M. as normal, so that the food would stoke my performance in the evening without making me feel full and sleepy. It was a nice airy restaurant with a lot of glass about, and I was the only person in the place. Since I usually ate on my own before a gig, I tucked myself away in a corner with a book for company. There was a flurry of noise, and a lady swept in with a retinue of the staff from the restaurant in her wake. I assumed she was a regular and that they must like her. Chatting to the staff, she moved many tables down the restaurant and sat down.

"Yes, I have had a good day and I am looking forward to lunch," she trilled. "And yes, what a good idea; I think I will have a drink." It was a bit like watching a grand entrance out of an old black-and-white movie, but I couldn't quite place her accent. "I'll have an Irish whisky," she decided. Before I could stop myself I called down the restaurant, "Oh, surely not—not *Irish* whisky?" There was a brief pause; then she looked up and said, "I'll have a Scotch."

That started a lively conversation, eighteen tables apart. There was nobody else in the place at that hour. Finally, I said, "I'm having a great deal of trouble with your accent; you're obviously not from here, but where have you come from?" She smiled. "No wonder you're having trouble. I was born in Australia, and then I studied in England, and I studied in Sweden. My accent is a mixture of all of these and would be difficult to place. What are you doing here?"

"I'm in town to do a concert," I replied. "Oh, how lovely. I used to be a singer." "Nobody ever *used to be* a singer," I told her. "Oh yes, my dear," she said. "It's true. I sang as a young woman in Australia, found that I had a voice, and finished up with a voice teacher in Sweden who said this was the voice she had waited her whole life to teach. I had a three-and-a-half- to four-octave range, but the self-confidence of a chicken. My Swedish teacher kept telling me—and it translates very poorly—'to sing, you have to have the elbows.' I didn't have the elbows, so I simply stopped singing." "What a shame," I said—and meant it.

I left before she did to get ready for the gig, but I always loved her quote. It's true; you do need elbows. To sing, you must have the ability to command the space you're in, then the confidence to produce the voice and the song, even if you happen to be rattling your heels off the floor with stage fright. If you have to, you fake confidence, then get on with it.

Looking back to these busiest ten to fifteen years of my career, my life seems spent in perpetual motion. A lot of the gigs were now return concerts. I usually tried to leave about two years between visits, but I was in and out of Chicago to the Old Town School of Folk Music a lot more often than this.

New York City was another place where I did a number of concerts—indeed, at the suggestion of a group of friends, and with Iddy producing, we set about organizing our own concert in Town Hall. One was normally invited to perform there, but we decided, what the hell, why wait for the invitation. We rented the hall and found a PR outfit to do the publicity. I can't remember if I got paid for that performance. Obviously, it costs a fortune to rent the Town Hall, but, again, that wasn't the object of the exercise. What I do remember was being royally pissed, because it was a union hall, and, under the union's rules, there were two young guys sitting around backstage reading paperbacks all night. They never lifted a finger to help us, and I was fried at the notion that I and everybody I knew were working our butts off to make the concert happen, while these two guys were getting paid out of the proceeds for doing absolutely nothing.

These years were busy, busy. In America I was moving far, moving fast, doing a lot of recording and branching into new ventures that kept me stretched. On top of this, I was still commuting back to Scotland twice a year, partly to keep in touch with my parents and also to perform in the gigs which Hetty had booked. The same pattern of dipping toes into new ventures was emerging in Scotland too. In Edinburgh, I worked for two or three years with the Saltire Society, doing concerts at Gladstone's Land on the High Street during the Edinburgh Festival Fringe. I also worked one year for Tom in *The Wallace* at the Assembly Rooms.* You were pretty close to the audience and the place was packed every night. I opened the

* Gladstone's Land is one of the oldest buildings in Edinburgh's Royal Mile, a unique high-rise tenement. "Tom" is Thomas Kelman Fleming (1927–2010), actor, director, poet, TV and radio commentator on state occasions for the BBC, founder of both the Gateway Theatre and the Royal Lyceum Theatre in Edinburgh, member of the Royal Shakespeare Company, director of the Scottish Theatre Company, and lay preacher for the Baptist Church.

evening by walking out and singing an unaccompanied song which had been specially written to introduce *The Wallace.* I was quaking in my shoes, but butterflies are always good—it's when you don't have them that there is cause to worry, because that means you are probably getting stale and losing your edge.

To sing that song, I had to wear a quasi-period costume, performing as a minstrel introducing the players and the story. I can't remember who wrote the song, and the melody was quite strange—it was by no means a standard series of notes that I could recognize, and I really had to work pretty hard to learn it. My job was to set the atmosphere. Tom, as always, was a joy to be with. He and I had also done a Burns concert together in St Cecilia's Hall in the Cowgate in Edinburgh. That old hall has a magical quality; it was where Burns's songs were first heard while he was still alive. It is an oval auditorium, built for sound to carry into every nonexistent corner, and it has the most glorious acoustics you will ever experience. One song in the Assembly Rooms was scarcely a set, but you still have to prepare each night, search for and find the mood, and then project it. It felt like a whole day's work.

Another new Scottish venture was going on a cruise ship with John Cairney* to perform during the Clan Macdonald HOMECOMING YEAR. In organizational terms, this homecoming year had been an on-again, off-again kind of thing.† They chartered a ship called the SS *Calypso* from a Greek company, and there should have been about 800 people aboard, but, because of the chaotic organization, we finished up with only 350. That, for us, was far better—not least because everybody could eat at the same time without us having to work our performances around staggered meal times. John had put together *The Scotland Story,* a combination of songs that fitted around his thread of history, with little sketches here and there which could be done with a minimum of rehearsal—which is just as well: I am no actress. It had worked pretty well when we did it at Hopetoun House‡ during the Edinburgh Festival , and he thought it would be

* John Cairney is a Glasgow-born actor, writer, painter, raconteur, and lecturer and a recognized expert on Robert Louis Stevenson, Charles Rennie Macintosh and Robert Burns, Robert Service and William McGonagall.

† So much so that the Highlanders rechristened the ship the SS *Collapso,* and it has never been anything else in my head ever since.

‡ I remember at Hopetoun House one performance where I stepped onto the stage and was looking out through the window, singing, with the audience at my back, and a whole herd of deer leapt across the path of light outside—quite magical.

ideal to use for the homecoming trip. On the ship things weren't quite so easy. It is difficult to remain focused and intense when you're taking two steps forward and two steps back as the boat pitches and rolls. Happily, I don't suffer from sea sickness,* because acting my way through the performance was a big enough challenge.

In one of my scenes I was to appear dramatically at the right moment, several steps up in a doorway. Once, on my way up I accidentally walked up the inside of my kaftan, and, with each step I took, I got more and more tangled and gradually dragged into a doubled-up shape. For that performance, all that finally appeared in the bottom of the doorway was my head. Ever tried to play it straight, like a trouper, when you look like a cross between St. John the Baptist's head on a platter and the hunchback of Notre Dame? How John kept a straight acting face, I will never know.

One of the years during my times in Scotland, quite fortuitously, I stayed on for almost three months. Partly it was to cover the work which Hetty had set up, but also my father had been taken to hospital and was quite unwell. More or less straight off the plane, I had gone with my mother to visit him. Walking along the hospital corridor with our leather heels, we sounded like a regiment and overshot him that first time and had to turn back to where he was waiting for us. When we came in, for probably the only time in his life, he got hold of me, and I would swear that he was weeping. He looked so old and frail, even scared. Any one of these images was frightening to me, compared to the hard-working and competent man I knew.

They nursed him through the crisis and sent him home again, but I kept dropping in between gigs, to check on him. Then, toward the end of my three months back home, one night when I finished a performance at the Queen's Hall in Edinburgh, I got a call that he had been rushed back into hospital. The call came from my mother. She and my aunt Elsie had been with him all day since he went in.

I drove straight from the theater to the hospital, where my mother said, "I will have to take Elsie home; she's on the point of collapse."

More than Elsie was at the point of collapse; I had never seen my mother look so drawn and exhausted. I think she knew what was coming, and it was too sore for her to bear. "There's not much more you can do here," I told her. "Why don't you both go home and I'll sit with my dad." That's what I did, until he was gone. I don't quite know why it was left to

* I'm a Fifer, and we part with nothing. . . .

me to be there for him as he lay dying, but I think my mother would have been in a hospital bed herself if she had stayed with him any longer. They came from a generation where affection was never shown in public, but they were close to one another. It must have torn her apart to watch him dying and to feel so utterly helpless.

After he died, I knew that it was my job now to tend to the living rather than the dead. I phoned back home with the news. "Are they goin' tae bring him hame?" my mother asked. "In his coffin?" "No way," I replied. The words shot out of me, but I was surprised that she had asked, when it was her decision. Maybe, from a lifetime of looking after myself in all sorts of situations, I just got bossy and took over. I have never bought into the thought of coffins in homes. Perhaps in the old days, when there were no funeral homes and the local joiner came in to measure and then produce the box, that was the only way to deal with the body. The corpse has to lie someplace. But in modern times, why bring a corpse into the house? It wasn't as if Jim Redpath was there anymore.

That's my view of things. I don't honestly know what my mother thought, but I have a feeling that she was relieved to have the decision made for her. For her to have said no, would have been tantamount to rejecting the man she had married. The death of someone beloved, and the sense of utter loss, comes to everyone in time. To find the essence of grief, first you have to live through it to project it properly into a song and bring that song alive. That night, more corners were knocked off me and more hard experience gained.

But there was one last thing that no one can ever take away from me. Just before he died, I had the chance at last to hold my father's hand and tell him that I loved him. In return, came the slightest of answering pressure from his hand.

CHAPTER 7

My Trusty Friels

For many years,* living on the road had become my way of life. An itinerant musician sets down no real roots, unless they grow in friendships. When I think back, it is the people I met along the road, rather than places and events, that I remember most clearly.

One of the things I quickly learned about people was that it is much easier to do one-night stands or two-night visits than to stay anywhere for a week. If you throw a flat stone and skim it across a pond, there is only a momentary connection with the water, and there is no real depth: you can be polite and amusing and as entertaining (or entertained) as you choose, then move on. For years my singing and traveling kept me skimming across the water like that stone. There is no real investment, not even over forty-eight hours, but, if you stay with someone for a week, that's a very different level of commitment and much more demanding.

Not everybody can skim. When my mother came over to America for a visit after my father's death, I planned things so that she wasn't being dragged around, arranging that we would stay for a series of four-night visits, which I figured was just about right for her. Wrong. She needed more structure in her life than I did and, after three of those visits, she found it a great relief to get to my cousin's in Toronto, where she could stay in the same place for a week and a half. I guess there is a technique involved in being on the road. If I can use another analogy, you keep your petticoat tails tucked in tight around your ankles and just keep moving on. Do not get involved.

Wherever possible I traveled in my beloved 1971 yellow Beetle. It's easier going places in a car, because you're not changing climates and time zones in the two or three hours of traveling. Plus you have your own

* The title of this chapter, "My Trusty Friels," meaning my well-loved and trusted friends, is drawn from "Auld Lang Syne," by Robert Burns.

space, and you don't have to talk to anybody or listen to anything unless you want to do so. That little car became one of the few fixed points in my firmament, my own private bubble of personal freedom, and I was always grateful to find it waiting for me in some strange parking lot after a concert.

Traveling between gigs is very much like changing radio channels: you have to retune, become adept at shifting gears. It turned me into a chameleon, learning to adjust constantly to different people and their different expectations. However, within this adjustment process, you must fight to preserve a firm sense of self, even if you're not terribly sure what that self is, because constant readjustment can become confusing. It is all too easy to become a stranger to yourself.

In each new meeting, you search for common ground, some sort of central anchor that will keep things stable and friendly. You sense quickly enough when that is missing—every once in a while I ran into an organizer or a host who had the same effect on me as sandpaper. Mostly, because of our shared taste in music, we found something in common almost immediately, and real friendships could develop from something as casual as an invitation to come and have a cup of coffee after a performance—as happened in New York. I wonder if Sylvia, CB, and Anne would have issued that invitation quite so spontaneously had they realized that it was going to make me a sporadic presence in their New York life for the next seven years—and provide a home base for me in Chelsea, or in Orient, Long Island, when I wasn't traveling at a flat run.

Doing your own driving, finding the club, and showing up for work without knowing for sure where you are going to be staying afterward can be exhausting. If you find hosts who are genuinely welcoming and a bed that is clean—and hasn't been used by dozens of itinerant musicians passing through—this can transform and save a trip when you feel utterly burned out after a concert. There is a downside. Through many kind offers, I have become intimately and painfully familiar with "kidney-killer" sleep sofas, the older variety which had a middle bar that ran right across at about kidney level. I lost count of the number of times I crawled out of bed crippled in the morning, and it got so that when I saw one of these sleep sofas I thought, "Damn, I'm not going to be able to walk tomorrow."

In the early days, there was no choice: without these offers to put me up overnight, I would have had to sleep in the dressing room at the theater, if that had been allowed. It was years before I could afford to pay for a motel room, and until then I got by on subsistence living. People's courtesy and generosity were essential elements in my survival, and it is unworthy of me to grade them by the beds I got. I am just so grateful that people helped me when I sorely needed help, and that often, when I was fed and watered, these incredibly generous folk also found me a dram.

That reminds me of a situation I got into in Southern California because of the presence of two longtime friends from the Folk Song Society in Edinburgh who now lived there. They had arranged a house concert for me, which turned out to be in the orange grove behind a neighbor's house. I got there and was introduced by Ella and John McEvoy to these neighbors. Everyone had a drink in hand and raised it to toast me, saying, "Keech!"

Were they judging me, even before I had given my performance? I spluttered, apologized for choking and, having got a severe warning scowl from John, held my tongue. In Scotland "Keech" is about the worst possible thing we can say when we are about seven or eight years old and still too afraid to say the real swear word. Yet here were all these lovely suntanned people in California who thought they were using an ancient Gaelic toast, and John had dared me to enlighten them. It was a wonderful moment. For all I know, they still think it's how you toast people in the Gaelic tongue.

To an itinerant musician, friends are not just important: they are also essential, because they are often all you've got. I have been lucky in my choice of friends; they have not only supported and shaped my career but have also influenced hugely my development as a person. To all of them, I owe something. To many, I owe a great deal, a debt which I will never be able to repay in full.

Looking back, my first experience of a casual act of kindness which ripened into deep and lasting friendship came in the form of Miki Isaacson, who opened house, heart, and arms to a total stranger on the strength of a phone call from some of her own friends who were driving me into New York City from Philadelphia. Or Everett and Marion Stanley, who invited me home after a Scottish Country Dance session, then nursed me in Berkeley when I fell over with some sort of a heavy-duty virus. Or there were Ken and Rochelle Goldstein, who rescued me from disaster when that first nightclub gig in Philly went belly-up. In all cases, there was an open invitation to drop in and use their home as my base whenever I was drifting through their area. For many years, even when I wasn't working in their hometowns, I was happy to drop in and stay in touch.

Turning back to Miki, her place wasn't just a bed for the night; it was a home, a real lifesaver, and a completely new start in life. Within it I found an adoptive family of other itinerants who became my professional support group for years, and it was always fun to sit down over a beer and have a blether if we happened to coincide. At the same time, from there I ran into most of the performing artists who had made or were making names for themselves, because all of them swung through New York and, if they weren't sleeping on Miki's floor, they would show up at one of the Village clubs or at a ceilidh.

The Clancys* were very much on the scene, and I remember, sometime in the late 1960s, sitting in the Limelight on Seventh Avenue in the Village after closing time (the door closed at 3:00 A.M., but a dozen of us stayed on to have a ceilidh there), thinking to myself, "What would I do, if I couldn't do this ?" On that occasion, I had just come back from a tour and, straight off the plane, was spending the night drinking and singing with the Clancys. But I was younger, then. Ten or fifteen years later, I would have been less enthusiastic—attitudes tend to change and what was great fun at thirty soon becomes an absolute killer chore. Carpe diem.

Yet it is odd, while I have formed many strong friendships over the years with musicians, I have seldom done so with my fellow performers. One of the reasons is probably that we seldom saw very much of each other even if we were in the same town, because, when we were working, we would all be pretty busy and keeping the same night-owl hours. Alasdair Fraser, whom I didn't meet until the 1970s, is probably the only person among performers who graduated into becoming a close friend. As a rule, the people I stay in touch with from these earlier years tend to be instrumentalists with whom I have worked both in concert and in the recording studio.

Working with instrumentalists involves tapping into yet another small circuit. For the first four records I made, musicians were provided, and I was simply told "This guy's going to play the guitar for you." It was some years before I got to the stage of saying what, or who, I wanted. "I need a cello, and somebody who can improvise. I don't want a written score behind this. I need somebody with a feel for traditional music," I told Bill

* The Clancy Brothers were an Irish folk and traditional music group who performed in Aran sweaters and introduced much of their music to America, becoming a huge influence on emergent artists of the early 1960s. They were Paddy, Tom, Bobby, and Liam, and they made a lot of LPs with Tommy Makem.

Schubart. "There's a cellist we've worked with before, in Woodstock," he replied. "Why don't we try her?"

That was how Abby Newton and I got together for the first of many recordings. For years, even when there was no joint work in the offing, I would still make a point of going to see her when I was in the area. She was always busy professionally, as well as with raising a family, but we met up whenever we could in New York City or Woodstock.

At the various festivals I met all the performers who were singing, including Bob Dylan with whom I shared a couple of gigs, and Joan Baez with whom I shared a manager for some years, plus a lot of the country music folk. Doc Watson was a great favorite of mine; although he was blind, all he ever had to hear from me was "Hello, Doc," and he knew who it was. His voice recognition was staggering, but no doubt my Scots accent helped. Then there was one memorable evening in Philadelphia when Gordon Bok,* whom I met sporadically and with whom I shared friends in New Hampshire, turned up in his motel room with John Hurt,† and about six of us piled in there. That Philly festival was where Mississippi John Hurt was rediscovered. He seemed to me to be an elderly man by then. Sadly, he was only on the scene again for about four years before he died. I loved the sound he made.

Recording gave me a break from being on the road, and I began to do a lot of work in recording studios. With peanut butter and jelly now a fond memory, I could take time to put the songs together, pre-plan and find the studio time, contact my cellist, pianist, harpist, fiddler—whatever combination we needed—and have them there at the same time. It was so much easier to do it this way, even if we had to do extra takes, when someone wasn't satisfied. This kind of live recording has its own creative dynamic and has always been a very different experience from the experimental and highly structured work we had done in layers for Serge Hovey.

* Gordon Bok is folklorist and singer-songwriter from Camden, Maine, who drew on his experience of working on boats in the Gulf of Maine for his song writing.

† Mississippi John Hurt was a sharecropper who picked a guitar and sung blues at parties and dances and then graduated to making some records in the late 1920s. These weren't successful, and he went back to working as a farmer until he was rediscovered; one of his blues songs was recorded in the Library of Congress in 1964. His new success and the fresh start to his recording career brought several other old blues singers out of anonymity.

Around this time I met Marty Streicher and Lynda Ciolek. When Freddie and Sylvia and some other New York friends persuaded me to do my own Town Hall concert, they brought in several PR teams to interview to do the publicity. After talking to the first of these teams, I said, "We don't need to see the others; this husband and wife team are perfect." They have been among my closest friends ever since and, although Marty is now dead, Lynda is still my manager.* They offered a combination of professionalism and personal interest and seemed to grasp very quickly what I wanted from them. Hiring them represents another crucial decision which almost made itself. I have always preferred to take side paths rather than the main highway, never going for the big companies who might get me big money, but rather for someone who took real trouble to understand what the hell it was I was trying to do. Not that Marty was any slouch on the money-earning front.

"We hear you are looking for management,"† he said, as soon as we had agreed on the PR deal. "So we are putting our names into the hat." I barely hesitated. "OK," I said. That was an easy choice—the instantaneous recognition of kindred souls which comes along now and then. I knew I would feel comfortable working with them.

"Right. What are you doing at the moment for professional fees?" he asked. "Well, I think I am asking 600 dollars," I replied. "What!" he exclaimed. "What's wrong with that?" I demanded. "Six hundred dollars for a concert, irrespective of the size of the hall, what they're charging for tickets, how many people are going there?" he asked. "You're nuts! Don't ever talk to anybody about money again . . . ever! I'll kill you!"

He was right, of course. Why should I be charging the same for a house concert to maybe twenty-five people and for a hall that would take twenty-five hundred and charge twenty dollars a seat? So long as I was solvent and not in anybody's debt, chasing money was never a priority for me, which isn't very businesslike. Which is why I needed a manager like Marty.

Early friendships sometimes merge with later ones—and the result isn't always a happy one. Take what happened to Miki, of all people, and which shows how casual chance can change, and maybe ruin, a life.

* Marty and Lynda's work in New York City was exclusively in the PR field and I believe I am the only person for whom they did personal management.

† Iddy was still making my bookings but had told me that she had jobs in her own field coming in, and so I needed to go out and start looking for another manager.

I was going out with a guy in San Francisco for a while. I think he was the one truly amoral person I have ever met, not so much a crook as a chancer—an opportunist of the highest order. He played the system, and it didn't seem to affect his conscience or his ability to sleep at night. I never really figured him out, but he wasn't somebody I was planning to spend the rest of my life with, so I didn't have to. He bought a VW van and outfitted it for camping, with good sound equipment; then he promptly left the state, driving his new acquisition. Back then, there was no legal reciprocity between states: he couldn't be sued in Illinois for what he'd done in California. He followed me to New York and showed up at Miki's apartment.

Eventually Miki married him. I suspect he married her because her parents were pretty well off, but she seemed to be happy, and they drove back to San Francisco. I hadn't been so keen on the guy that losing him affected our friendship in any way, so I saw a lot of Miki in San Francisco until eventually he took off and left her on her own on Ashbury Street. Miki died there, vastly overweight by then, and should probably never have left New York as and when she did. A restless spirit, she didn't lead a happy life, and I lost a close friend when she went.

Jean Weber is another friend who goes right back to that first trip east to the Caffè Lena, when I was starting out and she was raising a young family. Her husband was in the English Department at Skidmore College in Saratoga Springs, New York. On my second trip to Saratoga, they invited me to stay with them, and, after the camp bed in the middle of the tables, I was blown away by their house. Jean's background is artistic, so everything about their house and its contents was beautifully put together. To this day, everywhere she has ever gone in her museum management-directorship career, she has created a home which was exquisite—because that's the only way she knows. I was still fresh from Scotland, and the whole New England aesthetic of patchwork and handicrafts and the many other artistic furnishings she had collected made a huge impression on me.

I have long since stopped trying to head her off from being the perfect hostess when I drop in for a visit. There is always much thought goes into what's in the room when you get there, what you're going to be eating, and what you might like to do. The only thing I can offer in return is to try and straighten her garage door—she has a quirky habit of backing into it. So I usually start off my stay with her by borrowing a couple of tools and trying to take the dent out of the door and get it to open again.

Another longtime friend was Lisa Neustadt, right from our early work together in gospel singing. Lisa was a very funny woman, and it's hard to imagine her as a suburban housewife in Newton, Massachusetts, raising small children in a large house, because she was a divorcée and a teacher by the time we met.

Lisa was a large lady and someone whose quick responses I often envied. Through her, I met Helen Schneyer down in Washington, D.C., another powerful female who looked like a ship in full sail when she walked onto the stage. Helen had a great mane of gray hair and came onto the stage wearing yards of white *broderie anglaise* and about half a hundredweight of Navajo jewelry. She would pirouette and ask, "Has everybody seen this?" and then undo the concho belt and the squash blossom necklace and pile them onto the piano, because she couldn't possibly work under that burden.

Once Lisa, Helen, and I were doing a gospel workshop at a festival in Massachusetts with Barbara Carns, who had wonderful gray braids down both sides of her neck and a blues voice that could nail you to the back wall of the room. We were singing "When the Roll Is Called Up Yonder," which is a response hymn:*

> When the trumpet of the Lord shall sound, and time shall
> be no more,
> And the morning breaks, eternal, bright and fair; *(bright and fair)*
> When the saved of earth shall gather over on the other shore,
> And the roll is called up yonder, I'll be there. *(I'll be there)*
> When the roll (when the roll) is called up yonder, *(called up yonder)*
> When the roll (when the roll) is called up yonder, *(called up yonder)*
> When the roll (when the roll) is called up yonder, *(called up yonder)*
> When the roll is called up yonder, I'll be there.
> On that bright and cloudless morning when the dead in Christ
> shall rise,
> And the glory of His resurrection share . . .

Barbara's response came in absolutely straight in her deep voice with "erection share." The whole hall dissolved, and there is a series of photographs that somebody took. In one image, Lisa—never one to hold back from being expressive—had both feet off the ground and both arms in the

* In a response hymn the last few words of the line are echoed. This hymn was written in 1893 by James W. Black (1856–1938).

air as she fell backwards off her stool. Helen was in hysterics, while Barbara just sat there with a slight smirk and the hint of a canary feather sticking out of the corner of her mouth.* I have never been able to sing that response hymn since.

My work at the Old Town School of Folk Music meant that I spent a lot of time in Chicago. There, too, early contacts turned into lifelong friendships. The first time I was there, I was gathered in and taken home by Dawn Greening, one of the founding members. Dawn was another ship in full sail—about six feet tall and built accordingly. Nate, her husband, was a quiet guy, a construction engineer. We got on well, and I was spoiled rotten by him. I have told already of Dawn taking me to a gospel meet and coming out with a loud and heartfelt series of "Oh, yeahs!" that shook me rigid and started my culture change from being a dour quiet Scot. But that was simply Dawn: if she was ever enthusiastic, my God, you heard about it—all the way round the room.

Also in Chicago were Annie and Leon Bishop, other friends from a relationship struck up after a club performance. Leon was a wonderful painter, very quiet, very shy. He did all the driving, because Annie's eyesight wasn't too great. Annie was an editor with a textbook publisher, but in her spare time she wrote children's books and also a wonderful calendar in the style of "April 1st: On this day, 1632"—great fun to read.

They had a parrot called Macgregor who had the run of the house: he sat on Annie's shoulder at breakfast to be offered bits of toast with egg on them or a sip of orange juice. Leon wasn't quite so keen on the bird, and it was a miserable brute with anybody else. I walked in large circles round its perch, convinced it would take a lump out of me given half a chance. One night they both went out and left me in the house, parrot-sitting, with the bird securely in its cage. I was watching TV when I heard the sound of heavy footsteps coming closer. It was Macgregor; having done a Houdini, he was walking through on the linoleum from the kitchen into the living room. He hopped up to sit on the end of the couch, where I was sprawled back with my feet on the coffee table. I looked at him sideways and thought, Oh, I wish you wouldn't do that. Then he walked along the couch and climbed onto my knee, to sit there glowering balefully up at me for about an hour and a half. By the time Annie got home, both of my legs were locked to the point where I couldn't move, because I knew that

* One of Bluebell's favourite sayings when she was fed up with scrimping and scraping to make ends meet was "tae hell wi' poverty—gi'e the cat the canary."

if I made the slightest twitch, that bloody bird would go for me. That was one house pet I could have done without, but Annie was a constant source of support and encouragement, always egging me on to write, which seemed easy to her, given her background. Looking back, I wonder how much she was to blame for my jottings, like the hindsights in this book.

From that same broad period, another regular contact was Robert John Lurtsema, known universally as Robert J, the voice of classical music on WGBH Boston from 1971 until he died in 2000. His black-velvet voice was ideally suited to radio and to voice-overs, but he was a man of many talents who also composed music, painted, and wrote. Our friendship went right back to the early days, when Robert had a great deal more leeway than he did after the bean counters took over his broadcasting station. He had a finger in every musical pie in the greater Boston area, and, having heard me at a club or concert, he invited me to come and be interviewed on his radio program, where he worked as a classical DJ from 7:00 A.M. till noon. He was fairly stroppy, with a clear idea of his own priorities, and he refused to stop on the hour to make any kind of commercial announcement: the music ran until it finished. He also edited the news bulletin for his program, which he kept to a minimum, and on one famous occasion he told his listeners that "there is no news today worth reporting" and went straight back to his music, something only Robert J could have got away with. He was an institution.

From the start, we got along well. When I was passing through, I usually stopped by the station and wandered in—this was in the days when things were more casual, and you didn't have to wait for someone to shepherd you. He would wave me in to join him if he was on the mike and sometimes say, "We have a friend who has just stepped in; tell me, Jean, what you are up to." If he was marking St Andrews Day or Burns Day and had a Scottish theme to work through, I always tried to be in town and drop in for a couple of hours. He usually sent me through to the library with the instruction, "Find half a dozen LPs for me, and then tell me why you want me to play them."

Thanks to him, I became reasonably well known on radio, but the wretch got to the point where he wouldn't tell me if his mike was open when I wandered in. The second time he tried that, I knew by the look in his eye that he was hoping that I would open my mouth and put both feet into it. I didn't, not ever while we were on air, although it's something I am prone to doing. It was just great fun, very casual, very relaxed, because we knew each other well enough to take the conversation in almost any direction. He always argued that there wasn't such a gap between his classical music and my own, because classical musicians were steeped in their own musical traditions, and therefore it was a very small step from Felix Mendelssohn to a classic Scottish ballad.

Once we arranged to do a twelve day tour of Scotland,* and since he couldn't advertise this himself on air, he decided to bring me on to talk about the tour, provided that I added, "Oh, incidentally, Robert is coming with us."

The tour worked well but, being a screaming compulsive, I wanted to know in advance every milestone of the route we would be traveling, what sort of information I would be expected to give en route, and on which nights I would be singing. That generated a lot of planning work, until somebody said to me, "Why are you doing all this yourself? That's what you get a tour director to do."

We checked and discovered that we were two bodies short of the requisite number to get a tour director, so I was the one who finished up paying the bills in the tearoom, counting the suitcases as they were loaded and unloaded, doing the historical talks while we were on the road, and also performing. I never worked so hard in my life, not since my parents were in Gibraltar and I was running my mother's guest house. Robert, in contrast, seemed to think that lending his august presence to the tour was all that was required of him. It took two or three days before we got that one sorted out.

Finally, from those early days, comes one of my closest friends, Betsy Sandlin: I had known her from when she was a gangly all-legs-and-arms teenager at Skidmore College, and I was performing at the Caffè Lena. We kept in touch after her college days, although a couple of years would often pass when we never saw each other. She settled for a spell in California and often came down from San Francisco to visit me for the day, when she would clear up my correspondence while I made her a skirt. From my point of view, that was a good trade—there was nothing of her and her skirt was simply a tube, but that was the style back then.

In 1974, her mother Cel called her and said, "Let's take a cruise for my seventieth birthday." I got a letter from Betsy, wailing "Cel's taking me on

* The tour was basically just "Come to Scotland with Robert and Jean and see the home of some of these songs." The tour participants were all Americans, and it was a highly educational tour, mostly for me, in the form of "Don't ever do that again."

a *banana* boat." It was a freighter which took passengers, and that's where Betsy met Mathew, the first mate, who became her husband. She traveled round with him quite a bit until they had Charlie, after which they settled down on Long Island. When Mathew died in an accident on the Brooklyn docks, Betsy moved back to Tucson, where she bought property in the desert. Betsy's house is always open to her friends, and I started dropping in on a regular basis at the end of the winter, spending a month in the sun while doing my taxes—it takes some of the curse off taxes if you're sitting in desert sunshine while everybody else is freezing their butt off. That started a pattern which has gone on until now, so that I am almost part of the furniture, and these ever-changing wonderful mountains and desert cactus plants are my daily background.

So, even when you set out to skim, you still find and form attachments, to places as well as people. The biggest attachment of all for me is for Scotland, the land itself—the moors, the mountains, the islands floating in the sea mist—quite apart from its people and traditions. Scotland is my home, my touchstone, the link deep and indelibly in my blood. I puddle up every time I think of another expat, Eric Bogle, and the lines he wrote tapping into his memories of where he had grown up:

> You're still the bonny Border toon
> A grey and ugly housing scheme
> You're Castlemilk and Brigadoon
> You're part real and you're part dream
> You're Hogmanay and Auld Lang Syne
> And pints o' heavy at the pub
> Ach! You're just a state of mind
> But you're still singing in my blood.

Back in Scotland there was always Hetty, my manager and a constant friend until she died. Hetty was another forceful woman—there do not seem to have been any anemic women in my life—and one of the things I remember vividly about her was when I was singing at Eden Court. Something in the arrangements had displeased her, and she confronted the stage manager or general manager (certainly somebody who was not in the habit of being dictated to) and began to tell him that she wasn't happy. To drive home her point, she kept tapping him on the tie with her forefinger. I remember thinking, "Hetty, you don't have to bully the guy; he would probably do it if you asked him nicely," but when Hetty was in Rottweiler mode, you really didn't want to mess with her.

She was an appalling driver. The first time I went north to visit her in Thurso after she became my manager, I took a train as far as Inverness, and we arranged to meet up after she completed business of her own in the town; then she would drive me north, saving me many hours of waiting for my connection. However, when we were perhaps two miles out of Inverness, I said, "Henrietta, pull over please." She did so, looking puzzled. "Why don't you change places with me?" I suggested. "Either that, or just let me out and I will walk back to Inverness."

I could never understand how she survived as a driver as long as she did. Her technique for a roundabout was not to check for other traffic but simply drive straight onto it, hold the middle of the road, drive round it twice if necessary, then drive out—all without a single signal. She always traveled at the same sedate pace, and traffic simply swerved round her once they got over their heart attacks and absorbed the message that this lady was not about to make any detours of any kind for anyone.

She came over to America to visit me. Hetty was a wonderful traveler who truly appreciated everything that everybody did for her but, despite her time in London, life up north in Thurso had somewhat sheltered her from modern living. I remember with affection, two such occasions.

A couple of friends of mine in San Francisco took Hetty and me out for a drink to the Fairmont Hotel, which has a revolving restaurant at the top, and introduced her to a Mai Tai, which is fruit salad in a beer mug with a good deal of rum. It tastes pretty innocuous, but it can knock you onto your back in no time. She finished her drink and put it down on the window sill at which we were standing, admiring the view outside.

"Have another one," she was invited. "I couldn't possibly . . ." "Oh, go on . . ." "All right then." Hetty had another drink, got stuck into her fruit salad and the nice tangy juice, and then put the nearly empty mug down on the window sill again. After more conversation, as she reached down for the drink, she blinked and said, "Oh, my goodness. That building out there is moving; it's overtaking us."

The other time we were walking on North Beach and passed one of those adult shops with a whole window display of dildos. I walked on, but Hetty stopped, peered into the window, and said: "What's that?" "Henrietta, you really do not want to know," I advised. "But it looks . . . Oh! It never is?" Her face was a study. "All of them, yes, they really are," I replied. Encountering Hetty was another casual meeting in Scotland which developed into a profound friendship between two people, a friendship which ended only with death.

HINDSIGHT 7.1: *Written in the early 1990s on the West Coast of America, when my mind had obviously drifted back to my native Scotland*

Funny how deep friendships spring out of random meetings. I'm thinking of the time when I got an invitation to sing at Blair Castle amid the Perthshire hills. Knowing that the event was imminent, I decided to drop in and meet Alec Barbour, who had issued the invite, when I was showing off Scotland to Lisa Neustadt, who was visiting that summer. That way, he wouldn't be a total stranger when I arrived to perform.

He seemed to take a very long time to come out of his office to meet us: we discovered later that he had phoned home in a panic to explain that we had shown up unexpectedly and was told firmly by his wife Hazel that on no account should he invite us back for more than a coffee, because they had already company that evening. We left two days later, having slept on the lounge floor.

Actually, I left only to come back again and again until Alec died and Hazel had to move from their farm eyrie down into the village of Blair Atholl. There was little about Scotland that Alec didn't know, and we spent many glorious trips in the north and west hunting the phalarope. Their house became a second home to me in Scotland. I often wonder what would have happened, if I had left meeting Alec to the night of the concert . . .*

Other cherished Scottish links were John and Alannah Cairney, with whom I kept in touch even when they were gone for twelve years to live in New Zealand; Alannah comes from there and does a lot of radio work. While in New Zealand, John took time out from his acting and began painting again—he's a prolific writer as well, a man of many parts. He has always been an enormous source of information, inspiration, and encouragement to me over the years.

Once, I asked him, "Not a complaint, just an observation—why do you talk so much in company?" "I have found it is inevitable that you will have to meet people, either after a performance, or simply being introduced to them. If you talk, then you're in control of the conversation and don't have to come up with answers" was his reply.

* The phalarope is a thin-billed species of wading bird related to the sandpiper and the red- and greenshank; they breed in the Arctic Circle and overwinter in the southern seas and so pass over us in their migration path going north and south.

I remember sitting on a wall in the sunshine with John and Alannah on the Fife coast somewhere, talking about this same problem of public interaction. He and I decided that we were both studied extroverts—relaxed and confident in public, but if left to our own devices we would get along pretty well in our own company. We both need a lot of alone time. Being sociable in public is another form of performance and coming over as an extrovert is our way of coping with people.

Marcel Marceau, in *The Mask,* makes the point that if you adopt a mannerism for long enough, it ceases to be a mannerism. This is true in that, despite still being inherently shy, I no longer have to make an effort to talk to anybody, almost anywhere, when I am circulating in public. But if I am not out in the world, leave me alone; don't talk to me. This is not so much an affectation as a conscious adjustment which has to be made if you spend the bulk of your life interacting with people and responding to their expectations. You need the counterbalance of time spent completely on your own—it's a survival mechanism.

I love to watch John work because, as the consummate professional, he can step into and out of whatever he is doing. It is an approach I have always liked and has become a trademark approach of my own, whereby I can be very much inside a song when I am delivering it but am able to go somewhere entirely different two minutes later as I try to take the audience where I want them to go.

John is a master of that. I watched him work at the Edinburgh Fringe a couple of years ago, at 10:00 A.M., in "Coffee with Cairney," chatting to a room full of people at that unearthly hour. Within the chat, he had an agenda, a script, and he weaved effortlessly in and out of this as he chose. At one point, he stepped off the stage, gasped "Oh!," and grabbed at his leg. Half the audience rose to help him—he's in his eighties, after all. Then he looked up and said, "I'm acting, I'm acting!"

Another very private person I found myself drawn to after working with him was Tom Fleming. When I was driving through Edinburgh, I often stopped at his door and begged for a coffee. He was always very gracious, but I look back now and think that it might have been nicer to phone first to see if he really wanted company. After all, I hate it when somebody else barges into my alone time.

Tom was rather startled when we both got honorary doctorates from the Royal Scottish Academy of Music and Drama. I didn't know he was going to be there until he arrived for the cocktail reception. I hadn't seen him for a long time, so I leapt to my feet and threw my arms around him. After a split-second pause, he responded heroically. It was a reverse-cultural thing: showing affection in this way is something I have learned to do in America but, back in dour and self-restrained Scotland, it is not expected—least of all by people from my own or older generations.

Worse still, when we went to the formal presentation onstage, Tom was every bit as dignified and gracious as you would expect, whereas, when it was my turn to be presented with the honor by the principal of the Royal Scottish Academy of Music and Drama, I threw my arms round him too instead of shaking his proffered hand. Having broken out of these Victorian stays during my years in the United States, I have to remember to climb back into them when I go home. I was a bit of a loose cannon that day and didn't cover myself in glory.

Some friendships are cut short before they run their course. Arthur and Ruth Argo were other longtime friends of mine in Edinburgh. Arthur was from Aberdeen, where I first met him through the Aberdeen Folk Song Society. He worked for the BBC in Glasgow, where I frequently stayed with them. Arthur and I grew about as close as siblings, I think. He used to say of Hamish Henderson: "Hamish has got his Jeannie—and I've got mine."*

His, sadly, was too short a life: there is a lot that he could still have been doing. I think of Arthur often. Music was in his blood, from his forebear Gavin Grieg and his *Folk Songs of the North East.* Arthur sang as naturally as he talked, but I felt at times that he struggled to be a corporation man with responsibility for being a husband and a father when I think he was a gypsy at heart. Not a good combination.†

On a more cheerful note, I found a musical soulmate in Alasdair Fraser, who is young enough to be my son; indeed, if I had ever had one, I would have been thrilled if he had turned out like Alasdair. Our musical intent is pretty much the same, and it is something which has never had

* Jeannie Robertson, the ballad singer. It was through Hamish that I discovered Jeannie and her interpretations of the old songs.

† Arthur Argo (1935–1981) was a performer, collector and producer of Scottish folk music; his long-running radio shows such as *Fit like Folk* were used by him to help many emergent artists, not just myself but Barbara Dickson, Aly Bain, and Billy Connolly, who become more widely known. Argo was the great grandson of Gavin Greig (1856–1914), a writer, teacher, and collector who was jointly responsible with the Reverend J. B. Duncan (1848–1917) for compiling the Greig-Duncan *Folk Song Collection,* which covers more than one thousand songs and tunes and was first published in 1925.

to be discussed, because each is instinctively aware of what the other is trying to do, in both fiddle and vocal music. We work well on stage together and, when he was a session musician and working on CDs with me, he came up with some brilliant and spontaneous backings to songs. There is a great deal of affection between us, and it is always very easy to talk.

At one point, relaxing after a joint gig in America with a glass of wine in our hands, he asked me, "Have you ever written any songs of your own?" "No, not really. None that I would be particularly anxious to own up to, anyway," I replied. "Why not?" he demanded. I barely had to think. "Because, if there is something I really want to express, it has already been done better than I can ever do, in a traditional song. Whatever we Scots want to say, the chances are that there's a song which already says it." He shook his head. "I don't think you're doing enough," he said. "Right," I challenged him. "How old are you?" "Thirty three." This was some time ago. "Well, I'm old enough to be your mother. I'm tired of carrying the Fiery Cross*—*you* carry the bloody thing for a while," I told him.

Another powerful Scottish presence in my life was Donald Low, with whom I shared another siblinglike relationship. Donald was like a younger brother—in fact, he often introduced me to people as someone who should have been his big sister—and his was the Burns connection at Stirling University. A tall man, a lovely gentle soul, Donald was another linchpin in my wandering existence. I found myself working in parallel with Serge Hovey and then with Donald on his collection of Burns songs from the Scottish Musical Museum. Frequently I found myself singing the same song in two different tunes, which was enough to confuse anybody.†

* The Highlands was am area always torn by disputes between clans, even where there was no greater war or army raised from them. When a clan was threatened, the clan chief sent out runners carrying a burning wooden cross in one hand to summon all the clansmen to a named gathering point. It was simultaneously a call to battle, an icon of clan loyalty, and a sacred symbol which no one could ignore.

† In later years I often wondered wryly if this was a safe thing to do. There was a Burns scholar in Edinburgh whom I didn't know but who was known to Donald and who died at an early age. Then Donald, also Burns scholar, developed MS and died. Serge also died after a debilitating illness. I used to think that maybe I shouldn't be spending so much time studying Burns; it isn't healthy.

In our Burns work together, we got to know a Japanese scholar called Toshio Namba who was fascinated by the bard. We have pictures sent over to us by him with all sorts of Japanese writing on the board in which my name and Donald's name figured prominently. We got word that Toshio was coming over with his wife to be honored by the Lochgelly Burns Club and, at his request, we were asked to attend. In response to the invitation, I drove around in the half-dark in Lochgelly without finding anywhere which looked as if it might be holding a civic reception. The only place producing any noise was up above the Goth bar.* We found our way to the function room, where somebody was playing on a squeezebox, to discover a large congregation already there and waiting for us.

The president of the club was a young man of about six foot two inches, and the secretary was a huge ex-miner called Charlie who was even taller and had a voice like a foghorn. Now that we were all assembled, the secretary began the evening by welcoming Toshio Namba and his wife, inviting them to stand out into the middle of the floor while everybody clapped. However, they were only the start of a long list of invitees, ourselves included, and the foghorn voice boomed "and please put your hands together for" time after time. When he finally stopped, almost half the audience members were standing in a ragged line across the floor, while the remaining half were applauding us. At this point, Charlie unfolded a computer printout which was about ten feet long and on which had been painstakingly printed the greeting, "Welcome Toshio, proud to call you brother."

Charlie indicated that the line of invited guests, among which Toshio and his wife were both a diminutive four foot ten inches and standing in the center, should hold the banner across our front. Somewhat self-consciously, we held it at about chest level. There was a brief silence; then Charlie's voice boomed out: "Aw, come oan, haud it doon a bit—ye're coverin' him up, he's only wee." Toshio had disappeared completely behind the welcoming banner, which had rather spoiled its intended effect.

For a skimming stone, I have made and collected a lot of friends: unfortunately, having lived this long, I have outlasted many of them. The ones who have gone have left a lot of precious memories. The ones who

* Goth bars in Scotland were mostly in mining communities; they were owned by the community, drink prices were kept "fair," and any profits from them were channeled back into community needs and activities.

are here still kick ass when I need it—and I would not have it any other way. Those kicks have kept me going and have saved me from making many a blunder. That's what friends are for. To all of them I say, Thank you from my heart and bless you for being there; I could not have had either the life or career I have enjoyed, without you.

CHAPTER 8

Wherever I May Roam

I have been blessed with a natural singing voice and learned how to use it better as the years passed. However, there was a point, as I was approaching my forties, when I nearly lost it altogether. I came from a generation when everyone smoked, and it was good social manners to offer other people a cigarette. Under the excuse of performance stress my habit grew, until I was smoking seventy cigarettes a day. Sounds bad, but these were American cigarettes, about four inches long, where two inches of this was filter; therefore, the actual amount of tobacco was less than it might seem. However, it was still too much and what made things worse was that when I returned to Scotland on my routine visits, I simply switched onto the old-fashioned unfiltered "coffin nails" available there. Nobody can smoke seventy of these a day without some ill effects.

After one Scottish trip, by the time I returned to the United States, my voice had gone from husky into gruff and was threatening to become bass baritone. It was suddenly obvious that I had to change my smoking habit quickly or lose my chosen career. I had a ten-day gap before I was due back on the road to sing. When in trouble, phone a friend, and I contacted one in California who had recently been to a smoking clinic.

"I know where you can get a cure, but the decision to stop has to come from you yourself; otherwise going to a clinic won't work," I was warned. I phoned the Californian clinic from New York. "We're happy to help," they told me. "But you'll need three weeks for the full treatment, and it isn't going to be easy to find space in our treatment schedule." "You don't understand," I replied. "I have ten days before I sing. I need to do it right now—and within those ten days." Silence for a moment, then: "Well, if you are prepared to fly six thousand miles here and back, we assume you're serious. Come over and we'll fit you in somewhere."

I flew in to a friend's house in Modesto, California, on a Thursday, phoned the clinic, and was told, "Come over and see us tomorrow." So I went there on Friday and was ushered into a quiet sunny office papered with antismoking posters. The coffee tables where I waited had sections of healthy and smokers' lungs between the glass and the wooden table top. Nothing terribly subtle. I spoke with someone for a while, and he agreed that I was ready and serious about giving up; then he told me to come back on Monday and to try not to smoke over the weekend. Two whole days? OK, that wouldn't be fun, but if it was the start of the exit route . . .

On Monday, they began aversion therapy. They put me into a small cubicle with a glass wall; it was insulated, so that the person working with me was not exposed to cigarette smoke. Everybody who worked there was an ex-smoker, so they knew every trick in the book. The cubicle had a table which faced a mirror on the wall and also a very large glass ashtray. Neither the ashtray nor the table had been cleaned since the clinic started, leaving a mountain of butts of every conceivable brand, every possible length and every known shade of lipstick you had ever seen, with the tar from them running into the ashtray. The mirror not only played this twice, but also let you see what you looked like when you were smoking. Next, they placed a bracelet on your right wrist which sent an electric shock into you at the strength of your own choosing: you could have a pinprick, or a jolt, or have your arm flapping all over the place. Once you decided, they never changed the setting; therefore the receiving skin got more and more sensitive.

I was told to smoke, but not inhale. So I puffed right-handedly on a cigarette, and every time my hand went near my mouth, they pressed the button outside the cubicle, and I was hit by a jolt. About the fourth time, I reached unthinkingly with my other hand—the animal had said, that hurts; let's try something else—only to get a knock on the window: "No, no, no." Back to right-handed smoking, more jolts for about half an hour, and then you watched some videos to reinforce the basic message.

Come Tuesday, I had not inhaled for three days, so the nicotine was mostly out of my system. They took me into what they called the Green Room and handed me four cigarettes—the number being dictated by my age, my health, and my habit. My supervisor lit the first one and told me that I had to chain smoke all four cigarettes to a tape recorder which said, every seven seconds, "Inhale." Have you any idea how short a time seven seconds is? You barely breathe that quickly! After about four draws on the cigarette, the place was starting to swim around me. I soldiered on through two cigarettes and was lighting the third off the end of the second, when she said, "I think that's about enough."

I guess they call it the Green Room, because that was pretty much the color I was right then. She became quite alarmed when I slid onto the floor and lay on my back because I felt so damned dizzy. For a second she thought I had collapsed. "No, I'm fine, I'm fine," I tried to reassure her—then I began to projectile vomit. The treatment was sudden, savage, and very, very effective. Since that moment, I have never had the slightest desire to smoke. Just as well: without that cure, I wouldn't have been singing for very much longer.

Even switching more into concerts, traveling was still my way of life. Apart from the usual run of concerts and recording sessions, there were two major Burns projects, one on either side of the Atlantic. Recording Burns lyrics to the original tunes for which they were composed took twenty years of working with Serge Hovey, as has been described above. The second project involved working with Donald Low in Stirling to record Burns songs as preserved in print for the Scots Musical Museum. These parallel projects left me memorizing a great many traditional Burns songs, frequently to two different tunes. Not easy—I think the modern word is *challenging*.

However, I was very fond of Donald, so this additional Burns work wasn't in any way a punishment. Some of our recording sessions were unusual. We worked in a wee kirk which stands at the roadside outside Brig O' Turk in the Trossachs. Douglas Gray of Scottish Records had access to this location.* While I was singing, the cables were snaking out through the open door of the kirk, which meant that we had to stop work when traffic passed outside. Since the Trossachs are one of the main tourist routes in Scotland, that meant lots of stopping and starting. It was also pretty chilly, and it felt at times as if my backside was in a freezer, but the acoustics were good and we managed to cover a lot of territory.

At a later point we had to fill in a few more songs, because of problems in the original recording session. We did this at Douglas's house, in the most bizarre recording session of my life. We completed the new recordings in his living room, across a table littered with toast and breakfast dishes. He had an Irish setter which was so full of goodwill and

* Douglas took a first in economics at Aberdeen University, but he was a lousy businessman—one of a kind, though—and his archives have still to be properly plumbed. Described online as a "lovable eccentric," he died in 1997 at age seventy-four. I think I had his son Fergus's room once when I stayed with the Grays, and it was all black—walls, ceiling, rug, sheets; I thought I had gone blind.

enthusiasm that it knocked you on your back every chance it got. Douglas couldn't shut the dog outside, because it barked to get back in, which was even worse than passing traffic had been in Brig O' Turk. We finished up with the dog in the room beside us, along with Douglas's mother-in-law, an elderly lady, sitting in a wing-backed chair. As we got ready to record she stood up to leave and Douglas bawled, "Sit! Stay!" as if she too was a dog. The old lady sat down again immediately, while the dog took no notice of him at all.

The rest of us still twitching from the sudden roar, his mother-in-law sat rigid through an hour of recording, while Douglas operated the machine with one hand and hung onto the dog's collar with the other. The end result reflects none of this—just as well that second session wasn't videoed!

Over the next thirteen years, I rocketed back and forth to Scotland on a fairly regular basis, because my mother was now on her own, and it was easier to visit in several two- or three-month stints than to come over for a longer stretch. During this period, apart from concerts in the UK I was also doing the Stirling Summer School workshops and Saltire Society concerts on the High Street in Edinburgh during the annual festival—I loved these; they were intimate occasions at Gladstone's Land up near the castle.

My repertoire for these gigs had expanded from my early days in Edinburgh, because from the time I was at Wesleyan, when I was working with a ballad I not only researched it in depth but also tried to find and play as many different recordings of it as I could in order to contrast performance and interpretation. Gradually, I built up an extensive teaching library of LPs, providing a good range of material for any workshops I was running. Singing and teaching mixed well; they were good partners.

The grounding I had acquired at Wesleyan gave me a good solid base for discussing traditional ballads. "Scottish song" covers a lot of ground, and, apart from the old ballads, that umbrella allowed me to haul in any offshoots that came from them—for example, the songs which had been brought to the States or elsewhere by Scottish immigrants. I could analyze what happened to a Scottish song when it was adapted overseas by people who didn't speak the language or just how well it held up in a variant of the second language, as in Appalachia. Fascinating.

Ultimately, the Stirling workshops hit an unforeseen problem after we had been running the course for six to eight years. Many of the same people came back every year, which meant they had heard my pitch and had extensive repertoires from their notes of earlier years. Mostly what they wanted to do was sing, have a week-long ceilidh. This was wonderful—but the other half of the students had come for the first time, were usually non-Scots speakers, and didn't have a clue about what was going on. After ten years, this blend of regulars and newcomers became totally insupportable. I just plain couldn't do it. We tried running a beginners' week and an advanced week, which should have separated the two streams. But people came when they had their holidays and picked whichever week matched these, leaving us with the same mix and the same clash of interests. Nobody was happy. After much agonizing, we closed down the summer-school workshops, victims of their own success.

Some of the most powerful ceilidhs I have ever attended were at Airthrey Castle toward the end of these years, because we had Tom Anderson doing Shetland fiddling, Alastair Hardie doing Northeast fiddling, and Angus Grant doing Highland fiddling, with all of the people who had attended the classes chipping in, and many of the songs deliberately chosen for their choruses. We had a roomful of musicians when the ceilidh started, and the head of steam we built up during the program left some people quite emotional.

After a gap of several years, we tried to restart the classes, but this attempt wasn't successful. In the 1980s, nobody else had been running summer schools in traditional ballad, so anybody who wanted to do this came to Stirling. By the second time round, there were competitive courses and fiddling camps all over the place, splitting the market to the point where there wasn't enough interest to support any summer school properly. We never built up the same momentum. In any case, by then I had probably got past that kind of outlay of energy for the return involved, and I cannot honestly say that I was disappointed at this outcome.

HINDSIGHT 8.1: *Elie, Fife 2013, a somewhat different kind of Hindsight. We were sitting over a mug of coffee during a break in the interviews, watching the tide come in. Jean said, as the seagulls called outside,*

"I can remember so clearly, sitting down at that exam desk in Edinburgh and writing my rebellion onto the margins of that exam paper. What was it . . . yes . . . 'God knows, I'm not proud of myself, but I can't find it in me to be sorry. You can't please everybody, so if you please yourself it's always a start.'"

She paused, sipping coffee strong enough to strip the varnish off her highly polished dining room table—Jean was aye the house-proud Queen of Clean, even at this late stage.

"Why do we remember things like that so clearly, and in such detail—the daft impulses, the first few gigs, the first big folk festival and my knees knocking together on that stage? Then after we've made it, once we're established as professional performers, why do the coffeehouses, the nightclubs, and even the concerts blur together? Why do we remember the fight upward far better than we do the rewards for getting there? Why, in these later years, is it the people and the places which stand out more clearly than most individual performances?"

She looked at me. "Well, don't just sit there, say something."

"Maybe you remember best when you're hungry," I started. "Maybe when you're older and have made it to the top, it just becomes a job."

"No," she said firmly. "I haven't got old. Not yet. And it's never been just a job. Singing has always been the only thing which ever mattered. It's not just the songs which come to life; it's me as well."

However, as one door closed at Stirling, another opened in terms of my work schedule: two Aussies who came to my classes were largely responsible for me setting up a tour of Australia. They gave me the name of a booking agent in Sydney, who turned out to be a pretty good guy and, after many months of planning, I set off for Australia. One of the Aussies, Kel Watkins, met me at the plane at 3:00 A.M., which was very sweet. So nice to land on the far side of the world, where I didn't know a soul, and see a weel-kent (familiar) smiling face waiting for me. That was a journey I remember well, even though I am no stranger to jet lag. It was a trip from hell, sitting at forty thousand feet for twenty-four hours, changing countries, climates, and time zones. It left me completely disorientated in relation to time and sleep and took me a full week to recover. That memory has been enough to keep me from going back, although I would dearly love to see New Zealand.

I landed in Perth to sing at the Perth Folk Festival and do a couple of workshops there. That was a delight, because it was like California twenty years earlier, with a wonderful outdoor Shakespearean theater. The temperatures were just right, and I remember the thrill of seeing a lake full of black swans. Kel Watkins was a bush balladeer—the Australian bush ballads are not songs but are spoken in rhyming couplets, and to this day I am in awe of anybody who can memorize and recite fifteen minutes of story without a tune to hang it on.

From Perth, I went to Adelaide. This was where Moira Lawrie, my harpist buddy, worked with her husband, so I spent a few days with them and did a concert at the folk club there; then I went on to Melbourne and Geelong and the big festival down on the south coast at Port Fairy. Next I went to perform in Sydney, and during a tour arranged by my hosts for the concert, sneaked the chance to sing from the stage at the Sydney Opera House, when there wasn't a soul in the building. That was a lifetime experience, and the acoustics were wonderful. From there, I flew to Alice Springs to do a concert, and that too was like stepping back a century. While in Alice, I went back to the theater for the first Aborigine concert that had ever been held there, and I was one of the twenty-five white faces in the hall that night.* Everybody came to that concert in Alice, including babes in arms; I swear most people had picnics with them. It was an incredibly informal and exciting evening, and the crowd was wired beyond belief.

I hitched a ride out to Ayres Rock and climbed about halfway up the rock itself, thinking that I would never be back there again, so the least I could do was make the climb. Easier said than done. I stopped climbing when I realized that if I went any further, with its combination of heat and elevation, I would be taken out feet first—which was not the object of the exercise. At least I made it to where the chain, which is anchored into the rock, runs out and you have to start scrambling. I sat down and admired the view until I got my wind back. Returning to ground level, I took a small-plane flight to see the rock from the air. That was a shocker—Australia is a huge country with nothing in the middle. When you look down, the rock and its encampment are just a spit in the ocean, because there is simply nothing else as far as the eye can see in any direction.

I caught the bus back to Alice, then flew to Darwin, where I saw geckos in a house for the first time. They ran around the walls, taking care of mosquitoes and all kinds of bugs. It was subtropical, and the bird life was quite exotic. I would have liked to spend more time there, but I was back on a plane the day after the concert and returned to Sydney for a couple of days before flying on to China.

For once in my life, I was visiting a country as a tourist—although at one point I did sing for the Folk Club in Hong Kong. My friends Alec and Hazel Barbour were traveling with a British-based tour just as China

* It reminded me of my Apollo Theater experience in Harlem, but at the Apollo Theater I was one of three white faces—me and the two guys who took me there.

opened up at the end of the 1980s and before the Tiananmen Square massacre. I joined up with them for part of the tour.

If I had seen nothing other than the Terracotta Army, that would have been worth the trip on its own. I was absolutely transfixed by the scene, despite the fact that it was the early days of the excavation and the display was much smaller then than it is now. There was a large airplane hangar with a few walkways from which you could look down on the army. I still get goosebumps when I think about them, because they looked so real that I was waiting for one of them to move. The electricity of that place was fantastic—thousands of figures each with a different face.

We went to the Great Wall, once again almost too much to take in as you walked along it and saw it stretching out in front of you for miles, snaking over the hills. Then we did several boat trips on canals and rivers in the middle of China, where you saw life in the raw, everything from personal bathing to washing laundry, while others were tipping in garbage along the banks. In the cities, I saw a couple of things I wish I hadn't—like some nameless creature, probably a dog, being cooked at the roadside by a small boy tending the fire—and struggled to cope with the sheer weight of people. My lasting impression of that vast country is of a very simple world of people who were happy with their lot, while I, as one of many tourists, was likely to be instrumental in changing everything. Tourism invariably destroys what you have come to see.

I have a vivid memory of a village, where the smell was simply appalling—there was open sewage somewhere. We were invited into someone's house, which was as basic as it is possible to be inside four walls, with no luxury or trimming of any kind. Yet the people were so proud: it was clearly more than they had known up until then, and they were genuinely welcoming and generous. We also went into a school where the kids were impossibly well behaved, and, remembering my own teaching days in Kirkcaldy,* I found myself wondering where we had gone wrong.

Alec and Hazel were heading down to Guilin and the Yangtze gorges, but I had to fly back to New York for a concert. Another murderous trip. I know for a fact that I came back and did the concert, but I have no recollection whatsoever of the evening: my performance must have

* Kirkcaldy was the place where the headmaster had briefed me about the kids who were waiting to leave school at the soonest possible moment: "It's impossible to teach them; just try to stop them from tearing up the books and destroying the place."

been given on automatic pilot. The only thing that registered was that the lady who organized it was far more concerned with whether there were enough cups and saucers for tea afterward than about running a sound-and-lights check for the concert. The rest is a total blank. I was jet-lagged out of my skull.

HINDSIGHT 8.2: *Mid-1990s, written after I returned from the China trip. I love Chinese food in any shape or form, and the dinners that we had were wonderful, but I remember wishing that they would give us what the locals ate at breakfast time, because their attempts at a European breakfast were downright awful.*

Everything was so different, ranging from the awesome to the appalling. To have your mind blown by looking down at the patient and eternally waiting faces of the Terracotta warriors or by stumbling along the Great Wall and knowing that this could be seen from outside the Earth itself. To see priceless porcelain—and abject poverty. Yet, amid that poverty, to find that people who had nothing reached out to offer you kindness—unscripted, spontaneous.

While over everything hung the stench of raw sewage. Even in the cities, the plumbing was horrendous, usually holes in the floor. If you were looking for a ladies' room, you walked down a corridor until you saw a lady in a Mao suit coming out from somewhere, shaking first one leg and then the other. Then, you knew you were heading in the right direction.

Next I went to Norway, at the invitation of a couple of Vikings. I had met them at an anniversary of the Battle of Largs* when I was asked to come and sing as a representative of the Scots in the old battle, a group of Norwegians having come over to represent the Viking raiders. One was a well-known Norwegian radio personality and the other, Hauk Buen, a Hardanger fiddler and a real charmer. Both were easy to get on with,

* The Battle of Largs (1263) was the result of Scottish kings trying to take back into their realm land which had previously been held under the overlordship of Norway. King Haakon of Norway sailed to squash the claim with a massive fleet, which was badly damaged in a severe storm. Although the fighting on land was inconclusive, the Vikings retreated in the face of the threat of yet another storm, leaving the Scots to claim (a) the victory and (b) the fact that right was on their side because God had brought the storms to defend them against the far greater numbers of the Vikings. Winners write history.

although my lasting memory of the Largs concert was of being soaking wet. The event was held on the Kelburn estate in pouring rain and in a tent which had a solid floor with a carpet over it. The tent was leaking and I was wearing a long dress so, as the carpet got wet, the trailing ends of my dress acted as a wick, and by the end of the night I was sodden. Wet or not, the concert was a huge success, and I finished up with an invitation to go over to Oslo for a radio interview, which I did shortly thereafter.

It may seem strange that I did very little touring or traveling in Europe, but I suspect that is yet again on account of the Scottish psyche. Europe was too close to Scotland and therefore didn't have the appeal of more exotic venues. In Fife we have a wonderful saying: "Have ye done any traivelin'?" "Naw, but I aince kent a man wha had been tae Crail."* I managed better than Crail, but it was my mother who was the real European traveler, because she and her sisters used to take buses to the Continent on tour when she could escape from all her bed-and-breakfast and meals.

Back in the United States, I was working closely with Marty Streicher and Lynda Ciolek, and our relationship, which had started well, had blossomed. One of the things I warned them about at the beginning was that I didn't like singing out of doors, for the reasons already stated above. That warning was necessary because, as my profile rose, there came a steady flow of invitations to sing at Highland games. These had pretty much the same problems as open-air festivals, but with an additional twist. Many of the people who attended them had a cookie-tin notion of what Scotland is like—you know, with pictures of Edinburgh Castle on one side and Balmoral or a wee Scottish terrier on the other—and they wanted the populist music which goes with this vision. The whole genre of "My Grannie's Heilan' Hame" songs† is something I don't subscribe to; it reflects a nostalgic, heather-coated image of the country which is

* "Have you done any traveling?" "No, but I once knew a man who had been to Crail." Crail is a fishing village on the east coast of Fife, and the saying is an ironic observation that Fifers regard travel, even as far as the next village along the coast, to be a great adventure.

† Literally, "My Grandmother's Highland home," an idealized folk memory that many Glaswegians carried in their minds about when their parents migrated into industrial Scotland to find work. This genre of songs bore no resemblance to reality and degenerated into mawkish sentimentality. *Tartanalia* is another wonderful term for this kind of vision that Helen Schneyer came up with.

only minimally true. There are only so many times you can smile politely and decline to sing a "good old song" which is nothing more than piano-stool music from the 1930s or a tartan hit tune made popular by the White Heather Club on TV. Therefore I had warned Marty and Lynda that I wanted nothing to do with Highland games and singing songs like "Scotland the Brave."

As always, they took my wishes on board. Things went smoothly until one day Marty came back to me with a potential gig at the Maxwell Highland Games near Toronto, Canada. "I know, I know," he said. "But this lot are being very insistent. They very much want you to be there, and they're paying extremely well. They will fly you up to Canada and put you up locally. Sounds like a great booking. Anyway, when did you last do one of these Highland games?" "About ten years ago," I replied. "Well, things might have changed," he argued. "Why don't you give it a try?"

I capitulated, without ever being fully won-over. Beware of going against your instinct and better judgement. What followed wasn't Marty's fault. It simply showed just how far I had moved beyond that point in my career where I took all work regardless, and how my expectations had risen in terms of what I regarded as being a professional and courteous way of treating any performer.*

First, I was really pushed out of shape when there was nobody to meet me at the airport. How was I supposed to travel the forty miles to Maxwell? I hung about until finally someone showed up at the other side of the service counter, waved, and asked me who I was—then left me standing again. However, he had only gone to get his car, and he turned out to be the grounds keeper, a perfectly pleasant guy who talked endlessly about the Maxwell Highland Games of which he was obviously very proud, telling me that about forty thousand people would be there over the weekend. I listened, thinking, "Well, it can't be all bad; at least I can sell some CDs." He drove me to the ground, where they were still setting up, and pointed out where the various beer tents would be. Beer tents? It didn't sound as if things had changed all that much since the last time, but I was determined to give this a fair chance.

* Hopefully, I had not put on airs and graces—Fifers don't do divas—but I had just gradually grown accustomed to being treated nicely rather than having to tough it out on my own.

We met the pipe major, John, who greeted me through a haze of whisky fumes and offered to show me around and complete the tour. He took me into the middle of a playing field where they were erecting a platform and scaffolding. This embryonic stage was perhaps twelve feet off the ground. "How do I get up there, John?" I asked. "Oh, we'll find a ladder," he replied. I had a flashback to Doune Castle in Perthshire, many years before, when I had to leave my jeans on under my evening dress so that I could climb a ladder to reach just such a stage, and I thought, "I am getting too old for this."

"OK. Where do I change?" I asked. There was no screening under the stage. "Maybe in the Athletics Building?" he suggested. That was about quarter of a mile away. "OK, but how do I get from there to here?" I asked. Alarm bells were ringing; had nobody thought through these practical issues? "OK, we'll get a car to bring you over."

Think of your bank balance, Jean, I told myself as I was taken out to the bed and breakfast, a delightful old farmhouse about two miles outside the town which was run by a Swiss couple. Maxwell itself was a crossroads in the middle of fields, with practically nothing apart from one restaurant at its center.

"Do I eat there?" I asked hopefully as we passed. Pause; then, "Oh you won't get anything to eat at the restaurant. That's been booked out for weeks; it's the same, every year." "Fine, so where am I going to eat?" I demanded. Another pause. "Plenty of stands on the ground will be serving food." If they had thought about it at all, it had been assumed that I would show up and hang around the grounds before, during, and after my set, living on beer, hot dogs, hamburgers, and popcorn. Then go to the Athletics Building, climb into my evening dress, and sing. My heart sank: I had been here, done that, and worn the jeans underneath. Had I one more time left in me?

At the hinner end* the B&B couple saved me from immediate disaster and fed me lunch, after which I was to be picked up by Connie the organizer who had corresponded with Marty. She lived a little further out along the same road and was the one who would ferry me in for my performance next day. She did in fact drop in after I was settled, greeted me without ever getting out of the car, and ran me back to the ground. There, on my own, I checked the whole place out, established that some form of sound check would be made, and then returned to the farmhouse

* the hinner end: literally, the hind end, at the end of it all

where the nice Swiss couple took pity and fed me supper too. Indeed, they fed me right through the weekend, until I left—otherwise, I would have starved.

Nice people, but their organization was absolutely chaotic—at least in as far as I was concerned. To them, I was the sideshow for people who had come to see and enjoy the games. It can be lonely—and a tad unsettling—to be a sideshow and not know from one moment to the next where you should be or what you should be doing, because organizers hadn't thought of problems until you raised them.

I had been told repeatedly that the Maxwell games were the biggest Highland games in the world, with forty-plus pipe bands coming every year. Maybe so, but one of their pipe bands had three pipers and a drummer, so we are not talking about massed pipe bands on the Castle Esplanade at Edinburgh. Nevertheless, it was clearly their biggest event in the year, and all minds were focused on making the Maxwell games run according to the usual success formula.

The day of the performance rolled round, and I was made up, coiffed, and waiting in the farmhouse with my evening dress in a bag. Meanwhile, the sky got darker and darker, with spatters of rain hitting the farmhouse windows. Then the heavens opened, and the rain became torrential. Nobody could run a gig in the middle of a playing field in this kind of weather. In the event, it had to go indoors, and it did. The staff crammed the remaining spectators into the Athletics Building, hauled in the dripping bleachers and set them up around the sides, and then brought in the sound system and set it up at the side of the hall. Problem. The only lighting available was for basketball, with everything blazing down onto the playing area at the center and everywhere else in shadows. Instead of a spotlit stage, there was a microphone and a small space against the wall, all shrouded in Stygian blackness.

Meanwhile, I was sitting out at the B&B waiting for Connie. The Swiss couple became increasingly agitated, while I reassured them: "They know I am out here; they will come and collect me . . . surely." Finally, a battered VW bus showed up with some kids who had been working the Highland games circuit on board. It wasn't quite a stretch limo, but it was a whole lot better than walking in, so I went back with them and got dropped off near the back door of the Athletics Building, where I ran into a young woman who asked me if I had a ticket.

I looked at her and smiled. "No, I don't have a ticket," I said. "Well I'm sorry, but I can't let you in without a ticket." "That's fine," I said. "When

Connie asks what's happened to her concert performer, tell her that you turned me away because nobody gave me a ticket"—which wasn't terribly kind, but my sense of humor was wearing thin.

Someone confirmed that I was indeed the performer, and I found a place to change in the boardroom, sharing this space with an enormous shiny table which could have seated forty people. As I was changing, someone stuck their head round the door and called: "Can you sing for about half an hour, Jean?" "That's fine, yes." I tidied myself up. Time drifted by. Then Pipe Major John stuck his head round the door. "Do about a twenty-minute set, will you, Jean?" he asked. "Certainly, John. Just let me know when."

Abandoned again, I waited for ages; then I left the boardroom and eased my way down to the edge of the basketball pitch. In the dark I couldn't see what was happening or find anyone to tell me when I was due on. Out in the brilliant lights, marching bands were striding in through the front door, their cheerleaders strutting their stuff, parading across every inch of the floor. This was what people had come from miles around to see and enjoy. This was their annual fix of Scotland.

Eventually, someone materialized at my elbow, and we scuttled up along the front of the spectators toward the microphone when John stepped over. "Give us about ten minutes, Jean, will you?" he said. Not quite the concert I had been booked for but, by this stage, ten minutes was fine for me. I did my four songs on the run, watching the front door like a hawk, because I knew that the very second my time was up, I would have to sprint across the floor to the boardroom before I got mowed down by the next marching band. An interesting experience, singing with one eye on my watch and the other on the doorway.

When I got back and was berating Marty, he waved me down. "Ten minutes?" he said. "Hey, this is good! You're the only singer I know who makes more than a plumber." Maybe so but, man, that was one grisly weekend. Marty never again raised the possibility of singing at a Highland games.

I can think of only one more-miserable experience in my entire career, and, whereas what happened at Maxwell was entirely out of my control, on this other occasion I was directly and personally involved. Don't ever go against your better judgement. Once again, I let myself be bulldozed into something which I knew very well I was not equipped to handle. It was to sing a complex Serge Hovey arrangement *live*. I am not even sure that this has been done before—or since.

When we had recorded these songs, they were always "layered," so all I ever worked with was a piano or, at most, a couple of pianos. The finished piece and its studio-built recording I never heard until it was completed. To present any of Serge's songs live was way beyond my experience of the music, but this was to be done at the insistence of his wife Esther, who heard that I was going to be working with the Hartford Singers in Connecticut and felt that this was a great opportunity to have Serge's music performed live. Talk about being between a rock and a hard place. Every instinct warned me not to do it but, after twenty years of work and friendship, how could I now turn my back on Serge and his music?

It was an unmitigated disaster, a concert driven by single-minded love rather than one brought together under the tight professional control of any sort of production manager. We were simply contacted and booked, and we turned up. There were two pianos, one on each side of the stage: these were backed up by two string quartets, some French horns, and some extra basses. The stage was full of musicians who had never played the music together before. Worse, there weren't any monitors, so the two isolated pianos were playing with the equivalent of earmuffs and weren't in sync. I was standing in the middle. Responding to a conductor wasn't beyond me, but I could hear both pianos from there; they were at quite different points in the score, and I didn't know which one I was supposed to follow. The conductor had to stop the whole thing and start again. By then she was wild-eyed: I felt for her, but I thought, "I can't do anything to help you sort this out, so which group do you want me to sing with?"

It was awful, a dreadful evening. I still get cold sweats when I think about it—but it is also human nature that I can recall in total and intimate detail the performances which made my toenails curl, while skipping blithely over hundreds, if not thousands, of nights where I left a performance flying as high as a kite, having had a wonderful time and knowing that the audience had too.

One such was in Los Angeles, when John Currie took over from Roger Wagner as conductor of the Los Angeles Master Chorale and orchestra. He invited me to take part in a concert, and although plugging two songs in twice at a concert has never been my favorite thing, I agreed. John had organized an evening around a Celtic theme in the Dorothy Chandler Pavilion, and I wanted to help.

The evening started out well, then got better. Outside of the pavilion, the whole esplanade has fountains, which are jets mounted flush and set by computer to plume up sporadically, providing great fun for the youngsters trying to run across the stretch without getting drowned. I stood on a balcony watching them dodge the jets before the concert.

The auditorium holds 3,300 people, and I had a 250-voice choir behind me, plus the orchestra. I did my own thing during the sets, and then John said, "Come back on and do an encore." At that point I was using "Amazing Grace"* quite a bit (although I stopped that after it became hackneyed) and sang this for my encore. Three thousand voices in front of me and 250 voices behind made a spine-chilling and unbelievably exciting sound. Although a one-off experience, I will never forget it.

Back in Scotland, my Burns work with Donald Low had produced four fairly generous cassettes with eighteen to twenty songs on each. That was a lot of singing. I tended to do one collection/cassette at a time, timing the recording sessions to run over the summer when I was working back at Stirling. While still doing concerts in Scotland, my pace of life over there had gentled down, and I began to spend some of the time on holiday with my friends.

On one of these working holiday trips in 1985, I finally got round to buying my own front door. Freddie Wachsberger and Sylvia Newman were in Scotland with me, and we were staying in my mother's house. Freddie and Sylvia were great trencherwomen, and I had just been introduced to a restaurant called the Bouquet Garni run by the nephew of a friend.

We drove there on one of those crystalline Costa del Fife evenings, absolutely beautiful, calm, and sunny, and went for a walk because we were a little early for our booking. Our feet took us down to the harbor, and as we passed a little row of cottages one had a small handwritten sign in its window which said, "For sale, key at Number 4." We stopped to admire, both the house and the view which spread out in front of it.

* Lyrics by John Newton'an Englishman who was a captain of slave ships, left the slave trade to study theology and was ordained in 1764. Many different musical settings of "Amazing Grace" were used until 1835 when William Walkerer set the words to the traditional tune "New Britain," itself probably an amalgam of two others from oral tradition. From this early start, the hymn was adopted by revivalists and shape-note singers and traveled across the States. As of September 2011 more than seven thousand recordings have been made. It was first recorded in 1922.

"Gee, what a wonderful outlook," Freddie said, sighing. "Wouldn't that be a great place to live?" It was no more than a casual observation before we walked down to the end of the pier and back to the restaurant, where we had a lovely meal. On that particular holiday we were heading for Shetland, so a couple of days later we drove to Aberdeen, got on a boat, and drank our way to Shetland. We had a great time up there, but, oddly enough, the casual judgment of that harbor cottage wouldn't go away. At least once a day, we would see a cottage or a view or a bay and somebody would say, "Isn't that gorgeous?" To which somebody else, after a pause to admire, would reply, "Yep, but I would rather have that house on the harbor."

This became almost a routine. "What is this nonsense about the harbor house?" I finally asked on our way back to Leven. "It was such a beautiful house, and setting," Freddie said. "We should go back and look at it again." "What on earth for?" I demanded. "You live in New York City. You have a house out in Orient. Why would you want another house in Scotland?" "It would be an investment."

So we drove back along the coast next day, went down to the harbor, and found that the sign was still in the window. At that moment, I realized that casual liking had shaded into real excitement inside me. Maybe it was just the excitement of a treasure hunt, or maybe something else. We went to Number 4 and knocked on the door. No answer. I opened the door and shouted, "Is anybody there?" Still no answer. As we walked away, I thought, "How nice, the neighbor's door wasn't locked; that makes a pleasant change these days."

We went into the restaurant and told the owner: "We're interested in that house down in the harbor, but there's nobody at Number 4 to give us the keys." Having got there, it seemed a shame not to have another meal. So we ordered, and, in the middle of the soup course, an arm appeared over us and dropped a bunch of keys onto the table. "I'm Alec Macrae, the factor," the owner of the voice said. "When you've had a look at the house, bring back the keys—my office is up on High Street."

We rushed through our meal and went down with the keys, opened the cottage door, and stepped inside. My hair stood on end. "I think I'm home!"—I blurted out the first words which came to mind. That was on a Thursday, and we owned the house by Monday. I didn't know you could do business that quickly in Scotland, but we did. Two other lots of people were looking at the cottage, getting architect's surveys done and other checks carried out but, with a lifelong habit of jumping into the swimming pool from the highest board without first checking that there's water underneath, I never paused to think. Did the house's roof leak? I didn't know. Did the drains work? I didn't care. The energy in that cottage was, and is, wonderful. The house wrapped itself round me the minute I stepped inside and has continued to do so, ever since.

Buying was likely to be the easy bit. There we were, three women co-owners each with strong ideas about what a room should look like and what it should hold by way of furniture. Ground rules had to be set. "I don't want a one-third ownership," I said. "I will go for half or not at all."

My friends were OK with that, but before we spat on our hands and shook them on the deal, there was another issue to be resolved. "Before we get in too far with this, Sylvia," I said, "Freddie and I seem to be on the same page, but you haven't said very much. Have you any misgivings?" "No, not really," she replied. "Maybe just one." "What's that?" I asked. "Decoration," she answered.

I knew it—she is renowned for redefining every plan and concept, when responding to anyone who asked for help in redoing rooms. "That's not a small thing," I said. "We had better kick this around." "Right. No wallpaper; I hate wallpaper," she came back. "Then you have a problem," I replied. "In an old house, you *have* to use wallpaper. You cannot paint the walls, because they're not regular. You can paper them, and *then* paint them." "Fine. Let's go for woodchip paper and any color of our choice downstairs, then wallpaper upstairs? You get to choose your bedroom, I get to choose mine?" "OK."

From there on in, we sailed through everything without a single glitch, which was nothing short of miraculous. What helped was that the house was in a conservation area and had to be equipped and furnished according to its position and its age—there was no way we were going to go for Japanese simplicity in an 1880s stone-built cottage that had once been the harbor master's house. In any case, it is a C-listed building, which means that I can't even change the paint on the outside door without permission.

I have never regretted that move, although when my mother died I was tearing around America with two empty houses sitting in Scotland, because her house came to me as well. Which house should I hold, and which should I sell? For a while, I agonized. Should I, could I, sell my mother's house, the house in which I had grown up? But there really wasn't any choice: would I rather get up in the morning to look out at the shows* across the road when they were in Leven in the summer, or would I rather look out over the bay? I chose the harbor master's cottage, because that felt like my home and I was happy in it.

After my father died, I had taken over the repair and maintenance of the house in Leven, where a lot of things needed to be done. However, I was earning enough consistently to let me remove her coal fire and put in a gas fire, so that she wasn't sclatching around clearing out cinders to build a new fire on cold mornings. Next I had the old coal house gutted and added to the main house via a new porch, installing a freezer, washing machine and tumbler dryer there, giving her access to them in all weathers. I gladly took over the cost and responsibility for the maintenance of the old house, which is one of the reasons it came down to me.

Between my mother and me, things had become just fine. I had mellowed a lot, and so had she. Perhaps one of the reasons why we struck so many sparks off each other when I was younger was that we were too damn similar. I am grateful to have lived long enough to resolve most of the issues which left us with locked horns in those early years. The moment when I finally realized that we were completely at ease with each other was when I had been asked to go up to Scourie, near Lairg, in Sutherland and do a concert. I had grown up with a lifetime of guilt trips, and this one started off in the same direction.

"I was aye tae get tae go tae Scourie,"† my mother said. "But . . . *ah, hah!*" Nobody could do a shuddering sigh like my mother, laden with hurt, grief, and weary resignation. The implication was that the world in general, and me in particular, had let her badly down. My extremely unladylike response was, "You miserable old bugger! Who's stopping you from going to Scourie? You have a car and your driver's license, and you don't need to ask anybody whether you can go or not."

She burst out laughing. If I had tried that reply earlier, God knows what would have happened, but the old barriers had gone. We were getting on extremely well. I was sorely tempted to take her with me to Scourie, but I didn't. First, it was an incredibly long and exhausting trip, and, second, I had left finding myself a bed and breakfast somewhere until I arrived. This was fine by me but nosebleed territory to my mother,

* the shows: summer carnival, complete with noisy rides, dodgems, and so forth.
† "I always wanted to go to Scourie, but alas!"

who needed every detail settled before she went anywhere. In any case, she had reached a stage when she was a lot more comfortable at home.

However, I did manage to tempt her to a couple of other local concerts and also took her with me to the ceremony for the honorary degree I got at Stirling University. At Stirling, I was given the job of responding to the university on behalf of all the people receiving honorary degrees and the other graduates. Dunblane Cathedral had been chosen for the event. The only place in the cathedral from which I could make the response was the smaller of the two pulpits so I climbed up to do it from there. As soon as the official party left the cathedral, the heavens opened. Freddie and Sylvia were looking after my mother, who was now in a wheelchair. By the time they reached the shelter of the building where they were hosting the postgraduation lunch, Bluebell was wheeled in looking a bit like a drowned rat. She glanced up at me, water dripping off her nose. "You should never had gone intae that pulpit," she said accusingly.

A strong woman, one of the strongest women I have ever known, very much a product of her time yet, on many levels, not at all. I remember being part-shocked and part-impressed when she had two workmen come to stay in the house while she was still taking guests. They were absolutely stuck for somewhere to live, and after listening to their tale of woe, she told them, "All I've got is a double bed. If you can manage with that, I'm happy to give it to you, but the house is full."

One of the men was a black guy, at a time when we didn't see many black faces in Fife. A neighbor said to my mother, "Don't you mind . . . you know . . . his color?" Bluebell stared at her. "Why? It disnae come off on the sheets," she replied.

Time never stands still, and although my sister-in-law was doing heroic duty in looking after my mother, Bluebell was getting to the stage where she really couldn't be left in the house on her own. One of the last summers I was home, I spent every second or third night staying with her myself, because she was quite frail. It was increasingly clear that she couldn't look after herself anymore, and she had gone even beyond the sheltered-housing stage. Ultimately, she had to be put into a nursing home where she could be looked after all the time. It was heartbreaking the first two or three times I went there to see her. She was getting very vague and forgetful, not at all sure what was going on, and, every time we went to visit her, she would say, "I'll just come home with you."

That hurt so much. Then she drifted down even further, and it came almost as a relief when I realized that she didn't know who I was anymore. Commuting home between bookings in the United States, I had crossed the Atlantic eight times already that year, and both my back and my bank balance were creaking.

She died in 1993. Just because something is inevitable, it doesn't take away the pain. Yet, in a way, Bluebell never disappeared. I still sense her hovering, disapprovingly, when I'm about to do something I know she wouldn't like—too tangible to be imagination, too vibrant to be a ghost. Someone that strong and vital never truly fades away. She is there, not just in scraps of memory. She was, and is, a huge presence and influence in my life.

CHAPTER 9

Honors? Have They Got the Right Person?

Being invited to meet the Queen generally costs you money, because turning up in jeans and trainers isn't normally an option. The first time my bank account was depleted, it would be unfair to hold HM directly responsible. I had been touring in England, which was hard work, frequently quite depressing, and had finished up staying with Jacqui and Bridie, my friends in Liverpool.* I stopped off to visit them and to relax for a couple of days and was dragged off shopping, which is seldom high on my list of priorities.

However, I came across a dress—on sale, of course, I'm a Fifer—which looked more like period costume than anything else. It was in a color, medieval green, which has always intrigued me even if I don't look particularly good in it. It had all sorts of floating panels and over-capes with tassels.† Lord only knows what particular fantasy I was fulfilling, but I loved that dress on sight and bought it. Ten days later, I received an invitation to sing at Edinburgh Castle for the Queen's Silver Jubilee celebrations. I thought, "Ah, so *that's* why I bought the dress." And cut off the *Sale Price* ticket.

For this event, we performers were working across the Castle Hall from a small high platform setting us above the diners, who were still at their tables. I can't remember who was acting as MC, but I was grateful to see John Cairney sitting practically under my feet—in fact, if I had fallen off the stage, I would have landed in his lap. In such pressurized circumstances, no matter how long you have been a professional performer, it is

* Theirs was the house that had been made available to me, as described above in chapter 5, when I went down there to sing with the Spinners.

† over-capes: sleeves

always nice to see a familiar face and to feel their silently offered support.

Despite the formality and importance of the occasion, nobody contacted me to suggest which songs I should sing. The choice was left entirely to me, and I chose "Mary Hamilton" for my first song, starting my performance as a recitation and finishing by singing the traditional ballad "The Queen's Four Marys," unaccompanied by my own choice, because I could never have managed the steep wooden stairs to the platform in my long dress and carrying a guitar. I needed both hands to get up there in one piece, and even more to scramble down again.

That platform was seriously high. Bobby Watson, the Highland dancer, whispered to me, "I'm terrified to go up there and dance, Jean—I can't see a thing, without my glasses." We were all on edge, muscles tensed, while he was dancing, for fear that if he strayed a couple of feet out of line, he would land among the diners. He didn't; like a true artiste, he never deviated from the center of that small stage.

There was a reception afterward, where we lined up to be presented to the Queen. She passed me without stopping to talk—maybe my song had pressed the wrong buttons.* Did I bow or curtsy? I'm afraid I did neither; it simply never occurred to me.

The next time I had to raid my bank account for a royal occasion was when I was told to turn up at Buckingham Palace almost ten years later in the mid-1980s to be given an MBE (Member of the Order of the British Empire, an honour only the Queen can formally give). This kind of invitation borders on a summons. As I studied the wording on the

* An intriguing illustration of how the old ballads interweaved fact and fiction—then were repeated so often that it all became fact in the listeners minds. *Mary Hamilton* is an alternative title to *The Four Maries,* in which Hamilton as a lady-in-waiting to the Queen of Scots is made pregnant by the King of Scots, and is driven to kill the resultant baby; but she is seen and the queen demands that she is both charged with the crime and executed. The ballad is allegedly Hamilton's thoughts in the small hours before her execution. However, research showed no Mary Hamilton among the queen's (Mary of Guise's) four ladies-in-waiting, and it was assumed that Mary Hamilton was completely fictitious, as was her tale. Then further research showed that the *real* Mary Hamilton was a lady-in-waiting to Catherine I in the Russian Court, wife of the famous czar Peter the Great . . . and you've guessed the rest. The story fit. Either way round, I was singing about a very irate royal lady taking savage vengeance on a maid whom her husband seduced. Maybe a bad choice, to sing it to our own queen. Ooops!

expensive paper, my initial reaction was, "Oh my! No, I don't think so." Why, I'm not too sure, because I'm not overtly antiroyal. Perhaps it was a lingering echo of the old E II R problem, which infuriated many Scots at the time and still leaves a lot of us resenting her claim to be Elizabeth the Second of Scotland* and irked by this casual English dismissal of our country's history. While I'm not likely to put a bomb into a postbox in retaliation, I tend to reflect my irritation in whatever way I can—without making it a core principle to be held unto death.

It took good old Marty, from his New York base, to put me right. "Don't be foolish, Jean," he said. "Turn it down, and you'll get two lines in a newspaper. Accept it, and you can milk it for the rest of your professional career." His advice made hard-nosed business sense. I earned my keep on the other side of the Atlantic, and royal recognition was one of the biggest fillips I could ask for, with American audiences in mind. I accepted and began to enjoy answering the friends who asked me "Well, Jean, what do we call you now?" with "Call me Madam," in my best throaty Ethel Merman voice.

My acceptance decision triggered a few frenzied hours in New York. Clothing raised its ugly head, because an event at Buck House was obviously an occasion where I had at least to broadly conform. So I was taken over by Freddie and Sylvia and dragged round the shops. I remember fighting hard not to be dressed in what appealed to them, because that would simply have been New York City fashion. The last thing I wanted to do was to buy an outfit I would never wear again, so I dug in my heels and insisted that it must be something fairly practical, even if I was going to Buckingham Palace. The final grudging compromise on both sides was an outfit a bit more formal than I would normally wear, a blazer and a skirt with low heeled flat shoes.

I wish my mother had been fit enough to come with me as my guest, because she would have got a lot of mileage out of going to see the Queen. She would have dined out on it for the rest of her life, and I could probably have filled a whole chapter of this book with her caustic comments. But by then she was far too frail for any sort of journey.

*The E II R symbol appeared on both coinage and postboxes. A more accurate title would have been Queen Elizabeth the Second of England and the First of Scotland, which is, admittedly, a bit of a mouthful. Forget the technicalities, and let's just settle for me—and many others—being annoyed.

For the trip itself, I invited my friend Kate from Perth to come down with me and asked her to help me out by making the arrangements for the journey, while I was working over in the States. Expecting her to laugh, I told her that we were being allowed all of thirty-nine pounds each for bed and breakfast on top of travel costs. This was a bad mistake because, bless her teacher's heart, she assumed that this was all we should pay, and not one penny more. Therefore, she had a hell of a time finding any accommodation in London for that amount, but she finally managed to track down a hotel within this budget—which looked pretty much like what you would expect for thirty-nine pounds a night in London. We would have been better off in a Salvation Army hostel.

The "hotel" had been constructed out of a row of houses which had been taken over by the accommodation's owner. Inside its entry door you stumbled over an extremely unattractive and elderly plastic fountain, from which some sort of thick fluid oozed over grubby polystyrene rocks. A young woman receptionist waited for us in the hotel's cramped foyer. We were laden with hand luggage, each carrying a suitcase, garment bag, handbag, and a couple of plastic bags, but there was no porter to offer, "May I take that for you, madam?," not for thirty-nine pounds a night. The receptionist merely pointed toward the lifts. When we reached the fourth floor, we should have left a trail of breadcrumbs, because we wandered through a series of dogleg corridors and fire doors cut through between the different buildings until eventually we tracked down our room for the night.

First impressions count, and the one which hit me hardest when we pushed through the bedroom doorway was that there was a huge hole in the wall above my bed, where piping had been replaced. For most of that night I lay in mortal dread imagining what might slither or scuttle through this. The small room had two double beds crammed into it, leaving barely room to move. When you entered the room, you fell headfirst over my bed, which was sitting sideways across the door. Kate's bed lay beyond this, and, if she got out of it in too much of a hurry, she fell into the bathroom. To complete the thirty-nine-pound delight, every surface in the place, as is often the case in London, had its own film of urban grit.

My itinerant life had given me a lot of practice in surviving rooms from hell, but poor Kate was mortified to have booked us into such a place. Like all Scots, she took the entire guilt onto herself, and I spent most of the night telling her, "Don't worry; we can always eat out and we're leaving first thing in the morning, so there is only tonight to survive."

At this stage in my career, I traveled with a suitcase which split in the middle and opened flat, perfect for my kind of traveling life because you could keep all your tidy clothes—evening dress, and so on—in one half and all the other clothes and things you needed overnight in the other. But here the beds took up so much floor space that it was impossible to open, then leave open, the case. On top of the bed? Fine, but where did I sleep? That single case claimed as much room as a large human, challenging even my finely honed skills of changing to the skin while balancing on one foot. Meanwhile poor Kate, still guilt-ridden, could hardly move as she struggled to find enough space to get ready.

HINDSIGHT 9.1: *Written on the train back to Scotland*

The receptionist told us "Room 461, to the left," and we staggered with our luggage to the lift, then along a doglegged corridor that displayed neither rhyme nor reason in the directions it chose as it wandered under metal grills poised like a portcullis above the joins between the different buildings. We caught glimpses of stairs behind FIRE EXIT *signs and increasing evidence of rising damp on the façade walls "overlooking a quiet square" until at the end of a long corridor we found our room. At which point, we began to wish we hadn't.*

Room 461 might have been designed to strengthen the resolve of a faint-hearted suicide with its forty-watt bulb, muddy colored paint and wallpaper, and raw hole and partial patch on the ceiling, the legacy of some fifth-floor plumbing disaster. My first reaction was to turn and go somewhere else, but at 6.30 P.M. *on a dark evening, with no ready access to a phone, any search for new accommodation wasn't really on.*

Our morale rose after a leisurely and very tasty Nepalese dinner, within easy walking distance of the hotel. The two-foot long-stemmed roses in the bud vases on every table were a novel touch and the maître was quite the most innocently beautiful young man I have ever seen.

Then back to our grubby hotel for many sleepless and restless hours, then a deep sleep until the 7:00 A.M. *alarm went off, after which it took a certain measure of acrobatic skill to get washed and dressed without allowing bare skin to come into contact with either the carpet or the bedcover. First, we threw some clothes on and went in search of breakfast in the bowels of the building, then back up to the room to crank up the hair and climb into our "braws." Repacking and securely locking everything, we were delighted to escape the place by 9:30* A.M.

We had planned to get a taxi to the palace from the hotel, keeping the final leg of our journey simple, so we went down to reception, and I asked the young Indian man at the desk to call a taxi for us. He was pleasant and polite, but I don't think many people had made this particular trip from his hotel.

"Can you order a taxi, please?" "Sure. Where are you going?" "Buckingham Palace." "Oh, yeah, what are you going to do there?" Then, with polite Indian humour as he struggled to handle what were clearly crazy people. "The Queen, she is very busy, you know." "Yes, I do know," I replied. "She is entertaining Russian heads of state." "No, not today," I said. "Today, she is entertaining us."

Ultimately, he called a taxi but pointedly avoided giving them a destination; he left that embarrassment to us, and I glanced out the rear window to see him still looking after us, shaking his head. However it was a different story, when we returned later that day to collect our gear. By then, the penny had dropped, and he was phoning everyone he knew to tell them that guests of his had just been honored by the Queen. This news probably went into his marketing brochure. Good luck to him, but I would bet every penny to my name that we were the only people at that honors ceremony who spent the night before the ceremony in a hovel like that hotel.

Nothing fazes London taxi drivers, and ours headed without comment toward the destination we gave, dropping us off at one of the main gates to the palace. It was March and, dear God, it was cold!—both outside the place as we were fielded and gathered in and inside the palace, although I was better off than most, in my blazer and woolen pleated skirt. But no head gear, the absence of which had triggered outrage and consternation from my mother back in Fife. "Whit? Ye're no' wearin' a hat?" "I haven't worn a hat for the last twenty-five years. I'm not going to start now." "But ye're gaun' tae see the Queen!!" "OK, then let *her* wear the hat," I replied.

Everyone probably fantasizes about receiving red-carpet treatment, and here I was on the most famous red carpet in the world, sharing it with several hundred others. At the grand entrance we were separated into victims (or recipients) and guests, then ushered off in separate directions to meet up again almost immediately in the shared ladies' cloakroom, an elegant anteroom distinguished by some magnificent pieces of china in wall cupboards—and, on this occasion, a fine array of confiscated cameras on a central mahogany table, each with a check stub attached.

Clearly, when the palace had warned "no photographs" they weren't joking.*

This cloakroom was downstairs, down a magnificent steeply curving stairway with a central brass rail, those going down using one side and those coming up the other. I arrived to find myself in a lengthy queue of nervous ladies awaiting their turn for the loo. The stalls were presented as seven wall-to-wall doors, each going all the way discreetly to the floor and opening to reveal the most splendidly polished mahogany platform thrones—one holers incorporating fitted china bowls and a sunken handles which, when pulled, triggered a flushing process akin to opening the trapdoor under a gallows. The effect was fearsome. I always check that I have no loose glasses in a pocket before reaching over to work the handle of a strange toilet—in case they drop in and that's the last I see of them. A good precaution here, because the toilet flushed like an enormous vacuum cleaner; an owner, never mind her belongings, might have vanished without trace down there.

I struggled to get my serious head on and checked my person carefully: this was not the occasion to risk the dread scenario of a hitched-up skirt or a trailing streamer of toilet paper. Check completed, I took a deep breath and headed up the grand stairway toward civilization. On the return route, we were shepherded discretely by various court officials in morning dress past some handsome figures in high black boots, white breeches, gilded cuirasses, and drawn cutlasses resting on the right shoulder. At first, I thought they were stuffed, but then I realized that these were real people—the Household Guards, drawn from the regiment known as the Blues and Royals.

We were steered gently into the picture gallery, under its long and high vaulted ceiling with mirror double doors inset to their own depth and facing each other in the middle of the room. The pinkish walls were covered in oils, van Gogh, Rembrandt, and other artists whose names I couldn't read without my spectacles; I'm guessing that these weren't prints. Red ropes were looped on brass stands, separating the OBEs and CBEs from us lesser MBEs. And there we were left to stand for about forty-five minutes, which seemed more like an eternity at the time.

*Do they still do this, I wonder, or has the advent of tiny cellphones with built-in camera optics changed everything? Doing selfies with Her Majesty? Never mind the Queen, I would dearly have loved a photo of this ladies' cloakroom.

Some months later, a friend from the Lifeboat Service explained, with tongue in cheek, the different honors grades to me: "Oh, well done, Jean," he said. "I do hope you don't regard an MBE as any form of lesser recognition. You know what these letters stand for, don't you?" "Er . . . vaguely," I said. "Why?" "Well, an OBE means for Other Buggers' Efforts. And a CBE means that you got it for Corporate Bloody Efforts. But an MBE is for My own Bloody Effort."

With the bitter cold still biting even in this wonderful gallery, I headed for the fireplace and fell into conversation with the first Scottish voice I heard. This voice belonged to a lovely guy called Harry Rose who, like myself, was there for an MBE. He was a real lifesaver for me that morning—apart from an overpowering smell of mothballs which hung around him, strong enough to bring tears to the eyes. "It's from the minister's* morning coat," he apologized. "I borrowed it, because I was damned if I was going to buy one of these things"—a man after my own heart, even if the coat was many sizes too big for him.

As we chatted around the fire, I discovered that there had been an earlier ceremonial service for the sirs and dames. Now it would soon be our turn. Harry and I stood with our backs to the fireplace, turning fireside tartan on one side while remaining saltire blue† on the other. Most of the men—and I—were clustered round the solitary source of heat, chatting and waiting nervously. Finally, an official arrived and said, with a plum in his mouth, "Ladies and gentlemen . . . if I may have your attention. . . ."

He took us through what was going to happen, and how we must behave when we were called forward to be presented to the Queen, concluding with, "Ladies and gentlemen, when you are presented to Her Majesty, you will either bow or curtsy." "Oh, do we have the choice then?" I asked, and got a frosty stare. Smart-mouthing was not on the menu, it seemed. The air now thick with tension, we were shepherded a little further up the picture gallery where someone pinned a bar with a fixed hook onto my blazer, so that the Queen could simply drop a loop over the hook, and there would be no last-minute fumbling or potential puncture involved.

* minister: church pastor or vicar

† fireside tartan: skin turned blotchy pink and red from being too close to the heat of the fire. Saltire blue: the rich deep blue of the Scottish flag; the saltire is the diagonal white cross displayed on the blue background.

While we waited, I counted bodies and calculated that there was a ten-to-one male-female ratio for MBEs and a seventeen-to-one ratio for the OBEs and CBEs. I wonder if this is still true or if it simply reflected that single ceremony. I would hope that the percentage has changed a bit since then, but who knows.

Next, we were carefully lined up in order of presentation, ladies first rather than everyone simply being taken alphabetically. I had spent my time with the men around the fireplace, toasting my backside against the cold. This was my first real glimpse of my own species: most were wearing light dresses and shaking violently from a mixture of the bitter cold and nerves. The officials lined us up at the side of the room, from where a corridor took us right to the back of the hall, so that we could look down and see what was going on—and what was waiting for us. As we processed, I heard music being played from the minstrels' gallery down below, a selection from *Mary Poppins,* which didn't strike me as the sort of thing that any of us expected, least of all as it was played by a military band.*

From there we were ushered along another corridor, then fed down into the hall, to be processed one at a time, when our turn came. As we waited to be nudged forward, most of the ladies around me were in a terrible state, wringing their hands, adjusting their hats—some of them even practicing minicurtsies. Let's face it, we don't have to curtsy on a regular basis, and, added to this novelty element was the fact that some of the women were wearing tight dresses, not designed for gymnastics like this. The lady ahead of me seemed at the point of collapse in an absolute lather of perspiration. "Oh, my God," she kept moaning. "This is awful; I thought we were supposed to be having a good time." "No, I don't think anybody promised we'd have a good time," I told her. "Look on the bright side—it will be over soon."

Having watched actresses on stage with wide flowing dresses go into these floor-down graceful curtsies, with one knee behind the other, then rise again as elegantly as before, the vision this time wasn't quite the same. These actresses have yards of dress material around them, covering

* I was later told by Kate that it had been preceded by a selection from *The Sound of Music.* As a musician, the background music to the event probably registered more with me than with many of the others, some of whom were too far gone with nerves to register anything of their surroundings at that point. But why didn't they play something more stately and appropriate?

a multitude of sins, whereas most of these poor ladies had no room for maneuver or disguise and were left looking like jucks amang tar,* with their feet in the wrong place and their plump bodies dipped like half-shut knives. By now I was struggling with incipient hysteria—no doubt reflecting my own stage fright—and it left me wanting to giggle rather than cry.

As I waited for my nudge, I whispered to Sir David Slessor, the official at the starting gate, "Has nobody ever fainted at this stage?" "Madam, we have seen *everything*, at this stage," he replied solemnly. I was desperate to ask for details, but gentle pressure from his hand pushed me forward as my name was called. The measured paces straight out, as instructed, next a right-angled turn, then forward until the toes touched the stage where HM was standing. A curtsy of sorts, the best I could manage when stiff-jointed from the cold.

My God, but the lady looked tired: she was weary. "And what is your work?" she asked. For one wild moment, I wanted to answer in the style of one of the characters from *Scotland The What:* "Ach, weel, ah do a wee bittie o' this an' a wee bittie o' that . . . an' fit dae ye dae, yersel'?"†—but she wouldn't have understood me, or recognized the comedic source, and I would probably have been thrown into the tower. Suppressing the mad urge, I said, "I sing traditional Scots songs, like those of Robert Burns."

I remember vividly the regal handshake, which is with a bent hand, palm downward—otherwise the poor woman would have no bones left—then the slight push away at the end to let me know that my time was up. A couple of steps back, as instructed, and another right-angled turn, followed by marching off to be fielded and shepherded out of the hall. As I passed a miserable-verging-on-grim-looking equerry, I muttered, "Aw, cheer up, son; it cannae be as bad as that." Behind me, I heard him splutter.

We were marched out to the right and smartly along the corridor back to base, where the bar-and-pin was taken from us and the gong‡ slapped into a box and handed to us; then we were pointed back into the hall to

* jucks amang tar: ducks stuck in tar, leaning forward, bottoms sticking out behind

† "Oh, well, I do a little of this and a little of that—and what do you do yourself?" Scotland The What was a popular stage show which evolved into an ongoing series with droll Northeast rural characters poking endless fun at everything in their slow Doric tongue (original old Scots).

‡ gong: British slang for a military or any other kind of medal

join the audience and watch the rest of the proceedings. Well organized: we were much relieved, if not drained, humans, coming off a palace assembly line.

Afterward, we went outside to freeze our butts off and have formal photographs taken. Kate had bought herself a light dress for the occasion, something totally unsuitable for March weather; it was a miracle she didn't catch pneumonia. As soon as possible, we broke ranks and found a long line of taxis, then headed back to the hotel from hell to pick up our suitcases and leave.

HINDSIGHT 9.2: *Written later in 1988; the Lady in Purple*

We waited edgily for forty-five minutes in the picture gallery, at first in silence, then applying our social skills—"So what are you doing here?" In front of the solitary fire, I chatted amiably with Harry Rose of Queen's College and with a pleasant open-faced Englishman whose name I didn't catch.

Later arrivals dribbled in, looking strained and self-conscious. Then came a group of young people, much below the average age of fifty-plus, and they provided a welcome breath of normality.

"I've got new shoes on," the lass whispered to her male companion. "My feet are bloody killing me." These two were later decorated for bravery shown during the Manchester air disaster.

The woman in purple came into the gallery a good deal later than the rest of us. She was tall, thin, and pale, wearing entirely the wrong color for that particular complexion, a strong purple dress, hat, shoes, and gloves. I was about to go over and speak to her, but someone else started a conversation, so that I never had the chance to hear her voice or ask any questions. Something about her diffidence and inwardness piqued my curiosity, and I found myself providing her with a history of proficient work for its own sake, perhaps in a university library somewhere.

This image was later reinforced out in the bitter cold of the quad (where official photographers were raking it in) when I saw her having her picture taken with a tiny elderly couple who were clearly bursting with pride. Maybe she was an only child, and they didn't have her until her mother was in her forties?

Whatever her history, or her achievements, somehow or other she gave me a different perspective on the proceedings, and a counterweight to my own innate skepticism. Behind all these new clothes and borrowed morning coats lay an enormous amount of sheer hard work and worth.

Amid the excitement of my royal visits, honorary degrees from the Scottish universities had begun to trickle in—almost as if, after one had honored me, the others felt that maybe they should do the same. I have already mentioned the Royal Scottish Academy and the University of Stirling awards—with my mother's immortal line as she sat sodden in front of me in Dunblane: "I telt ye that ye shouldnae have gone intae that pulpit."* Both St Andrews, and Glasgow awarded me honorary doctorates for my services to traditional music. From St Andrews, I got an honorary Ph.D. from the music department after the music department had been closed—I hope its closure had nothing to do with my nomination! I remember this particular ceremony as being tremendously formal, far more serious than the others, and the document awarded was a large medieval-looking manuscript, which I still have framed at home. However, beneath the fine robes of that occasion, I was wearing the same skirt I had used to receive my MBE—told you, I was going to get my money's worth out of it, like any good Fifer.†

Looking back, perhaps part of the perceived formality of the occasion at St Andrews was owing to the fact that I didn't know anyone in the platform party, in sharp contrast to both the University of Glasgow and the Stirling occasions. At Glasgow, I knew my fellow awardee Ross Roy, who is always great fun. Also, my lifelong friend Betsy was there, along with John and Nancy Cameron and Hazel and her daughter Jeannie. It makes such a difference to have friends around you, just as I had really enjoyed the Stirling occasion because Donald Low was there and presented me,‡ while Freddie and Sylvia were over on holiday and there too—they looked after my mother and her waterlogged wheelchair. On each of these occasions, the edge was taken off the formal ceremony by the presence of so many close friends, unlike at St Andrews.

My underlying problem is that there is a part of me which has never really taken these honors seriously. Of course I'm fully conscious of the recognition of both my music and my contribution to traditional song,

* This translates loosely as "This is our punishment for you going into that cathedral pulpit."

† In fact, that was the last skirt I ever bought, and I got a lot of mileage out of it. I have a sneaking feeling that it was worn under more than one set of formal university robes.

‡ From Stirling, I received a doctor of the university degree, as I did from Glasgow.

but there is part of my mind that always asks, "Are you sure you've got the right person and you're not making a mistake . . . and what am I going to do with this anyway?"

Then came the portrait which hangs in the National Gallery. How did that kind of recognition ever come about? I'm not sure of the exact detail, but I heard through a friend, who had been present at the crucial meeting of the Fife Arts Council, that there was a conversation which went along the lines of, "Something should be done about that wumman. She's been working away on the other side of the Atlantic and nobody here pays any attention to her." "Well, what do you suggest?" Mutter, mutter, mutter. "We could maybe put a plaque on the wee school she went tae?" "Ye cannae—they've ca'ed it doon."* "Well, we could put a plaque on the High School she went tae?" "Ye cannae, they've ca'ed it doon tae." More mutterings, then, "What about a portrait?"

True or not, I cherish that account of the proceedings. Having my portrait painted was finally decided to be the council's course of action, and they chose Alexander Fraser to be the artist. Sandy was mostly known for his portrait work on CEOs, so I must have been a bit of a comedown as well as a challenge. The Council gave him a classroom in Cowdenbeath as his studio for the project—a room facing east, with good light. However, the school itself was an absolutely soulless building, one of these draughty 1950s or 1960s constructions with rusting metal-framed windows and faded institutional colors inside.

I don't quite know what they thought he would be doing with his paints, but they covered all the well-worn fitted carpet that ran up the wall for about six inches with sheets of black plastic. When I met Sandy that first time, I walked into the room to find a rather slight, good-looking man with an easel set up. I looked around me and said, "God, Sandy, what do they expect us to be doing—mud wrestling?" He looked fairly startled at this entry line, and I thought, "Whoops, at least you should have said that it was nice to meet him before you started smart-mouthing him, Jean."

From memory, I sat for five two-hour sessions. At 10:00 A.M., this wasn't much fun, but I drove from my home to Cowdenbeath and went along to the girls' toilet—there was no ladies' room in that abandoned school—and pulled an evening dress over my head, leaving my blue jeans

* ca'ed it doon: knocked it down—and the following *tae* translates as "too"

and trainers on underneath, because it was freezing cold in that classroom-studio. After all, it was a three-quarters-length portrait, and nobody would see what my legs and feet were wearing.

Sitting still and behaving myself was boring. After a while I asked: "If I keep still, does it matter to you if my mouth moves? Would it bother you if I talk?" "No. Actually, it's quite helpful to have some idea of who I'm painting," he replied, glancing up and down between me and his canvas. "Talk about myself? I can handle that," I said, and began to motormouth.

Even after the first day, the result of Sandy's work was staggering. I am in awe of anybody who can draw anything—even a straight line without a ruler—but when he allowed me my first look at what he was doing, the likeness was already recognizable. There came a point, as he was working on my face, when he sighed and put down his brush, "Jean," he said, "could you bear to keep your mouth shut for just a minute?" I tried—honest—but my biggest surprise when I see that portrait is how on earth he managed to paint me with my mouth shut and not as a blur.

The unveiling of the portrait was a formal occasion at the front of the Scottish National Gallery in Edinburgh, with Alec and Hazel there to give me support, as on many other occasions. Normally, I deal with situations as they happen and ad lib my way through them, but there are times when a little forethought on my part might have saved me a lot of discomfort, and this was one. In truth, I didn't really know how to handle the unveiling formalities and was uncomfortable throughout. My strongest memory is of wanting it all to finish and wishing that I could escape from there and buy myself and my friends a cup of coffee.

That sounds ungracious, but it's a national characteristic and flaw. We Scots are cursed: we can accept anything but fulsome praise. The portrait was a nice thought, and I appreciated the honor but, oh dear, I have never squirmed in such total discomfort before or since. I just can't handle people going on and on and building me up as some sort of Scottish icon. I'm a singer, and I have done my best—let's leave it at that. However, when I got home, it let me wind up Bluebell. "Well," I told her, "your mither's no' the only one tae get hung in the Scottish National Gallery."* The last I heard of my one-and-only portrait was that it was gracing the cafeteria. A friend told me, "It was strange to go in there for a coffee and have you glowering down at us."

* "Your mother isn't the only member of the family to be hung in the National Gallery."

For many of the other awards, such as being made a member of the Saltire Society, I was working in America and unable to come back for the ceremony—in this case a luncheon—so that the award was made in absentia without involving me in any great pomp or formalities. The same was true of other honors, including membership in the Scottish Literary Society and in the Scottish Traditional Music Hall of Fame: these awards came through the mail, because I couldn't be around, and they were relatively painless.

One of my more exotic honors was being made a Kentucky colonel by the governor of Kentucky. That honor has triggered a lot of questions, and it came after a concert as a complete surprise to me. Flora Macdonald (the great-great-great-great-great-granddaughter of the original Flora Macdonald who helped Bonnie Prince Charlie escape the pursuing English)* had proposed that I and another person should be made Kentucky colonels. In my case, the proposal was occasioned because of the obvious link to traditional Scottish songs, some of which might well have been known to the original Flora Macdonald. On the stage after my concert, I was presented with the Kentucky Colonels scroll and award—only to discover later that they were a charitable organization and I was now placed on their hit list for donations. Americans are more direct at putting the bite on you than are ancient Scottish universities!

Unfortunately, the first thing that springs to people's minds when the award of Kentucky colonel is mentioned is the KFC version of the brand. However, the work of the charity is a great deal more serious than this, and I am happy to be involved in some small way.

*Separating truth from legend, this Jacobean heroine was in fact a staunch Presbyterian and would as readily have helped the duke of Cumberland, who was pursuing him, as the Catholic Prince Charlie himself. Fleeing from the Scottish mainland after his defeat at Culloden, Charles found it difficult to land, because the islanders were afraid that they would be punished for helping him. Flora Macdonald, then age twenty-four, was asked by the Jacobean Captain O'Neill for help. A kindhearted and impulsive young woman, she hesitated, then agreed. Getting a military pass to sail from the Outer Hebrides to the mainland, she left with two servants and six boatmen on June 27, 1746; Charles was disguised as one of her servants, an Irish spinning maid. This act of sympathy and natural kindness saw her imprisoned in the Tower of London. After her release, she returned home to Flodigarry in Skye and married at the age of twenty-eight, to have five sons and two daughters before immigrating to North Carolina in 1774. "The Skye Boat Song," written more than a century later, commemorates the escape.

Obviously, I didn't choose to be a singer so that I could earn awards: they came as something of a surprise in the later stages of my career, and at first I didn't really know how to handle them. Being honored for your work is not something to be dismissed lightly—even if there is still part of me which is Scottish enough to flinch in acute embarrassment, as with the portrait. Given my upbringing, that gene will never be fully removed, but I am now sufficiently Americanized to take issue with anyone who suggests that a given award was indeed a mistake and that I didn't deserve it.

From a wider and more objective viewpoint, it has always been a burr under my saddle that so very few other Scots, particularly those who stayed in Scotland, have ever got the recognition they deserved for the work, passion, and commitment they have given to their culture. Do we have to go overseas to get recognition? Do we need to be accepted by others first—and be somehow therefore authenticated? It infuriates me that our Scottish culture is so negative, so reluctant to give praise of any kind where it is due that recognition has almost to be dragged from it.

Looking back at these honors from this later point in my life, I am grateful for the recognition they implied both for the traditional music which has been my life and for the implicit judgement on the work I had put into it, stating publicly that this was both valid and worthy of an award. Where this came in the form of academic recognition for my research, as well as for my singing, so much the better, because this is a currency that not even the snobbish will dispute.

In summary, no, I don't really think these honors were given by mistake. If nothing else, it was almost impossible to ignore me after forty years of performing Scottish traditional song—I have been on my feet and on the boards for half a century now, so I'm bound to have made a dent of some kind.

Honors do matter: looking back, the MBE awarded to the Lady in Purple was clearly the high point of her parents' lives and probably of her own. My various honors probably mattered every bit as much to my parents, although they would never have admitted this was so. Who knows; it might finally have proved to them that I made the right decision back in Edinburgh, when I opted to be a singer rather than the first member of our entire family to get a university degree. And perhaps, or is this still too much to hope, they might even have forced the family optician in Leven to accept that indeed I had a proper job.

CHAPTER 10

What Do You Mean "We Have a Problem"?

We all feel immortal and think that life will go on as it always has up to now, until one day we discover this isn't necessarily true. So I wasn't the first, and won't be the last, to be given a reality check—whether I wanted one, or not.

Retirement wasn't something I ever really considered. People with more conventional lives look to a particular age when they will no longer be employed and must therefore find something else to do with their time. However, performers and musicians are different: we go on until nobody wants to listen to us anymore.* Therefore, if I thought about it at all, I simply planned to work on either until somebody told me to stop or, more realistically, until I drifted into doing something slightly different and less taxing as I got older.

After all, over the course of fifty-odd years some things had already changed in how I gave performances. From working every night except Monday—which is the dark night in most clubs—and doing up to three sets a night, I had gradually switched into giving concerts. These involved more money for less effort and a lot less travel—a sensible move and something which happened without being planned, fitting nicely to that stage of my life and career. So I assumed that other changes would arrive in the same natural and evolutionary way, when the time was right for both them and me.

Then, somewhere around 2004 I was given my first intimation of mortality. It came when I was standing on top of a turf wall at Skara Brae

* In one of my later concerts, I was walking down through the audience to reach the stage when I overheard a woman say to her friend, "Jean Redpath? I thought she was dead"—to which I replied in my best John Wayne growl, "Dead? Not scarcely yet, ma'am."

in Orkney,* taking a photograph. I went to climb down, and realized that I couldn't move. My hip joint had seized up completely, leaving me in excruciating pain. From later reports, I had reached the bone-on-bone stage of hip deterioration. I needed help, both to get myself out of this emergency situation and to deal with the condition as soon as possible. However, this was one of the occasions when I have to admit to being thrawn. Somehow I crawled back to the B&B, having first collected and then driven the car there—not a lot of fun with a seized-up hip. Then, instead of going to a doctor to get medical diagnosis and treatment, I fought the condition for almost two years longer than I should have—crazy, because it quickly got to the point that if I found a comfortable position, I was terrified to change it for any reason. Worse, I couldn't lie in bed for any length of time and began to sleep in a chair.

In fairness, one of the problems of a peripatetic existence is getting immediate access to a doctor, dentist, or any of the mechanics who keep the physical plant on the road. For primary health care, I looked to the Mayo Clinic in Rochester, Minnesota, where I dropped in for a pretty extensive health check, while I was staying in the area with my friend Julie. She and her husband Allen were accommodating hosts for many years, and provided a routine central spot in the country for both friendship and shared musical interests.†

Urged by Jean Weber, another friend who already had had a hip replacement, I asked the clinic to check out my hip. In January 2007 I had the hip replaced and the result felt nothing short of miraculous, once I got over the immediate aftereffects of surgery. Once back on my feet, I thought, "Well, that's taken care of," and I returned seamlessly to my normal life of doing a concert here, a workshop there, and commuting back and forth across the Atlantic.

What did this first warning teach me? I guess it made me realize that I could no longer expect always to be a hundred percent fit, as my body began to show signs of wear and tear from all those years of traveling and performing. No big deal, I thought. If something like that happens again

* Skara Brae is an ancient Neolithic stone-built settlement first exposed by massive Atlantic storms in 1850 and then more fully revealed in 1925. It is one of the most complete and regularly visited historic sites in Europe.

† Julie is the conductor and founding member of the Chorale, set up in 1982 for individuals who share a love for singing and performing, so we found much common ground in music.

and my body malfunctions, then the solution will be to get myself fixed, recover, and pick up my working life again. A simplistic view, but I have always had the constitution of an ox and shaken off various minor health problems before.

I began to make plans to celebrate or at least mark in some way the fact that I had been on the boards for fifty years—which seemed worth at least a long service award. After designing a poster of my LPs and CDs and setting up a series of concerts for the spring of 2012 to mark my half century, I went up from Illinois to the Mayo Clinic to get my usual annual check. The first three days were taken up with the normal routine of blood tests and so forth, the equivalent of checking the oil and water in a car. On Wednesday, the doctor suggested an ultrasound test, and on Thursday morning he came back to me with the lovely line, "We have a problem. You have a lump."*

It turned out that I had malignancy of some kind, but nobody could tell me what, at this stage. "What about keyhole surgery?" I asked. The surgeon to whom I had been referred replied, "Well, I could probably find somebody who could do it that way, but I wouldn't advise it personally, because there is no way of knowing what we are dealing with until we get in there." "That makes perfect sense to me," I answered, trying to sound practical and calm about this routine check which had suddenly produced a cancer result. It wasn't easy. The Big C was something that happened to friends. Not me.

Once I came out of the initial sense of shock and disbelief, I had no choice other than to stay practical. My first priority was to stop and rearrange concerts in the immediate future. I got in touch with Lynda, my manager, to tell her that I doubted I would be fit enough to accept any concerts over April, May, and June and to ask her to cancel anything we had planned too close to my hospitalization. I knew the upcoming surgery was likely to be bigger than the hip replacement and might involve a longer recovery period—but it never occurred to me that full recovery from this surgery would be any less smooth and certain than it was the first time. Therefore, I didn't want it to become widely known that I had cancer and would be going into a period of chemotherapy. I retreated mindlessly to the mantra "Get yourself fixed, recover, then go back to work as normal, just like you did last time."

* I love the way doctors share your problem—and then leave you on your own to suffer it.

Sure, it was naive, but I'm not a quitter, never have been. Throughout my career I have always held up the example of Alicia Ann Spottiswoode, who began to collect traditional music at age sixteen and was still riding out to the hounds at age eighty-one. "See," I tell people. "Traditional music is good for you. It makes you live longer." So, with Alicia as my role model, I was pushing straight ahead. Why not? I firmly intended to emulate her and be doing something fairly active and disreputable at the age of eighty-one. However, I draw the line at riding to the hounds: me and horses don't get on all that well.

Therefore the plan was that, having been hit by this unforeseen cancer scare, we would do what it took to sort it out, then I would get on with my life. Lynda called the people involved in our bookings, some of whom I had worked for in the past, and they were all very understanding and told her to let them know when I was back in circulation. All that I had left to do was wait for the surgery to take place.

On Monday morning, five days after the ultrasound test, I had a radical hysterectomy—it turned out that I had two primary cancers—and about a week later I flew back down to my friend Julie in Illinois to spend three weeks recuperating, not doing very much but sleeping a lot. From there, I flew on to Betsy's house in Arizona, as I had been doing routinely for many years, spending from January to the beginning of March with her and doing my taxes in the warmth and sunshine while other people were avoiding snowdrifts back east and up north. Betsy and I go right back to my beginnings as a performer—almost to my first gig at the Caffè Lena. She too offered a routine annual habitation base and, just as I had picked a point of primary care near one close friend in Illinois, I had my tax accountant at this other one.

Friendship sometimes comes without conditions. Most people would run miles to avoid taking on the responsibility of looking after someone still recovering from major cancer surgery, but not Betsy. When I crawled out of the plane in Tucson, apologizing and worrying about how I would fit the upcoming chemotherapy course into my stay here, she snorted: "Why on earth would you even *think* of going back to Minnesota for chemo in the winter, when there's a Mayo clinic up in Scottsdale, Arizona, just east of Phoenix? You can easily reach that from here."

This was no routine annual stay. For well over a year, I commuted back and forth on a round trip of 250 miles between Tucson and Phoenix, most of the time doing my own driving. At the start, they hit me with all their big guns in chemo. That was brutal. I lost my hair, just as the surgeon had predicted. At the time, he had asked me, "Is there anything that you want to know?" "I have two questions," I replied. "Life expectancy?" "What you have is treatable," he said. That was a side-step, but it was better than being told "three months." After all, nobody knows: some people tolerate the treatment better than others; some people go into remission for no apparent reason; and some people don't make it. I was asking the man a question for which there is no real answer.

I drew a deep breath. "Do I lose my hair?" Ridiculous, I suppose, but suddenly that was important. "Yes." This was clearly a guy who didn't dodge hard answers. "When?" I asked. "Ten to twelve days after the first treatment." He was right. My hair came out on cue, leaving me like a Buddhist nun. Overall, that first summer was pretty heavy going. There is no point in dwelling on things that are past and can't be changed, particularly unpleasant ones, so I will not even try to recall every miserable afternoon I spent after chemo treatment. From where I stood, it was doing what it was supposed to do and getting my blood test numbers down to seminormal, touching on a broadly acceptable range. Even so, I spent a week after each treatment as dead meat in the bunk, very grateful that I didn't have to get up from the horizontal more than once in a while. However, I was never, thank God, made physically sick like so many others on chemo. As I keep telling people, I'm a Fifer and we don't part with anything.

The end result of that chemo hammering was that I got home to Fife for six weeks in September 2012 and then went back, quite cheerfully, to America and my normal visiting routine and began planning again. But in February, when I returned to the Arizona clinic for a checkup, the news was not good. There were metastases in the chest cavity and in the paratracheal lymph nodes, and I had a spot on my right lung. To tackle these, this time the clinic decided on radiation treatment.

While I was getting radiation, I was lucky to have friends of Betsy's who lived in Phoenix and who were doing their best to avoid the summer heat by living elsewhere. They gave me access to their empty house, which saved me from having to book into a motel: for three weeks of five days a week of radiation, that would have been horrendously expensive.

As someone later described it to me, first they remove the offending organs, then they microwave you. In the process of discouraging the bad bits, the radiation did some damage and left me with scarring on the lung. Any lung damage is bad news for a singer, but when you consider the alternative, without this treatment I might well have been pushing up daisies by now.

Again, I was lucky in that there was no sickness involved, but after the bad report in February, I became aware that I was going to be with Betsy in Arizona for probably the best part of another year's extended treatment. In these circumstances, one's priorities become clear. Sure, there were concerts planned, and another year's absence might well damage my career, but I could scarcely tell the doctors, "Sorry, but there are concerts I have to do. Let me think about this later." The survival instinct is very strong. I had to get myself properly fit again before I started thinking about giving concerts. So I canceled all concerts and braced myself for what was clearly going to be a long drawn out war rather than a couple of savage battles.

By now I was a very different animal from the one who had just been told that she had cancer. It had been a pretty steep learning curve. First of all, it is tremendously difficult to have to admit that you need help when the modus vivendi of your entire life has always been "I would rather do it myself." Second, I felt driven to fill the enormous gaps in my knowledge of what the hell was going on inside my own body, which was something which had never raised its head before.* Then, it had been a case of "OK, whatever it takes, just fix me." Now, my mind was full of questions for my doctors. What are you suggesting? What are you giving me? What is it going to do? What are its side effects? Which of these should I worry about? Is there any alternative? If this doesn't work for me, where do we go from here?

The Internet gives access to a wealth of information. Further, I was under the roof and care of someone who was herself a cancer survivor and had done her own research and was already in touch with many bodyworkers and complementary medicines. Therefore, I had access to a whole new world of information and to someone I had known for a long time and trusted implicitly. I studied and learned, probably better and faster than I had ever done at university.

I started the second phase of chemotherapy, and, after three wasted months of treatment, they discovered that the drug they had chosen to use

* With regard to questioning doctors, this was unheard of during my childhood in Fife. There, our local doctor's normal advice ultimately became a family catch phrase: whatever the problem, this old guy would simply say "Jusht keep taking the bottle," which we did without question about what the illness was, or what was in the bottle, or how would it help. God walked at the doctor's right hand in Fife, and nobody would have dreamed about questioning either of them.

on me was doing sweet damn all. Again, there's no point in bleating about it. How is anyone, even an experienced oncologist, going to know how the patient will respond to a drug until they try it and give it time to work?

They changed the chemo drug and started again. Over this period I was still commuting between Tucson and Phoenix. The previous drug had been relatively gentle and left me able to drive there on my own, but this new treatment included Benadryl among its premeds. At the mere mention of Benadryl, I fall asleep; therefore, it was a poor idea for me to come out of the session where I had been in a drug-induced sleep for a couple of hours, then face a grueling two-hour drive back home on busy roads. Post-Benadryl, the visits to Phoenix now involved another person, usually Betsy, who had to hang around for four hours while I was going through the treatment session and then drive me home.

This didn't sit too well with me. I didn't mind the regular treatments, so long as I was the only person involved. However I hated the thought of anyone else having to spend four hours of their day on a round trip to Phoenix, then twiddle their thumbs between the road trips for another four hours while I had chemo. As soon as the blood test numbers began to come down again, I raised the subject of transferring the treatment to the oncology clinic in Tucson. Now that we seemed to have a protocol which was having the desired effect, the Phoenix clinic agreed. The transfer of treatment center left me or, more correctly, my driver with a seven-minute drive from the house. This lifted an enormous load off everybody, because I could be dropped off then collected later, when I called back to base that I was ready.

These treatment sessions took me through to April 2014, by which time there could be a discussion about quality of life—now that I seemed likely to have enough life to worry about its quality. Cancer is a disease, not always a death sentence. By now I had been gone from Scotland for eighteen months, which was longer than I had been away since 1963. I felt strongly that homesickness was probably doing me more damage than anything else. With my condition now stabilized, I began to argue that I should be turned loose to go home for a visit. The doctors agreed, even if I didn't look all that great for traveling five thousand miles—and doing a concert. Yes, doing a concert. Performers are like donkeys; we need carrots, and this was one concert that I would have crawled on my hands and knees to reach.

I was a singer long before I became an invalid, and it has always been a good idea for me to sing, no matter what kind of state I am in or whether or not there is anyone around to listen. Singing to me is a sort of emotional release, a way of expressing myself, and an activity which always seems to recharge my batteries and keep my personal energy lines fully functional. I need to sing almost as much as I need to breathe, but I had felt so low over the previous eighteen months that I had forgotten this basic truth. Before my cancer episode, I had never stopped performing long enough to become aware of the effects of not singing or not performing.

What I am talking about is a great deal more complex than "star need"—or getting your fix of applause. Yes, applause is good: you would have to be less than human or less than honest if you didn't admit to getting a real charge out of being able to bring a hall full of people into total silence, or, alternatively, to foot-stomping approval and a standing ovation. Getting such a large number of people to appreciate the material I was working with was always a tremendous high. So, yes, there was an element of missing being in the spotlight. But what surprised—even shocked—me, was the realization that it was the singing, rather than the performing, which was the very breath of life to me. Not singing hurt was hurting me a hell of a lot more than not performing.

First time round in chemo, I simply didn't have enough energy to sing. When singing came back to me, it was spontaneous and surprised me every bit as much as it did Betsy. She had returned to Scotland with me on that 2012 visit, and I took her to see the old kirk at St Monans, which has always been a favorite of mine. She was wandering around, looking at the centuries-old interior when she suddenly heard my voice in the empty church—I was singing an old Scots psalm, which seemed appropriate, and this was a place where I always sang when I had it to myself. It has excellent acoustics and lots of happy memories, and this was the first time I had felt moved to sing again. Why not? I had gotten home again and, to my surprise, after eighteen months of silence, my voice was still there, rusty but recognizable.

After that autumn break in Scotland, I picked up my guitar* and tried to sing on a more regular basis. Even when I felt too low to do a proper practice and had to quit, the fact that I had sung always made me feel a whole lot better. It was around this time that the concert invitation came from Benjie, who's among the people who have become constants in my life, even when I see very little of them.

* Ouch! The hard skin from fifty years of playing had gone on my fingertips, and I had raw fingers on both hands until I built it up again.

I had met Benjie and his wife while teaching in Wesleyan in the 1970s, and he was working within the school system in a program which gave him a select group of bright kids with the remit to keep them stimulated rather than treading water and bored in the usual classes of thirty kids with mixed abilities. He offered to help me with the schoolwork that I was doing there, not only with advice and suggestions but also by making me a kit-house, drilled and numbered for assembly, so that the kids themselves could build it. This was the shop, or post office, or bank, or simply play center that I mentioned earlier.

Then Benjie moved back to his home base in Cambridge, New York, a farming village out in the middle of nowhere, about an hour from Albany, just across the border from Vermont. Single-handedly, over many years, and literally with a hammer and a saw, he started to restore the town's late-nineteenth-century opera house, a typical of old wooden building with the auditorium on the second floor.* Hubbard Hall, as the building is known, is now a thriving concern, and the adjacent old railway buildings have been bought to be turned into dance studios, craft centers, and art studios.

Benjie and I had stayed in touch as friends, and when he started out I went up to do a concert for him. That first concert was in the basement, where they had just opened a coffeehouse on recently poured concrete over what had been a bare earth floor. I went back every two years or so, and each time I would nag him, "Have I to keep coming back here until you can afford stairs?" Then after he refurbished the hall, my comment escalated to, "I'm not coming back until you put an elevator in, because I can't handle these stairs with a long dress and a guitar. No way."

After he had worked on the place for thirty-six years, Benjie wrote to me that he was retiring, and he asked if I could possibly be in his final concert at the end of May 2014. In the throes of second-phase chemo treatment, I told him what was going on but finished, "I see no reason why not. I'm coming, even if I have to crawl."

The need to perform at Benjie's concert became the carrot which kept me going. Yes, I knew it was pushing things, but I was also aware that his audience knew me well enough to cut me a little slack, so that if all I could manage was a couple of songs, they would be comfortable about

* These buildings were called opera houses to make it respectable for ladies to go there; if they had been called music halls, you would never have let your daughter go.

me saying, "OK folks, that's all I've got in me tonight. What can we talk about?"

As it was, friends from all over the continent turned up at the hall to support me—which was an enormous shot in the arm—and the tiny place that only holds about 150 people was jam-packed. Sure, it was nerve-wracking and I was running on my reserve tank, but I got up on stage and did my promised concert for Benjie.

Before going on, I warned him, "Look, I have no idea how this is going to go, and whether I will have enough stamina to last. If I signal, be ready to come on and take over for a bit, until I get enough energy back to talk to them." "Sure," he replied. "Just do what you can. I'll cover." Benjie does a lot of theater himself and could easily hold the stage for an hour on his own, I knew. With my safety net in place, I braced myself and wondered just how long I could keep going.

I had never been this nervous before. Sure, I knew there was a voice of some kind there, because I had been working on it—but I didn't fully trust it. I was desperately short of practice, because only a couple of weeks before I had collapsed in a shopping mall in Tucson and was looked after by a couple of nice snowbirds from London until the paramedics came to collect me in their meat wagon. It turned out to be severe dehydration, which should never have happened because I had been long enough in the desert to know to keep hydrating. However, the symptoms had been very gentle to start with, and so similar to how I usually felt after each chemo session, that I ignored them. In the ER they pumped me full of fluid, and then because I was still struggling to breathe, they X-rayed me. A young doctor who didn't know my health background came back to announce both scarring and some fluid on the lung which could be pneumonia but was treatable.

The scarring I knew about; the other wasn't welcome. I was weak as the proverbial kitten, with dodgy lung capacity, and I was badly under-rehearsed—not the best preparation in the world for my first concert in two years. "Be professional, Jean," I told myself while waiting to go on. "You don't have enough energy to be scared, so talk to them while you get your bearings."

Taking a deep breath, I walked onto the stage and began to recite "McAllister Dances before the King," said to be a favorite of the old Queen Mother. The recitation surprised them—after all, they had come to hear me sing. However, the poem by D. M. Mackenzie worked beautifully, as it always does. At first, when the boastful old dancer struts his stuff and describes how his youthful prowess brought him an invitation to dance in London before the king, the audience didn't quite know how to react—they never do. Then, as he describes how he started dancing slowly, then faster and faster until the clouds of dust rose high around him, they relaxed and began to enjoy the story. It's a good story. The final two verses, as always, are the killer and left them laughing.

And then the gracious queen herself
Came shyly o'er to me
And pinned a medal on my breast
For everyone to see
Her whisper I shall ne'er forget
Nor how her eyes grew dim
"Ach, where were you, McAllister,
"The day I married him?"

Right, Jean, while they're clapping, pick up your guitar and go for it! I did and loved every minute, drawing energy from an audience who had come not just to listen to me but to give their complete support. The pipeline was rusty, and maybe the occasional verse was missed or the odd line improvised, but I have always been so studiedly casual that I doubt anyone noticed. I had hoped to do a minirecital which would last less than an hour, but by the time I got cranked up and hit my stride, we went for the full concert. I did forty-five to fifty minutes, took a fifteen-minute break, and then went out and did another forty-five minutes. As it turned out, Benjie never had to come on and pick up the pieces, but I refute absolutely what Betsy claims, which is that they had to hook me off the stage, leaving Tom-and-Jerry claw marks along the floor. Not true—but close.

Bizarre. Onstage, it felt as if the last two and a half years of fighting cancer had never happened. These were only two years out of fifty, and it was unbelievably easy to slip back into harness. I have no idea what I sang that night, other than my performance was off-the-cuff as usual, giving the audience whatever seemed to be right at the time. What I sang didn't matter, because the concert wasn't about me; it was about celebrating Benjie's hard work and the very long and deep friendship between us. I honor both of these.

For every action, there is a reaction. It came in waves. After the high of the concert and the round of meeting all my old friends, I returned to the hotel, thankful that I'd had enough sense to leave myself a day to recover, and my energy level hit the floor. Then Betsy, who had flown over for the concert, her son Charlie, and his wife Jen drove me for five hours from Cambridge, New York, to Newark airport. There I sat in my preordered wheelchair for five more hours—and damn nearly missed the plane because United staff forgot about me and ultimately had to hold the plane to wheel me onto it. On top of that, there were six and a half hours in the air, followed by an hour and a half to get from Edinburgh back to Elie. When I crawled into my own home at last, that's when the final tsunami hit me, and I don't believe I opened my front door for a week.*

For eighteen months, I had dreamed of coming home; now, here I was. Even on an empty and echoing tank, when I wakened many hours later, the cold sea air was like a bucket of water thrown over me. Rejuvenating. But I was still tired and jet-lagged out of my skin, and I knew that it would take at least a week to recover, because that's how jet lag always hits me. Indeed I suspected that this time it might be different, worse. Alongside the energy deficit from the long haul of travel and the concert, there were other problems to be factored in, problems which were going to take a lot of time before they went away.

So it would be rougher than usual, but the truth was simple. I needed to be back in Scotland. I needed to be under my own roof for a while. And I needed to be beside the sea. The only long-term problem about the desert with its constant sunshine is that it's too far from any ocean: there are no seabirds. Here in Scotland, as soon as I got off the plane in Edinburgh, I could smell the sea. Try as you might, you cannot get more than about one hundred miles from the ocean in Scotland.

I had been raised beside the sea and was consciously aware of it every day of my life. Now I was back, in my own house which I love, beside that same sea again. I would awaken to the noise of seagulls, then watch the waves through my bedroom window and help the tide come in. I was home and, for the moment, that was plenty good enough for me.

* The code I have established with locals is that if I leave my front door open, I am happy to have visitors; if the front door remains shut, I want to be left on my own.

CHAPTER 11

So Where Did My Journey Take Me?

People often ask me, how many songs I know. My usual answer is "About a thousand," which seems a nice round figure. However, it is such a BIG round figure that people tend to reply, "Aye, right," which is polite Scottish for "You must be joking." Not really—the number could be even higher.

Part of the problem lies in the precise definition of what is meant by the word *know*. Does it mean how many songs I know of, or how many songs for which I can sing the chorus and hum the tune, or how many songs for which I can sing all the verses and choruses? If it is simply how many songs for which I know the tune and some of the words and can easily put my hand on the rest of the words, then it is well over one thousand. With the Internet, a performer need no longer be utterly dependent on memory—in my case, oral memory.

Ultimately I had to keep a list of my recordings on a spreadsheet. Once I got past my first five or six records, I had no clear recollection of what I had put on the different LPs. Then, when I started producing CDs, things got even worse. In an LP you really shouldn't go beyond twenty-two minutes on each side or the sound can become distorted. This problem doesn't exist on a CD. On these, you can put down an enormous amount of material—which I did, being a Fifer and determined to get my money's worth. With both LPs and CDs stretching out behind me, it soon became impossible to remember what I had recorded and where—hence the formal list on a spreadsheet, and this shows that I have recorded 667 songs.* There may be a few apparent duplicates, for example, in those cases where I recorded a Burns song twice, one to an original melody that

* The rest of the thousand plus songs, either I haven't got around to recording, or I felt that they didn't merit recording, or, in many cases (which is normal with traditional songs from rural areas), they were too bawdy and explicit to record. There are worse lyrics around than "Tail Toddle."

Serge had found through his research, the other to a melody drawn from the Scottish Musical Museum when I was working with Donald. Do these count as one song or two? I would argue that they should count as two, because I had to learn and memorize two different tunes.

Recordings provide concrete evidence of knowing the songs—even if there are some songs which I could no longer sit down and sing from start to finish without a quick refresher look at the words. As I have become older, my memory of songs peripheral to my repertoire has faded. Oddly enough, the songs which have stuck the longest are those which were learned earliest, presumably because they went in when the page was blank and they left deep tracks. To get these clear and sharp again, all I have to do is run them through my mind a couple of times to get rid of the cobwebs and stour. I never lose a tune, but words get more and more difficult to remember clearly as more and more songs are added to the pile.

Most of these early songs, perhaps even the core content of my repertoire, I got from my family. Not because I was consciously memorizing the traditional songs my mother and her siblings sang; I just heard them so often that I could sing them through without thought. I have inherited my mother's flypaper memory—anything I hear tends to stick—but learning by listening created the occasional problem in our home. My mother had a wide range of tastes, from Victorian piano-stool music through the most ancient of ballads to pure bawdery. One of the last appeared often enough for me to start singing it on my own at around the age of six or seven. "Here! Whit are ye daen'?" my startled mother exclaimed. "That's no' for the likes o' you." Bluebell and her double standards.

Back then, we never thought of songs as "traditional" or "folk"; they were just what we enjoyed singing within the broader family. Pigeonholing or categorizing songs is an academic exercise. Most people, whether they are listeners or singers, simply say "It's a good song; we like it." And it might be from *Phantom of the Opera* or from *Cats* or it might be from the seventeenth century, but what is important is how it appeals to the individual, what associations the song strikes up in one's mind. Music is like all of art; appreciation is down to subjective taste and appeal.*

This thought brings me back to my inability to sing what many people see as the "guid auld sangs"—something which has plagued me

* This perhaps excludes pop music, where it is down to a must-have to remain a member of the pack.

throughout my professional life. For the speaker, it means "a song that I have known most of my life" or "my father's favorite song" or "the song my mother always sang—but she had to have a dram before she could do it." There is usually an intensely personal link involved which makes the song special to that speaker. But that was *that person's* link and *that individual's* personal taste. Maybe I plain simply don't like the song or, more normally, what they think is a traditional song is no more than a music hall–Harry-Lauder-type catchy tune or something modern which is totally false and exploits the "marching through the heather" vision of a Scotland which never existed. Yet if I refuse to sing it because it is so clichéd and ersatz, people can be puzzled or even deeply offended—when no offense is intended. Sorry, folks, . . . but I just can't do it. These songs make my skin crawl.

Even so, the range of what I like and do is nearly limitless, covering many hundreds of songs in several languages—some of which I don't speak. I sing what appeals to me or moves me, and in that too I have possibly inherited my mother's liking of singing anything that appealed to her through its lyrics or its tune. There was so much she taught me simply by encouraging me to sing along with her while we were doing the housework, learning through multiple repetition until I was note- and word-perfect. She even taught me two duets—the only duets I have ever learned, because I have no ear for harmony—and she must have taught me both lines of each duet. One was "Gin I Were a Baron's Heir"* and the other was "O Wert Thou in the Cauld Blast,"† which of course is Burns—although whether or not my mother knew it was Burns, I have no idea.

Everything I know was grafted onto this original broad base. As a student, when I returned home there were always new songs to hear and learn from the family repertoire. Then when I joined the Edinburgh Folk Song Society, that gave me access to a whole world of new material. I learned quite a few songs from Ella Ward/McAvoy, presumably songs that she herself had chosen to memorize; both her choice of songs and

* "Gin I Were" (pronounced with a hard G as in Guin): If Only I Were. I remember at a workshop I had great difficulty explaining to a student that we didn't do gin, only whisky, in Scotland. The Scots language does create linguistic problems at times, such as when I asked a hotel clerk to "knock me up at three next morning." He looked very surprised, until I hastily revised to "knock on my door, I mean."

† "O Wert Thou in the Cauld Blast": If You Were in the Cold Blast [of Wind]

her voice, which was much higher than most of the traditional singers I have been drawn to, appealed to me. She rang all the right bells in my head and in my heart. Likewise, I picked up many new songs from Arthur Argo, because he was steeped in the Northeast tradition.

From there everything spread outward. When I went to a festival or a club, there might be somebody singing a song I really liked. If we never coincided often enough for me to memorize it, then I would buy an LP with that song on it, and count this as money well spent.* Nowadays, collecting new material is so much easier: you can track the song down online and make sure that you weren't just particularly receptive (or not quite sober) when you heard it first and that you still like it enough to want to learn it. Song access is unlimited now, through sources such as DigiTrad,† where many thousands of song lyrics have been contributed by a diverse group of people, some of whom have researched the matter properly and give references, while others just quote from memory—which can result in some pretty mangled lines.‡ Always be careful with new lyrics: double-check your source's version whenever possible.

On the odd occasion, I have asked another performer for the words of a song—notably Archie Fisher, who blew my mind with one particular song during a tour of some malt whisky distilleries. We were having our own ceilidh after the concert, sitting around with a last dram after everybody else had gone home, when Archie launched into the most beautiful tune, one that I had been hooked on for a long time. His mother, who was a Gaelic speaker, had translated the original air into English as "The Eternal Surge of the Sea." Until then, I had never heard an English version of the song that I could tackle—a bit like "Róisín Dubh"—where the gorgeous tune was matched with words which didn't make me cringe.

A surprising source of new material has been my audiences. Asking them during a performance if they know a missing verse or if they have heard a different version of the song not only makes them feel more

* There was no point in me buying the sheet music, when that was available, because I couldn't read a note of music and could only learn from listening.

† You will find DigiTrad at Mudcat.org.

‡ I stumbled over a text recently for "Mhairi's Wedding" that had been printed out for someone's wedding, and it was an oral reading bearing very little relationship to the English translation from the Gaelic. The result was really quite funny, especially the line "dance to the scribes and the far out seas"—or the Pharisees, as it should have read.

involved in the performance, but often brings surprising results as well. It also opens a fascinating door when you ask the same question in the United States or Australia and still get a response. Had these people Scottish parents who brought this song with them when they emigrated? Or were the people who brought the Scottish song to that distant land their grandparents, even great-grandparents, and has the song changed as a result of its journey through space and time?

I have folders of scribbled notes and of material that came through the mail in response to my asking, "Do you know any more verses of this?" Most fascinating are the purely local ballads; I am constantly finding new ones—or tantalizing glimpses thereof. I am still chasing a song I heard down in Dumfries and Galloway when somebody got up and sang it at a ceilidh.

Collection of songs, like breathing, becomes a lifelong habit. Nevertheless, I have never seen myself to be a collector or preserver of songs and lyrics, as portrayed in the film *Songcatcher*. My emphasis is on collecting for performing, as opposed to collecting for its own sake, and is driven almost entirely by personal interest: I have heard something and liked it, and I am trying to chase it down.

Despite what many people think, traditional music is not a store of dead songs carried through to the present, but it is a living organism, constantly gathering in new ballads which over time will become "traditional." Sure, there is a put-down argument which has raged for many years, as in "Well, that's not traditional, of course." How exactly should we define traditional? Does it mean only eighteenth-century songs? Of course not. Traditional is anything which has the quality and appeal to last over many years, during which time it becomes an accepted part of any traditional singer's repertoire. I would say that "Yellow on the Broom" comes pretty close to this, because there are now several generations of people who have been singing this without knowing that it was written fairly recently by Adam McNaughtan. I would argue that if a song survives an arbitrary number of years in the oral tradition, then it becomes traditional. Such songs are still being produced.

Eric Bogle, for example, has an inspired touch with the language and in finding the perfect tunes to go with it.* It is far from easy finding a

*Eric Bogle was born in Peebles, Scotland, wrote poetry from the age of eight, taught himself to play guitar, and joined and ultimately led a rock and skiffle band before turning to folk. He immigrated to Australia in 1969. His work as a

melody which fits naturally with the lyrics of a song. Davey Whyte in Glasgow is another who has shown a brilliant touch in setting to music the poetry of others, such as the Angus poets, as well as in finding melodies for his own lyrics. It isn't easy to come up with a melody that somehow fits naturally with the Scottish vernacular. Too often I have been left hesitating, thinking, "I could learn that, and I love the words, but the song itself doesn't really *sound* Scottish."

The first Eric Bogle song I heard was sung by June Tabor, an English singer working at the Inverness Folk Club. She sang "Willie McBride," which is probably one of the most powerful antiwar songs in the contemporary repertoire. I thought what a wonderful touch with the words and what a great tune.* Gradually I stumbled over other people doing Bogle songs, then finally bought an LP of his. Song for song, he covers most of the territory that I would be interested in singing about, better than anyone else has ever done—an enormous range of quality songs. At one point he and Judy Small, who is Australian-born (Eric is a naturalized Aussie now) provided me with most of the material for a program I did a couple of times in America on the subject of old age; a social-worker friend dealt with the academic side, and I illustrated with songs. Eric and Judy, between them, came up with some incredibly powerful stuff for us—indeed, there was one song that I don't think I have ever been able to sing since. If there is something that Eric feels strongly enough about, it emerges sooner or later as a real killer of a song.† Music is highly subjective, and I'm not sure I can explain what it is about any given songwriter that appeals to me, but I don't think there is anyone else—apart from Burns—who has written so many songs that I have committed to

---

singer-songwriter includes powerful antiwar songs such as "And the Band Played Waltzing Matilda," "The Green Fields of France," and "Willie McBride" and also covers poignant subjects such as land depopulation, as in "Leaving the Land," and the plight of older women left by their men, as in "Harry's Wife."

* The song is about a soldier who was nineteen years old when he was killed in 1916. It has all sorts of references, including one in the chorus to "The Floo'ers o' the Forest." This was a traditional lament for the many young Scots slaughtered at the battle of Flodden by the English, and the reference is to the line 'the floo'ers o' the forest are a' weed awa', meaning the flower of Scottish youth, the very heart of the country, had been torn out.

† *Killer* is defined as something that not only moves an audience deeply, but also leaves the performer struggling not to burst into tears and gulping silence.

memory and which I sing to myself as well as for audiences. That is the greatest compliment I can pay the man.

As is true of so many performers, it is not easy to make contact with one another when you are both busy and on the road. In Eric's case, I met him briefly in Australia when I dropped in on part of one of his performances after I had finished my own, and he invited me home for a blether and a cup of tea. Yes, two Scots in exile, and we drank tea—while the whisky industry mourned. What a wonderfully gifted and genuinely nice man he is.

Which of his songs is my favorite? That depends on which kind of mood I am in, but it would probably be "If Wishes Were Fishes." While I don't actually agree with its sentiments, I know where he's coming from in this one.

> I wish I were young again
> My songs still to be sung again
> Sweet tunes of my life
> Have gone sour and off-key.
> Writing my precious rhymes
> Trying to hold back time
> If wishes were fishes
> I know where I would be.

It is so difficult to quote the words of any song—I have to sing it to be sure of them—but his melodies are always a delight.

Recently, I have been thinking of doing a collection of songs which deal with the inevitable, with loss, with death, with grief—none of which has to sound either depressing or morbid in its treatment. There are three of Eric's songs which are in my mind to be part of this collection. Why such a bizarrely dark theme? The answer, at its simplest, is that these are all issues which everyone has to deal with, and we are often not well-equipped to handle them. Particularly for a Scot, strong emotion is not supposed to be expressed or shared with anybody else: thou shalt not weep, wail, or gnash thy teeth in public. You don't do any of the things that one is tempted to do in extremis, unless you are in the privacy of your own home. Even there, you draw the curtains before you start.

Crazy: no one can internalize these sort of emotions without damaging the soul. This is where music can help, if only by showing you that—as with every other human emotion—you are not the first person, nor will you be the last, to feel this way. Others have been there before, hurting just as badly, and they have survived. One of the things contemporary songs do, which traditional songs can't, is give you permission to let go. Even if you cannot speak the language, they provide you in a song with the words and melody which set out these emotions that you cannot bring yourself to express. Your words, or the songwriter's words—Does it matter, so long as they bring release, let you cope with the problem, help you move on?

Knowing how much music has meant to me over the years when I had really no other outlet for handling my feelings, I am still toying with the idea of compiling a collection of songs that might help people handle the crises in their life—even if an irreverent friend of mine reacted to my proposal with, "Jeeze, what are you thinking of calling it, Jean? Songs to die for?"

I have been asked many times if I ever got tired of singing. Yes, but it wasn't so much that I got tired of singing as that I got tired of performing. A couple of times, I have grown heart-weary of the grind of traveling and performing, and each time, thankfully, I have been able to take a break. However, when I took these breaks, I kept on singing, whether or not anyone was listening. Singing is as much part of me as breathing: it is my whole being, my main way of expressing myself, my feelings. I couldn't live without singing, and, equally, I couldn't live without song.

Another thing people ask me is why I never went down the route of many of the musicians with whom I shared Miki's floor and become a singer-composer. My answer has always been the same: "Because anything I would ever want to say or write has already been done, and done better, in the songs I sing." Expanding on that, I would add that this is true, not just in traditional ballads which have stood the test of time, but also in the songs of many contemporary writers. When you see what you want to say already set down so beautifully and effectively, why even try to compose?

Music is the driving force which has shaped my life. Yet the path I followed hasn't always been easy to discern. I am perfectly capable of making instantaneous decisions, but these are seldom on the basis of no previous thought or previous information. I'm a slow burner, and apparently sudden turning points generally come at the end of a long thinking process. For instance, back in my student days at Edinburgh, it took me four years to reach the point where I finally recognized that I had really tried, that I was not lacking in intelligence, and that degree would have been awarded had I applied myself, but I just couldn't do it anymore. My cry of protest in writing on every margin of that exam paper was a dramatic exit, perhaps—but by no means a sudden impulse. A woman has the right to choose, and I chose, taking all responsibility on my own shoulders. That was a major decision which reshaped my entire life, and it came after long, hard thinking—even if the final decision and its timing were based on instinct.

Looking back, trusting and following that same instinct has been the catalyst which triggered many of my main turning points. It was on instinct that I accepted Manny as my first manager, then Iddy, when my career was developing arms and legs, and finally Marty and Lynda, when I had worked myself into a position to be successful in monetary terms, as well as mindlessly busy. Each brought exactly what I needed at that time, encouraging me to step forward into the next stage in my career.

I often think there has been something strange, almost predestined in that career. It evolved so naturally that I have often been left with the feeling that I must have come down here with a brief, an agreed job to do in life as a singer. Sure, I thought things through and picked the right people at crucial moments to guide me along my path, but, equally, there was a huge amount of luck involved, serendipitous moments when things fell into my lap as if Someone Out There was smoothing the way for me, taking good care of me. Like the whole adventure of going on a whim to the Big Apple and being steered to Miki's floor, then finding myself at the very place where folk music was taking off, and getting a review in the *New York Times* from what was effectively my first real gig. Or being invited to teach at Wesleyan, and discovering at Stirling that I enjoyed teaching and research almost as much as I did singing, fulfilling another side of me. All through my life, things have happened at crucial moments when I hesitated, and these have helped to make up my mind.

Not all my decisions have been good ones; I have made some bloody awful ones too. Nobody gets it right all of the time. But when it really mattered, the combination of slow-burning thought and trusting my instinct and recognizing and accepting luck when it came along, has given me what has always seemed to me to be a charmed existence. I have been so lucky. A major part of this luck has been in and through the people I have met. As I have said before, I have been blessed in my friends.

A traveling existence means that I have regularly been in a town for forty-eight hours and have been grateful when total strangers put me up. From many such casual contacts came people with whom I have kept in touch, developing friendships that go back even to my university days.

I have leaned on and learned from them, and each, in turn, has played some part in influencing me, shaping me, helping to turn me into the person I have become.

Songs, endless travel, and friends have been my life. What have I learned, from the journey? If nothing else, it is that life is a process of constant experience and change—and that I would do exactly the same thing again if I were dropped back at the beginning. That makes me one of the very fortunate few for whom, unlike the one described in Eric Bogle's verse, things have not gone "sour and off-key."

I think I have mellowed considerably in response to the process of living—I am a lot less prickly than I was as a young woman. Probably I have become a great deal more opinionated, but a lot less interested in making other people think the same way as I do. That is the benefit of having lived through so many decades.

Where has all this left me? Probably more comfortable in my own skin than I have ever been before. Life hasn't left me with many regrets. Along with anybody who has ever addressed the question, I would much rather say, "I sometimes wish I hadn't," because that is not nearly as sad as the alternative, "I wish I had," for no other reason than even if the idea was a piss-poor one and got you into all sorts of trouble, at least it provided an experience of some kind, and the knowledge of "Well, don't do that again." I did what I wanted to do and made my share of mistakes, and there are very few moments in my life to which I now look back and say, "I wish I had," You do it, then collect your prize—or limp away with your bruises and get on with the rest of your life.

There is always another dawn, another day out there, waiting. For as long as this is so, life continues to be a journey, an ongoing process. I'm still in motion, changing, developing, planning new ventures—and I expect it to remain that way.

On this plane, or another one . . .

Postscript

Within ten days of speaking these final words—yes, they were hers—Jean Redpath was dead. Her cancer flared up during her return to Fife, forcing her to cut short her visit and return to the clinic in Tucson as an emergency. There they carried out surgery to ease her immediate pain; then she was transferred to a hospice, where she died peacefully a few days later, her life complete.

Apart from getting back in touch with friends and family, she had used her last visit home to Scotland to revise and agree to the content of the first eight chapters of this book and to give the draining interviews that would form the basis of the final three chapters. Of these new chapters, she saw and commented on earlier drafts of chapter 9 ("The Queen will throw me into the Tower for sure, this time," Jean muttered.) and chapter 10 ("Oh God, I hate doing organ recitals," Jean sighed).

The only chapter she never saw in print is the final one; we planned to redo this via Skype. She was so weak by then that she wasn't really sure if she had managed to say what she wanted. The interview for that chapter was run, against my wishes and advice, on the day before she returned to the United States. Her exhaustion, coupled with several interruptions from family and neighbors as they dropped in to wish her bon voyage, resulted in some uncharacteristic unfinished thoughts and drifting, wandering sections in the recording. At that advanced stage of her illness, it was a miracle that she managed to say anything coherent at all. I have done what I could to mend the gaps, using previous conversations, and I have edited out sections which I felt she would have wanted to scrap herself.

What's in this book are almost entirely Jean's words—not all of them or we would have needed at least two more volumes. She would want me to say that she was working from memory, and that, if there are any errors or omissions, we are jointly sorry for these.

Jean has left a wonderful legacy of recordings and meticulous research notes on the historical context of the songs, to be split between the University of Glasgow and the University of South Carolina. These are currently being assessed and catalogued in both universities. It was her intention that they should provide resource bases for international students studying traditional music.

She has also left a huge, gaping hole, which she used to fill with gusto. Those of us who were and are her friends miss her sorely. For my own part, she was a joy to work with . . . even if she was frae Fife. Nobody's perfect. However, as both singer and loyal friend, Jean came close.

Mark Brownrigg
April 2016

GLOSSARY

Auld: old
Aye: yes; also, with a slightly different intonation, always
Bairn: baby, child
Beastie: animal
Blether: chat
Bobby: policeman—so nicknamed for Robert Peel, who set up the police force
Braws: best clothes—literally, "beautifuls"
Budgie: budgerigar, pet bird; reminds me of one of my mother's sayings—"Tae hell wi' poverty, gi'e the cat the canary" (Never mind our poverty, give the cat the canary)
Bumbaleerie: bottom, posterior
Burn: stream
Ceilidh: (pronounced kay-lay or kay-ley) any social gathering, but particularly one involving song and dance
Chancer: opportunist, on the margin of crooked while hoping to get away with it
Couthy: sharp, pithy, earthy, pulling no punches—the antithesis of politically correct
Dent: impact mark or worn hollow
Disnae: doesn't
Douce: polite, restrained, living always with one eye to one's dignity
Dram: glass of whisky
Dreich: gray, lifeless, miserable
Fae: from, as in "We're fae Fife"
Frien': friend
Froak: frock, dress
Glowering: frowning, glaring
Grotty: dirty, disgusting, unsavory
Guid: good
Hame: home
High jinks: fun and games
Jotters: notepads, memo books

Keech: shite, ordure
Kirk: church
Lug: ear
Lum heids: chimney tops
Moothie: mouth organ, harmonica
Navvy: laborer in heavy industrial work; the term came from the Irish laborers who came over to Britain to dig the canals and railway lines out by pick and shovel
Perjink: smart, proper, well-turned-out, and much concerned with "What will the neighbors think?"
Puggy: in Fife, a slang term for a monkey; in industrial Scotland, it meant the small pug engines which ran on narrow track lines and hauled coal and stone up gradients from mines to the nearest railway station. Take your pick—but that kid could climb.
Sclatching: scraping around
Skelp: smack, slap
Single end: a house designed with one room which serves many purposes, including living, eating, and sleeping
Stour: dust
Tarry chips: fresh blacktop on the road; literally, tar with stone chips scattered on it
Tatties: potatoes
Tawse: a teacher's leather strap, or belt—a hard strip of leather finishing in two "tongues," which hurt and was normally used more often on the boys in the class
Thrawn: stubborn, unheeding
Trusty: trusted, loyal, dependable—in modern parlance, "always there for me"
Weel-kent: well-known, familiar
Whaur: where
Wifies: older women, a generic term, even if some are unmarried
Wrang: wrong

DISOGRAPHY

This listing was compiled from Jean Redpath's own records and notes for the most part. It is incomplete and may contain some inconsistencies or inadvertent inaccuracies.

TITLE	RECORDING	ID NUMBER
	Ain Countrie, Legacy Records, 1973	FSS 0049
A' the Week Yer Man's Awa'		
Bonnie Gallowa'		
Eileen Aroon		
Farewell He		
Gairdner and the Plooman		
Gairdner Child		
Hishie Ba		
I'll Lay Ye Doon Love		
Johnnie o' Braidiesley		
Kilbogie		
London Ba' etc.		
Matt Hyland		
My Ain Countrie		
Rantin' Dog, the Daddie O't		
Silver Tassie		
Wars o' High Germanie		
	Angels Hovering Fretless, 1978	FR 138
Angel Band		
Have Thine Own Way		
Jesus, Won't You Come by Here?		
Land Where We'll Never Grow Old		
Precious Memories		

TITLE	RECORDING	ID NUMBER
There Are Angels Hovering Round		
Where the Soul of Man Never Die		
	Anywhere Is Home	
	Philo, 2009	FR 154
Grey Funnel Line		
Just as the Evening Sun		
Precious Lord		
Life's Railway to Heaven		
Jesus Hold My Hand		
Let the Lower Lights Be Burning		
Anywhere Is Home		
Near the Cross		
Face to Face		
	Ballad Folk	
	BBC Records, 1977	
Caller Herrin'		
Keach in the Creel (cf. Wee Toon Clerk)		
Love Is Teasin'		
Marnie (with MIRK)		
Plooman Laddies		
Recruited Collier		
Ten and Nine (see also Jute Mill Song)		
	Burns 1 (Hovey)	
	Philo, 1975	PH 1037
Amang the Trees		
Cauld Kail in Aberdeen		
Charlie He's my Darling		
Corn Rigs		
Country Lassie		
De'il's Awa' wi' the Exciseman		
Johnie Blunt		
Lady Mary Ann		
Logan Water		
My Tocher's the Jewel		
To the Weavers Gin Ye Go		
Winter It is Past		

TITLE	RECORDING	ID NUMBER
Wantonness		
A Red, Red Rose		
	Burns 2 (Hovey)	
	Philo, 1980	PH 1048
A Parcel of Rogues in a Nation		
Auld Lang Syne		
Beware o' Bonnie Ann		
Cooper o' Cuddy		
Dusty Miller		
Had I the Wyte		
Hey How Johnie Lad		
It Was A' for Our Rightfu' King		
Mary Morison		
Nine Inch Will Please a Lady		
Sae Flaxen Were Her Ringlets		
Steer Her Up		
Sweetest May		
	Burns 3 (Hovey)	
	Philo, 1981	PH 1071
Banks o' Doon		
Belles of Mauchline		
Deuk's Dang o'er My Daddie		
Duncan Davidson		
Green Grow the Rashes, O		
Lass o' Ecclefechan		
O Fare Ye Weel My Auld Wife		
Phillis the Fair		
Ploughman		
Reel o' Stumpie		
Slave's Lament		
Song, Composed in August		
Will Ye Go to the Indes, My Mary?		
	Burns 4 (Hovey)	
	Philo, 1982	PH 1072
A Long Winter Night		
Address to the Woodlark		

TITLE	RECORDING	ID NUMBER
Behold, My Love		
Here's His Health in Water		
I'll Ay Ca'in by Yon Town		
O Can Ye Labor Lea?		
Rattlin' Roarin' Willie		
Tam Glen		
Taylor Fell through the Bed		
There Grows a Bonnie Briar Bush		
Thou Hast Left Me Ever, Jamie		
Wha Is That at My Bower Door?		
	Burns 5 (Hovey)	
	Philo, 1985	PH 1093
Battle of Sherra-Moor		
Fragment		
German Lairdie		
Lament of Mary Queen of Scots		
Lea Rig		
Mill, Mill O		
My Collier Laddie		
My Nanie, O		
O This Is No My Ain Lassie		
O Were I on Parnassus Hill		
Posie		
You're Welcome, Willie Stewart		
	Burns 6 (Hovey)	
	Philo, 1987	PH 1113
Cardin' O't		
Fornicator		
Galloway Tam		
Gloomy December		
Here's to Thy Health		
Hey, Ca' Thro'		
Jamie Come try me		
Killiecrankie		
Last May a Braw Wooer		
Sandy & Jockie		
Strathallan's Lament		
White Cockade		

TITLE	RECORDING	ID NUMBER
	Burns 7 (Hovey)	
	Philo, 1990	PH 1126
Bonny Lass of Albanie		
Gallant Weaver		
Mauchline Lady		
My Father Was a Farmer		
My Love She's but a Lassie Yet		
O for Ane-and-twenty, Tam		
O Guid Ale Comes		
O Merry Hae I Been		
Ode to Spring		
Peggy Ramsay		
Where Are the Joys?		
Young Highland Rover		
	Burns SMM CD #1	
	Rounder, 1996	JR 103
A Rosebud by My Early Walk		
Banks o' Nith (2 versions)		
Birks of Aberfeldy		
Birks of Abergeldie		
Blythe Was She		
Day Returns		
Dusty Miller		
First When Maggie Was My Care		
Gae Fetch Tae Me a Pint o' Wine		
Gardener wi' His Paidle		
Green Grow the Rashes, O		
I'm O'er Young to Marry Yet		
Jamie Come Try Me		
John Anderson		
Jumpin' John		
Laddie Lie Near Me		
Landlady Count the Lawin'		
McPherson's Farewell		
My Love She's but a Lassie Yet		
My Wife's a Wanton Wee Thing		
O Tibbie, I Hae Seen the Day		
Of A' the Airts		

TITLE	RECORDING	ID NUMBER
Ploughman		
Rantin' Dog the Daddie O't		
Rattlin' Roarin' Willie		
Tam Glen		
Tibbie Dunbar		
To the Weavers Gin Ye Go		
Up in the Morning		
Whare Are Ye Gaun?		
Where Braving Angry Winter's Storm		
Whistle an' I'll Come tae Ye, My Lad		
White Cockade		
Young Highland Rover		
Winter It Is Past		
	Burns SMM CD #2	
	Rounder, 1996	JR 104
As I went Out ae May Morning		
Ay Waukin' O		
Bairns Gat Oot wi' an Unco Shout		
By Yon Castle Wa'		
Ca' the Yowes		
Craigieburn Wood		
De'il's Awa' wi' the Exciseman		
Fareweel to A' Our Scottish Fame		
Flow Gently Sweet Afton		
I Hae Been at Crookieden		
Killiecrankie		
Now Westlin' Winds		
O for Ane-and-twenty, Tam		
O Leeze Me on My Spinning Wheel		
O Love Will Venture In		
O Meikle Thinks My Love (cf. My Tocher's the Jewel)		
On a Bank of Flowers		
Parnassus Hill		
She Sat Down below a Thorn (cf. Fine Flowers)		
She's Fair and Fause		
Taylor Rell through the Bed		
Turn Again Thou Fair Eliza		
Weary Pund o' Tow		

TITLE	RECORDING	ID NUMBER
Where Cart Rins Rowin' to the Sea		
Willie Wastle Dwalt on Tweed		
Ye Banks and Braes o' Bonnie Doon		
Ye Jacobites by Name		
Ae Fond Kiss		
	Burns SMM CD #3	
	Rounder, 1996	JR 105
Comin' through the Rye		
A Red, Red Rose		
Auld Lang Syne		
Auld Man's Mare's Dead		
But Lately Seen in Gladsome Green		
Does Haughty Gaul Invasion Threat?		
Gude Nicht and Joy be wi' You A'		
Had I the Wyte		
Here's a Health to Them That's Awa'		
I'll Ay Ca'in by Yon Town		
It Was A' for Our Rightfu' King		
Leezie Lindsay		
Louis What Reck I by Thee?		
No Churchman Am I		
Now Nature Hangs Her Mantle Green		
O Gude Ale Comes		
O Lay Thy Loof in Mine Lass		
O Leave Novels, Ye Mauchline Belles		
O That I Had Ne'er Been Married		
Out over the Forth		
Peg o' Ramsay		
Robin Shure in Hairst		
Sae Flaxen Were Her Ringlets		
Tam Lin		
There Grows a Bonnie Briar Bush		
Wilt Thou Be My Dearie?		
	Father Adam	
	Philo, 1980	PH 1061
Willie's Rare		
A Slee One		

TITLE	RECORDING	ID NUMBER
Bonnie Susie Cleland		
Father Adam		
Highland Laddie		
Jock o' Hazeldean		
Rigs o' Rye		
Roy's Wife o' Aldivalloch		
Shearin's No for You		
Sir Patrick Spens		
Trooper and the Maid		
Twa Brothers		
	A Fine Song for Singing	
	Philo, 1987	PH 1110
Annie Laurie		
Broken Brook		
Broom o' the Cowdenknowes		
Capernaum		
Captive Song of Mary Stuart		
I Will Make You Brooches		
John o' Dreams		
Now the Die Is Cast		
Rohallion		
Song of the Wandering Aengus		
South Wind		
Tryst		
Up the Noran Water		
Wild Geese		
	First Flight	
	Rounder, 1989	Rndr 11556
Barbarry Allan		
Caller O'u		
Clerk Saunders		
Crookit Bawbee		
Dainty Davy		
Day We Went to Rothesay		
Gin I were a Baron's Heir		
Gypsy Laddie		
Inverey		

TITLE	RECORDING	ID NUMBER
Johnnie Cope		
Johnnie Lad		
Kirk Swaree		
Lassie wi' the Yellow Coatie		
Nicky Tams		
O Wert Thou in the Cauld Blast		
Ploughboy, O		
Quiet Land of Erin		
Rantin' Laddie		
She Moved through the Fair		
Tae the Weavers		
Wae's Me for Prince Charlie		
Wee Cooper o' Fife		
	Haydn: Scottish Songs	
	Philo, 2009	PH 1082
Fy, Let Us A' to the Bridal		
Gardener wi' His Paidle		
How Long and Drearie Is the Night		
I Had a Horse		
Leader Haughs and Yarrow		
Mary's Dream		
My Ain Kind Dearie		
O Let Me in This ae Night		
Oh, Onochrie!		
Robin Quo' She		
Todlen Hame		
Widow Are Ye Wakin'?		
Woo'd and married an' A'		
Braw Lads o' Galla Water		
Up in the Mornin' Early		
	Jean Redpath	
	Philo, 1975	PH 2015
Blackwaterside		
Captain Wedderburn's Courtship		
Dancing at Whitsun		
Faithful Johnny		
Grey Silkie		

TITLE	RECORDING	ID NUMBER
I Live Not Where I Love		
Lady Dysie		
Lagan Love		
MacCrimmons Lament		
Ned of the Hill		
Rambleaway		
Terror Time		
	Jean Redpath Live! Jean Redpath Records, 2CDs, 2000	JR 111
Absent (1 verse)		
Auld Lang Syne		
Banks o' Red Roses		
Dance Tunes Medley		
Davie and Jeannie		
Donald Came across the Heather		
Endless Surge of the Sea		
Eriskay Love Lilt		
Fife Overgate		
Help Me Make It through the Night (1 verse)		
Highland Lad		
I Know Moonlight		
I Will Make You Brooches		
Jock o' Hazeldean		
Kirk Swaree		
Lambing to the Wool		
Love Is Teasin' Medley		
Mary o' Argyle		
Mickey's Warning		
Nancy with the Golden Hair		
Of A' the Airts		
A Red, red rose		
Rigs o' Rye		
Saw you my Maggie?		
Scarborough Settler's Lament		
School Dinners		
Shenandoah		
Thora (1 verse)		

TITLE	RECORDING	ID NUMBER
Wee Wee Tot		
Wild Geese		
Willie's Rare		
Woo'd an' Mairrit an' A'		
Yellow on the Broom		
	Laddie Lie Near Me	
	Elektra, 1966	EKL 274
Robin Adair		
Ca' the yowes		
Dainty Davy		
Dream Angus		
Gin I Were a Baron's heir		
Johnnie Cope		
Johnnie Lad		
Laddie Lie Near me		
O Wert Thou in the Cauld Blast		
Ploughboy, O		
Quiet Land of Erin		
Rothesay Bay		
Sleeps the Noon		
Tha Mi Sgith		
Crookit Bawbee		
Lassie wi' the Yellow Coatie		
O Wert Thou in the Cauld Blast		
	Lady Nairne	
	Philo, 1986	PH 1087
Auld Hoose		
Caller Herrin'		
Charlie's Landing at Barodale		
Laird o' Cockpen		
Lament of the Covenanter's Widow		
Lammie		
Land o' the Leal		
Lass o' Gowrie		
Lass of Livingstane		
Regalia		
Rowan Tree		

TITLE	RECORDING	ID NUMBER
Strathearn		
White Rose of June		
Will Ye No' Come Back Again?		
	Leaving the Land	
	Philo, 1990	PH 1131
Hallowe'en		
Last Minstrel Show		
Leaving the Land		
Maggie		
Next Time Round		
Now I'm Easy		
Scarborough Settler's Lament		
Snowgoose		
Sonny's Dream		
Un Canadien Errant		
	Love Is Teasin'	
	Minnesota Public Radio, 1984	JR 101
Banks o' Red Roses		
Barbarry Allan		
Bonnie George Campbell		
Fine Flowers in the Valley (cf. She Sat Down)		
Jacobite Lass		
King's Shilling		
Love Is Teasin'		
Rosie Anderson		
Saw You my Maggie?		
Singing Bird		
	Love, Lilt and Laughter	
	Elektra, 1963	EKL 224
Caller O'u		
Day We Went to Rothesay		
Kirk Swaree		
Love Is Teasin'		
McFarlane o' the Sprots		
Nicky Tams		

TITLE	RECORDING	ID NUMBER
Paddy McGinty's Goat		
Peat Fire Flame		
She Moved through the Fair		
Song of the Seals		
Tae the Weavers		
Mouth Music		
Wae's me for Prince Charlie		
Lewis Bridal Song		
	Lowlands Philo, 1986	PH 1066
A Wee Bird Cam' tae My Apron		
Bonny at Morn		
Clerk Saunders		
Faraway Tom		
Gallowa' Hills		
Lassie wi' the Yellow Coatie		
Lichtbob's Lassie		
Lowlands		
Mary Hamilton		
Riddles Wisely Expounded		
Rose of Allendale		
Who Shall Count for Thee?		
	Maiden Voyage Jean Redpath Records, 2002	JR 112
Barrin' o' Oor Door		
Bonnie Lass o' Fyvie		
Caroline of Edinburgh Town		
Clerk Colven		
Cruel Mother		
I Aince Loved a Lass		
Islay Reaper's Song		
Lewis Bridal Song		
Lichtbob's Lassie		
McFarlane o' the Sprots		
Paddy McGinty's Goat		
Pawky Duke		

TITLE	RECORDING	ID NUMBER
Peat Fire Flame		
Rob Roy		
Rue		
Skippin' Barefoot through the Heather		
Trees Are Growing High, The		
Twa Corbies		
Wee Toon Clerk		
West Virginia Mine Disaster		
	Midlothian: Songs of That Area by Jean Redpath Midlothian District Council, 1989	
Captain Wedderburn's Courtship		
Clerk's Twa Sons o' Owsenford		
Collier Laddie		
Collier's Song		
Green Plaid		
Laird o' Cockpen		
Lord Roslin's Daughter		
Robin Tamson's Smiddy		
Willie's Gane to Melville Castle		
	Miller's Reel BBC Records, date unknown	BBC REH 737
Mill, Mill O (with Rod & Ed, String 4)		
My Ain Kind Dearie (with Ensemble)		
Green Grow the Rashes (with Rod & 4		
O Can Ye Labour Lea? (with Ensemble)		
Ploughman Lad (with Ensemble)		
Corn Rigs (with Rod & 4)		
Jamie Come Try Me (with Ensemble)		
Lass O' Ecclefechan (with Ensemble)		
Collier Laddie (with Rod & 4)		
Laddie Lie Near Me		
A Red, Red Rose		
Here's His Health (with Ensemble)		
Thou Hast Left Me Ever		

TITLE	RECORDING	ID NUMBER
	Moon's Silver Cradle Jean Redpath Records, 1996	JR 106
All through the Night		
Baloo Baleerie		
Birnie Bouzle		
Bonnie at Morn		
Can Ye Sew cushions?		
Connemara Lullaby		
Coulter's Candy		
Dance to your Daddy		
Dream Angus		
Fairy Lullaby		
Gartan Mother's Lullaby		
Hush-a-ba, Birdie, Croon		
Manx Lullaby		
Moon Man		
October Winds		
Shetland Lullaby		
Soontree Lullaby		
Spinning Wheel		
Victoria Blue		
	Now and Then Jean Redpath Records, 1999	JR 110
A Lum Hat wantin' a Croon		
Davie and Jeannie		
Gairdner and the Plooman		
Gilderoy		
Kilbogie		
Kirk Swaree		
Lass o' Patie's Mill		
Lum Hat Wantin' the Croon		
No, Sir		
Oggy Man		
Pull Down, Lads		
Quiet		

TITLE	RECORDING	ID NUMBER
Railway Porter		
Rothesay Bay		
Sheath and Knife		
South Side Blues		
Susan's Song		
Windmills		
Yellow Yorlin		
You're Braw wi' Your Pearls		
	Scottish Ballad Book	
	Elektra, 1962	EKL 214
Barbarry Allan		
Bonny Boy		
Clerk Saunders		
Gypsy Laddie		
Inverey		
Lichtbob's Lassie		
Rantin' Laddie		
Sir Patrick Spens		
Twa Corbies		
Wee Cooper o' Fife		
Wee Toon Clerk		
	The Scottish Fiddle	
	Lismor Folk, 1985	LIS 7009
A Wee Bird Cam' to Our Ha' Door		
Birks o' Aberfeldy		
Cradle Song		
Flower o' the Quern		
Highland Harry		
I'm A' Doun for Lack o' Johnnie		
Lowlands of Holland		
Through the Wood Laddie		
	Shout for Joy	
	Philo, 2009	PH 1068
Adeste Fideles (with Group)		
Away in a Manger (with Lisa)		
Christ Child's Lullaby		

TITLE	RECORDING	ID NUMBER
Flower of Jesse (with Lisa & Jim)		
Go Tell It on the Mountain (with Lisa et al.)		
Holly Bears a Berry (with LisaJimSar		
It Came Upon a Midnight Clear:		
Joy to the World (Group)		
O Little Town of Bethlehem (Group)		
Rorate Coeli Desuper		
Shout for Joy (Lisa & Group)		
Still the Night (with Lisa)		
Green Street (Group)		
Shephers Arise (Group)		
Sheburne C.M. (Group)		
	Skippin' Barfit Prestige International, 1962	Pr/Int 13041
Banks o' Red Roses		
Barrin' o' Oor Door		
Bonnie Lass o' Fyvie		
Cruel Mother		
Fife Overgate		
I Aince Loved a Lass		
Islay Reaper's Song		
Lum Hat Wantin' a Croon		
Maggie Lauder		
Pawky Duke		
Rue		
Skippin' Barfit through the Heather		
Willie's Rare		
	Song of the Seals Philo, 1978	PH 1054
Birnie Bouzle		
Johnny Lad		
College Boy		
Davy Faa		
Dowie Dens of Yarrow		
Highland Harry		
Johnny My Man		

TITLE	RECORDING	ID NUMBER
Logie o' Buchan		
Mill o' Tifty's Annie		
Muckin' o' Geordie's Byre		
Polwarth on the Green		
Poor Rovin' Lassie		
Song of the Seals		
	Still the Night Jean Redpath Records, 1999	JR 109
Balulalow		
Child in a Manger		
Christ Child's Lullaby		
Christmas Carol (Reading)		
Coventry Carol		
Dona Nobis Pacem		
Gift o' Gowd		
I Salute You (Reading)		
Il est né, le divin enfant		
Kings from the East		
Lord of the Dance		
Matthew's Gospel		
New Testament in Scots (Reading)		
Poem at Christmas (Reading)		
Rorate Celi Desuper		
Still the Night		
Two Thousand Years Ago		
Vieux Noël		
We Three Kings of Orient Are		
What Child Is This? (Greensleeves)		
	Summer of My Dreams Jean Redpath Records, 1995	JR 102
Alas! Poor Queen		
Andy's Gone with Cattle		
Blackbird		
Bonnie Bessie Logan		
Come by the Hills		

TITLE	RECORDING	ID NUMBER
Dark-eyed Molly		
Dumbarton's Drums		
Farm Auction		
Gipsy Lass		
Maggie Lauder		
Mally Lee		
Parlez-moi d'amour		
Sailor's Sweetheart		
Summer of My Dreams		
Sweet Thames Flow Softly		
Willie's Gane to Melville Castle		
Yellow on the Broom		
	There Were Minstrels Trailer, 1977	LER 2106
Caroline of Edinburgh Town		
Clerk Colven		
Davie and Jeannie		
Gilderoy		
My Love She's but a Lassie Yet		
No Sir		
Rattlin' Roarin' Willie		
Rob Roy		
Robin Shure in Hairst		
Sheath and Knife		
West Virginia Mine Disaster		
Yellow Yorlin		
Dumbarton's Drums		
	Think on Me Jean Redpath Records, 1998	JR 108
Absent		
Auld Robin Gray		
Birks of Invermay		
Castle Grand		
Eriskay Love Lilt		
Eternal Surge of the Sea, The		
I'll Walk beside You		

TITLE	RECORDING	ID NUMBER
Lochnagar		
Love's Old Sweet Song		
Mary o' Argyle		
Open the Door Softly		
Robin Adair		
Then You'll Remember Me		
Think on Me		
Turn Ye to Me		
We'll Go No More A-roving		
	Woman of Her Time Jean Redpath Records, 1997	JR 107
A' the Week Yer Man's Awa'		
An Auld Man Cam Coortin' Me		
Blue Blazin' Blind Drunk		
False Bride		
From the Lambing to the Wool		
Gardener		
Glasgow Lullaby		
Guidwife Speaks		
Harry's Wife		
High Jeanie High		
Jute Mill Song		
Lodger		
Lunderston Bay		
Mhairi's Song		
Mistress		
Nancy with the golden Hair		
Retirement		
Tecumseh Valley		
Why Should I a Brisk Young Lassie?		
Women of Our Time		